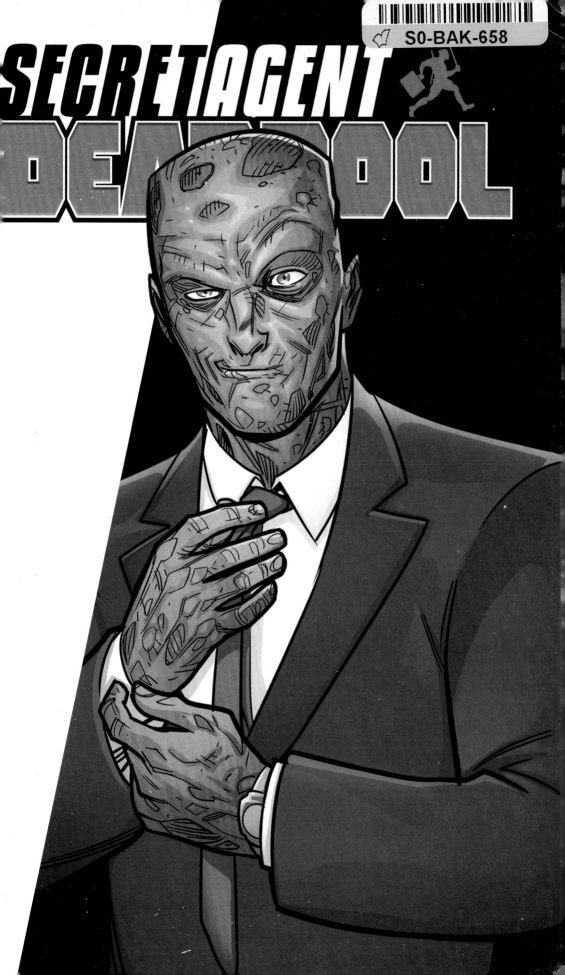

SECRET AGENT

DEADPOOL

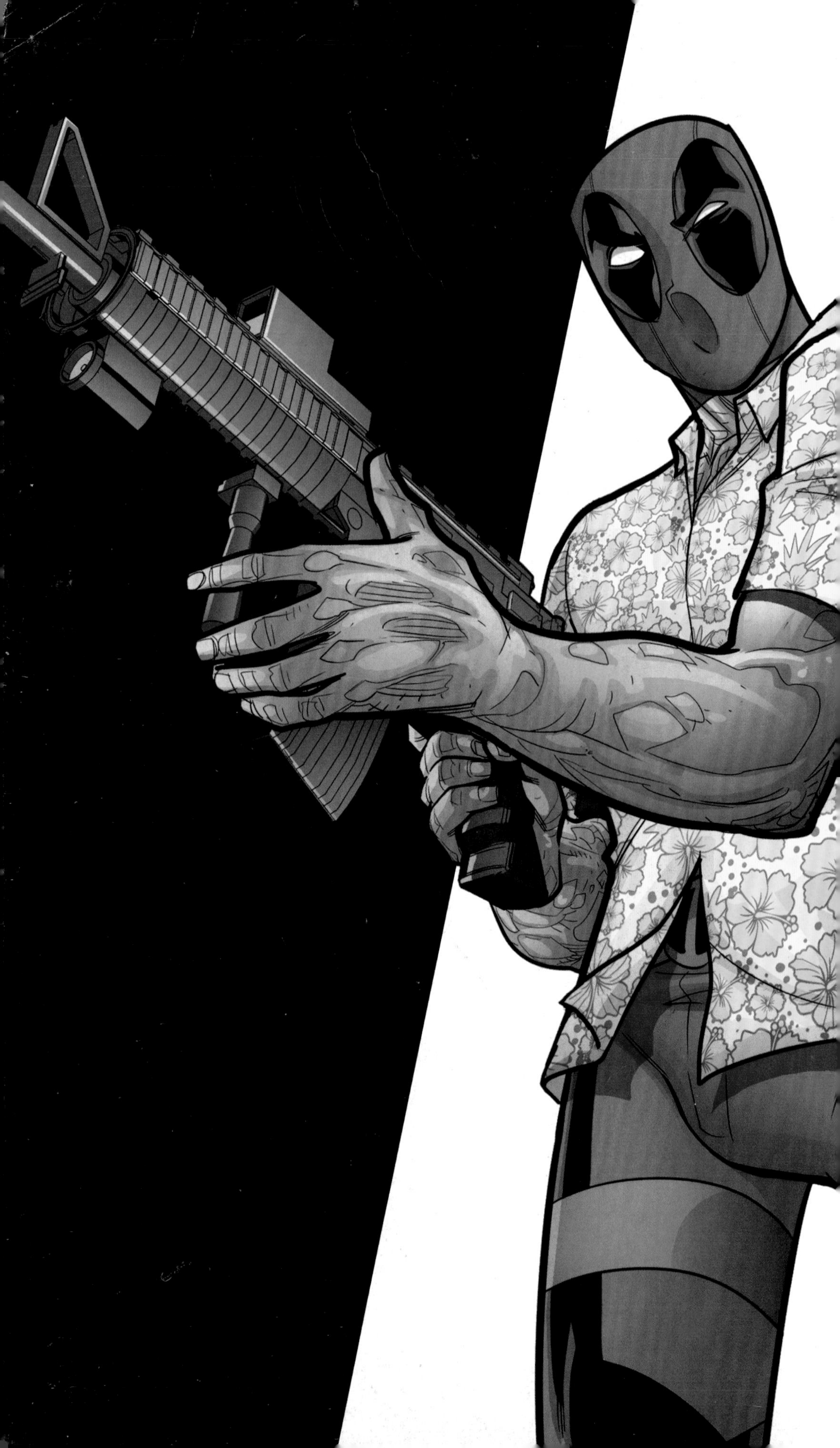

SECRET AGENT
DEADPOOL

WRITER **CHRISTOPHER HASTINGS**
ARTIST **SALVA ESPIN**
COLOR ARTIST **MATT YACKEY**

LETTERER **COMICRAFT'S JIMMY BETANCOURT**
COVER ART **DAVID NAKAYAMA**

ASSISTANT EDITOR **LAUREN AMARO**
EDITOR **DEVIN LEWIS**

DEADPOOL CREATED BY **ROB LIEFELD & FABIAN NICIEZA**

COLLECTION EDITOR **JENNIFER GRÜNWALD**
ASSISTANT EDITOR **CAITLIN O'CONNELL**
ASSOCIATE MANAGING EDITOR **KATERI WOODY**
EDITOR, SPECIAL PROJECTS **MARK D. BEAZLEY**
VP PRODUCTION & SPECIAL PROJECTS **JEFF YOUNGQUIST**
SVP PRINT, SALES & MARKETING **DAVID GABRIEL**
BOOK DESIGNER **ADAM DEL RE**

EDITOR IN CHIEF **C.B. CEBULSKI**
CHIEF CREATIVE OFFICER **JOE QUESADA**
PRESIDENT **DAN BUCKLEY**
EXECUTIVE PRODUCER **ALAN FINE**

DEADPOOL: SECRET AGENT DEADPOOL. First printing 2018. ISBN 978-1-302-91343-4. Published by MARVEL WORLDWIDE, INC., a subsidiary of MARVEL ENTERTAINMENT, LLC. OFFICE OF PUBLICATION: 135 West 50th Street, New York, NY 10020. Copyright © 2018 MARVEL No similarity between any of the names, characters, persons, and/or institutions in this magazine with those of any living or dead person or institution is intended, and any such similarity which may exist is purely coincidental. **Printed in Canada.** DAN BUCKLEY, President, Marvel Entertainment; JOHN NEE, Publisher; JOE QUESADA, Chief Creative Officer; TOM BREVOORT, SVP of Publishing; DAVID BOGART, SVP of Business Affairs & Operations, Publishing & Partnership; DAVID GABRIEL, SVP of Sales & Marketing, Publishing; JEFF YOUNGQUIST, VP of Production & Special Projects; DAN CARR, Executive Director of Publishing Technology; ALEX MORALES, Director of Publishing Operations; DAN EDINGTON, Managing Editor; SUSAN CRESPI, Production Manager; STAN LEE, Chairman Emeritus. For information regarding advertising in Marvel Comics or on Marvel.com, please contact Vit DeBellis, Custom Solutions & Integrated Advertising Manager, at vdebellis@marvel.com. For Marvel subscription inquiries, please call 888-511-5480. **Manufactured between 12/14/2018 and**

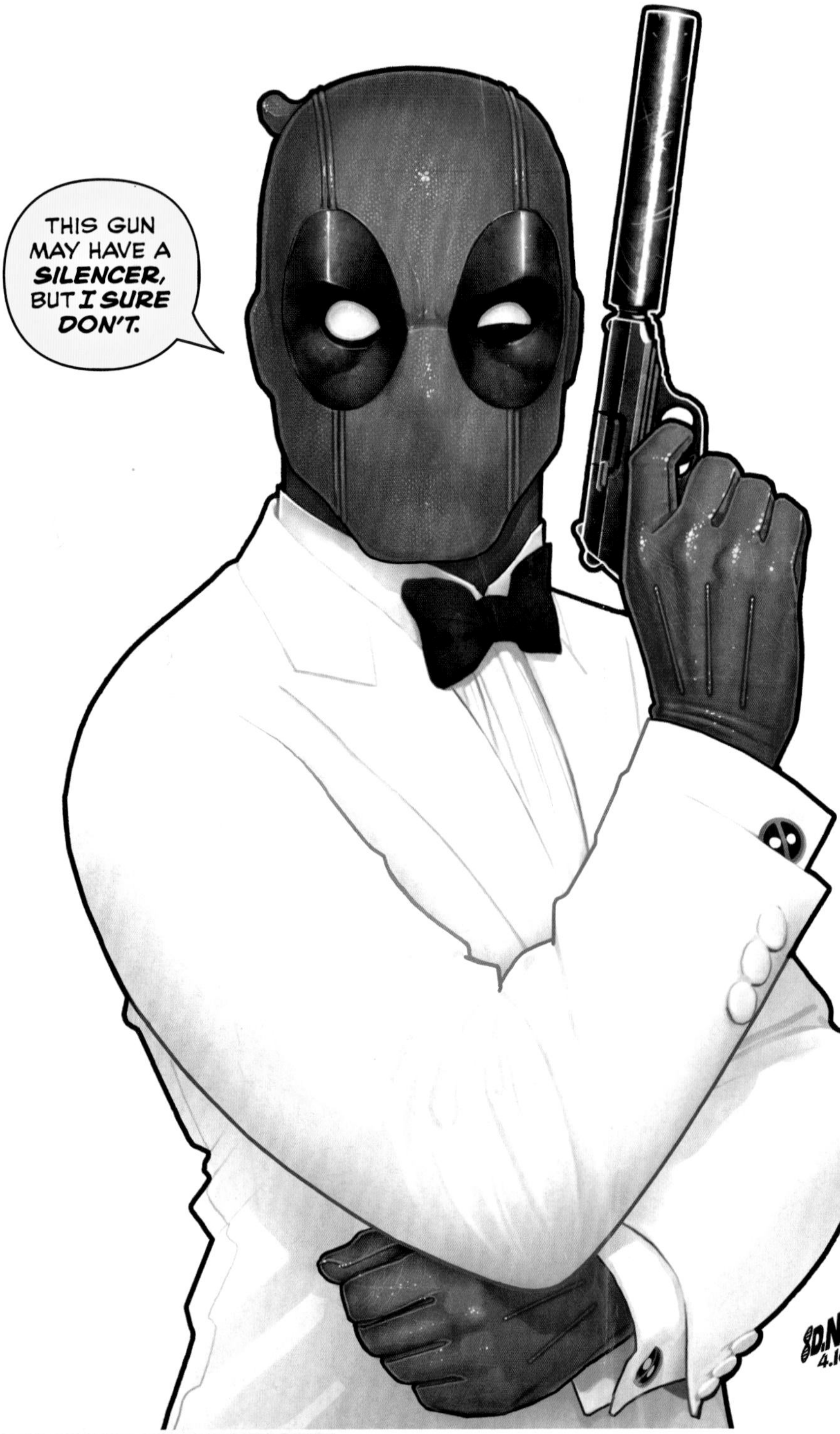
THIS GUN MAY HAVE A SILENCER, BUT I SURE DON'T.
D.NA 4.18

1

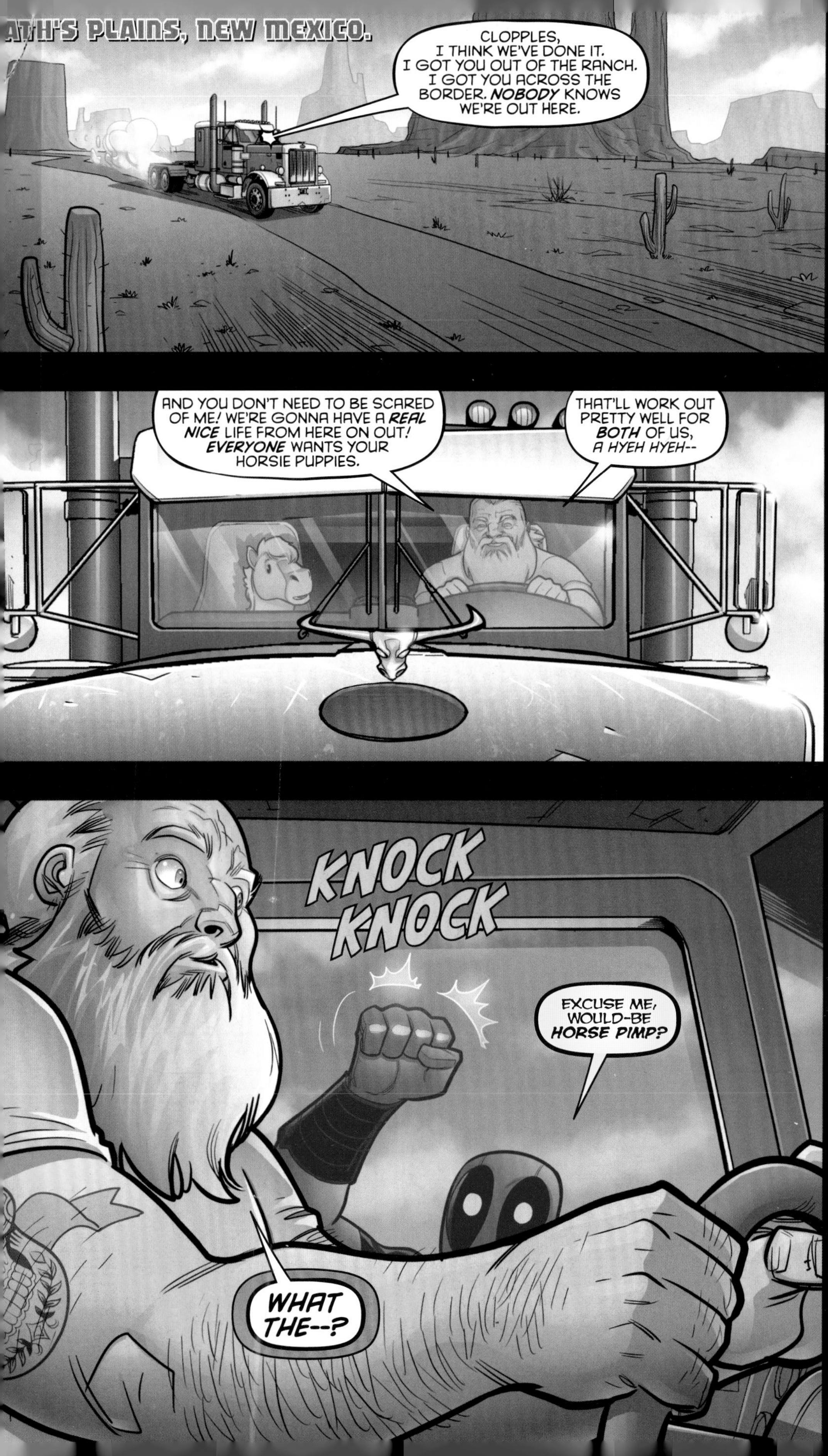
ATH'S PLAINS, NEW MEXICO.
CLOPPLES, I THINK WE'VE DONE IT. I GOT YOU OUT OF THE RANCH. I GOT YOU ACROSS THE BORDER. NOBODY KNOWS WE'RE OUT HERE.
AND YOU DON'T NEED TO BE SCARED OF ME! WE'RE GONNA HAVE A REAL NICE LIFE FROM HERE ON OUT! EVERYONE WANTS YOUR HORSIE PUPPIES.
THAT'LL WORK OUT PRETTY WELL FOR BOTH OF US, A HYEH HYEH--
KNOCK KNOCK
EXCUSE ME, WOULD-BE HORSE PIMP?
WHAT THE--?

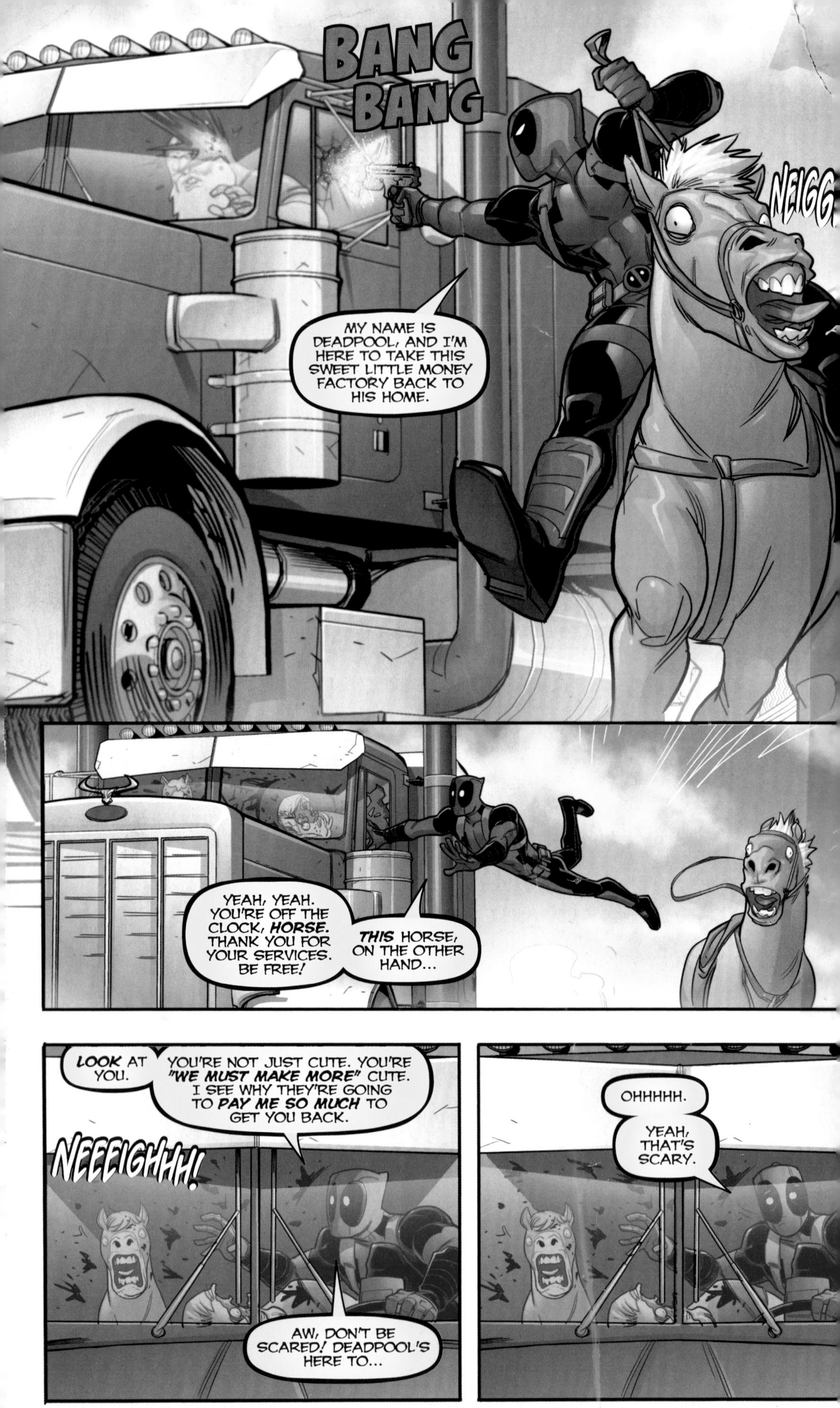
BANG BANG
NEIGG
MY NAME IS DEADPOOL, AND I'M HERE TO TAKE THIS SWEET LITTLE MONEY FACTORY BACK TO HIS HOME.
YEAH, YEAH. YOU'RE OFF THE CLOCK, HORSE. THANK YOU FOR YOUR SERVICES. BE FREE!
THIS HORSE, ON THE OTHER HAND...
LOOK AT YOU.
YOU'RE NOT JUST CUTE. YOU'RE "WE MUST MAKE MORE" CUTE. I SEE WHY THEY'RE GOING TO PAY ME SO MUCH TO GET YOU BACK.
NEEEIGHHH!
AW, DON'T BE SCARED! DEADPOOL'S HERE TO...
OHHHHH.
YEAH, THAT'S SCARY.

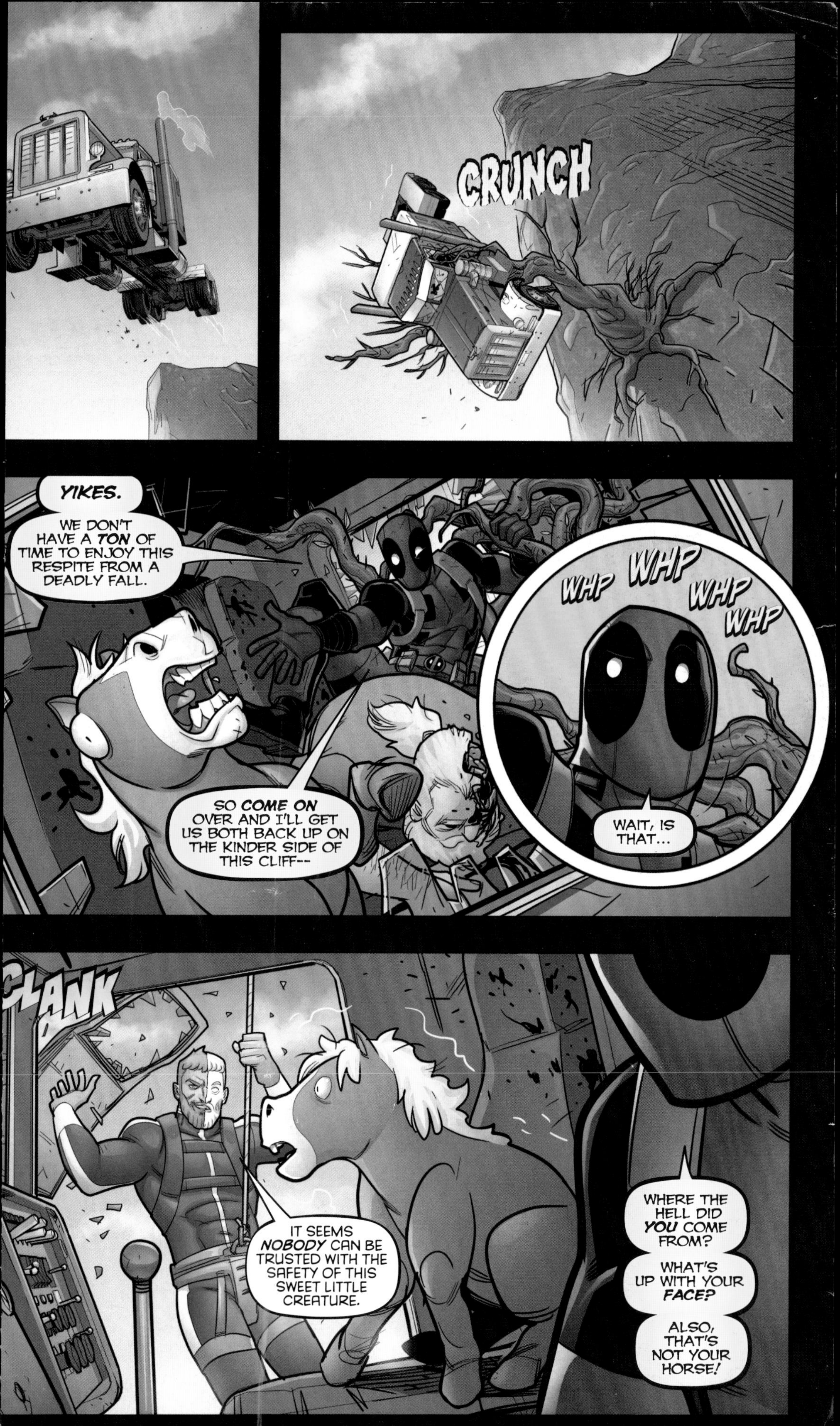
CRUNCH
YIKES.
WE DON'T HAVE A TON OF TIME TO ENJOY THIS RESPITE FROM A DEADLY FALL.
SO COME ON OVER AND I'LL GET US BOTH BACK UP ON THE KINDER SIDE OF THIS CLIFF--
WHP WHP WHP WHP
WAIT, IS THAT...
CLANK
IT SEEMS NOBODY CAN BE TRUSTED WITH THE SAFETY OF THIS SWEET LITTLE CREATURE.
WHERE THE HELL DID YOU COME FROM?
WHAT'S UP WITH YOUR FACE?
ALSO, THAT'S NOT YOUR HORSE!

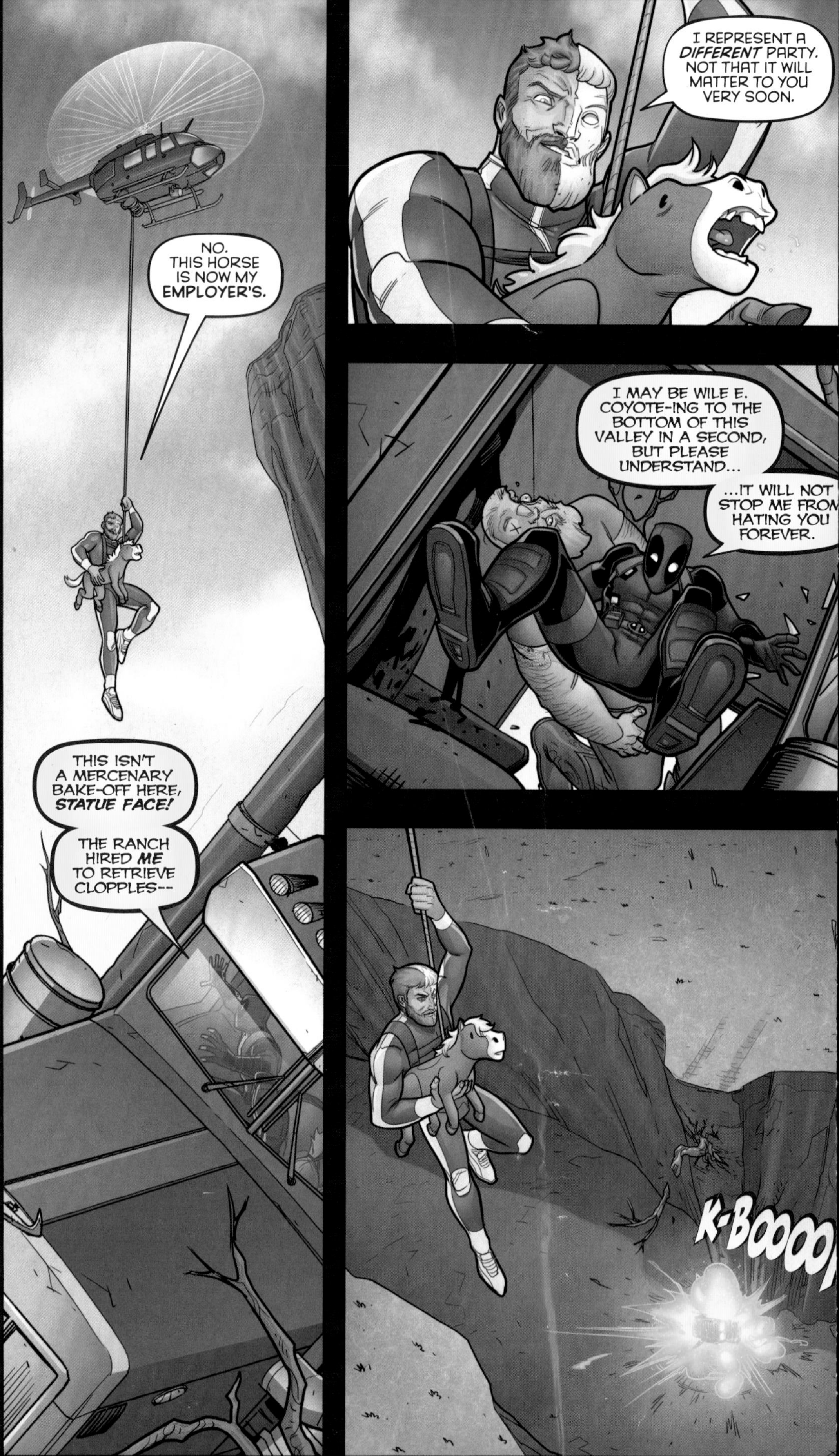
NO. THIS HORSE IS NOW MY EMPLOYER'S.
THIS ISN'T A MERCENARY BAKE-OFF HERE, STATUE FACE!
THE RANCH HIRED ME TO RETRIEVE CLOPPLES--
I REPRESENT A DIFFERENT PARTY. NOT THAT IT WILL MATTER TO YOU VERY SOON.
I MAY BE WILE E. COYOTE-ING TO THE BOTTOM OF THIS VALLEY IN A SECOND, BUT PLEASE UNDERSTAND...
...IT WILL NOT STOP ME FROM HATING YOU FOREVER.
K-BOOOO

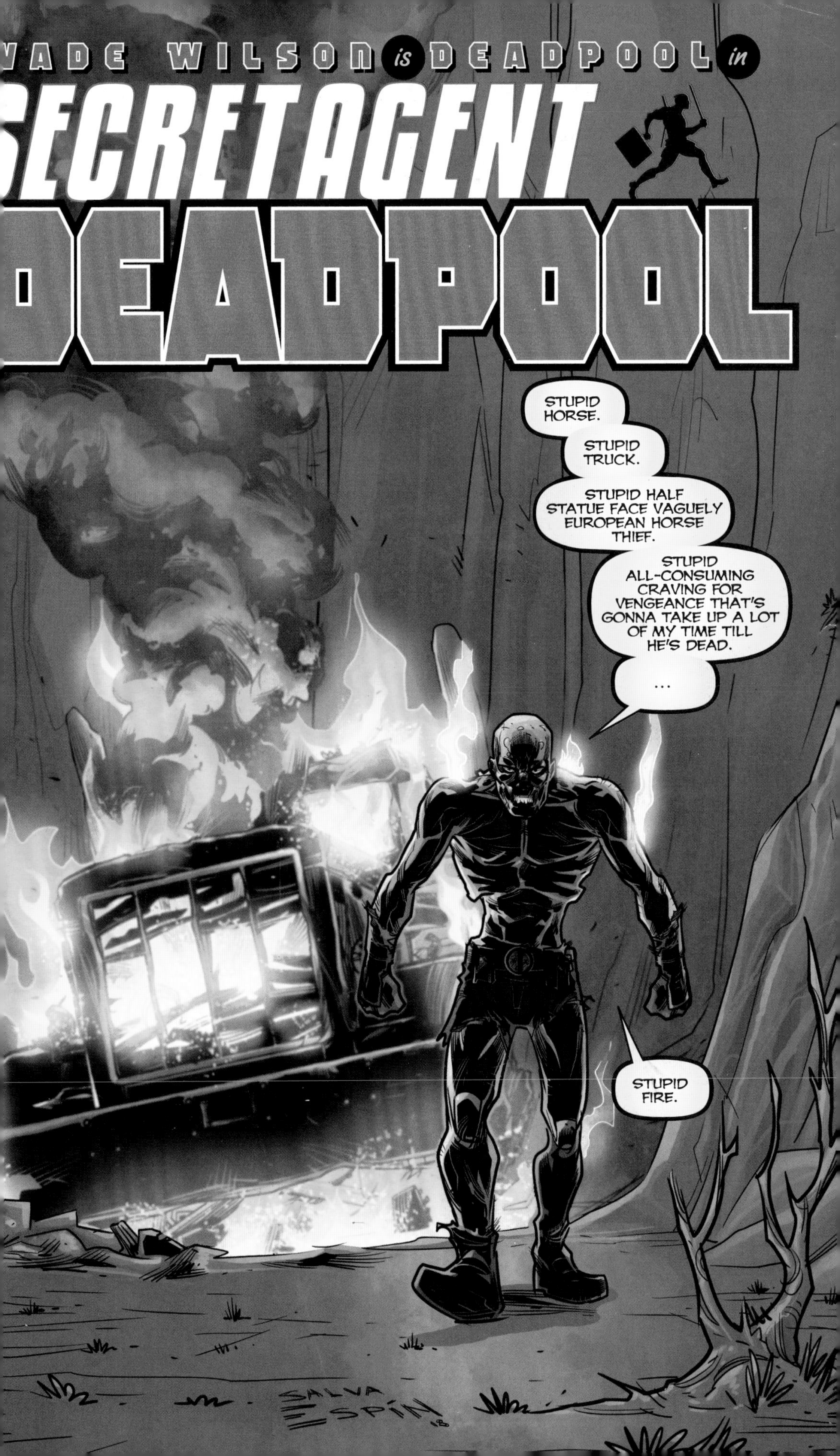
WADE WILSON is DEADPOOL in
SECRET AGENT DEADPOOL
STUPID HORSE.
STUPID TRUCK.
STUPID HALF STATUE FACE VAGUELY EUROPEAN HORSE THIEF.
STUPID ALL-CONSUMING CRAVING FOR VENGEANCE THAT'S GONNA TAKE UP A LOT OF MY TIME TILL HE'S DEAD.
...
STUPID FIRE.
SALVA ESPÍN '18

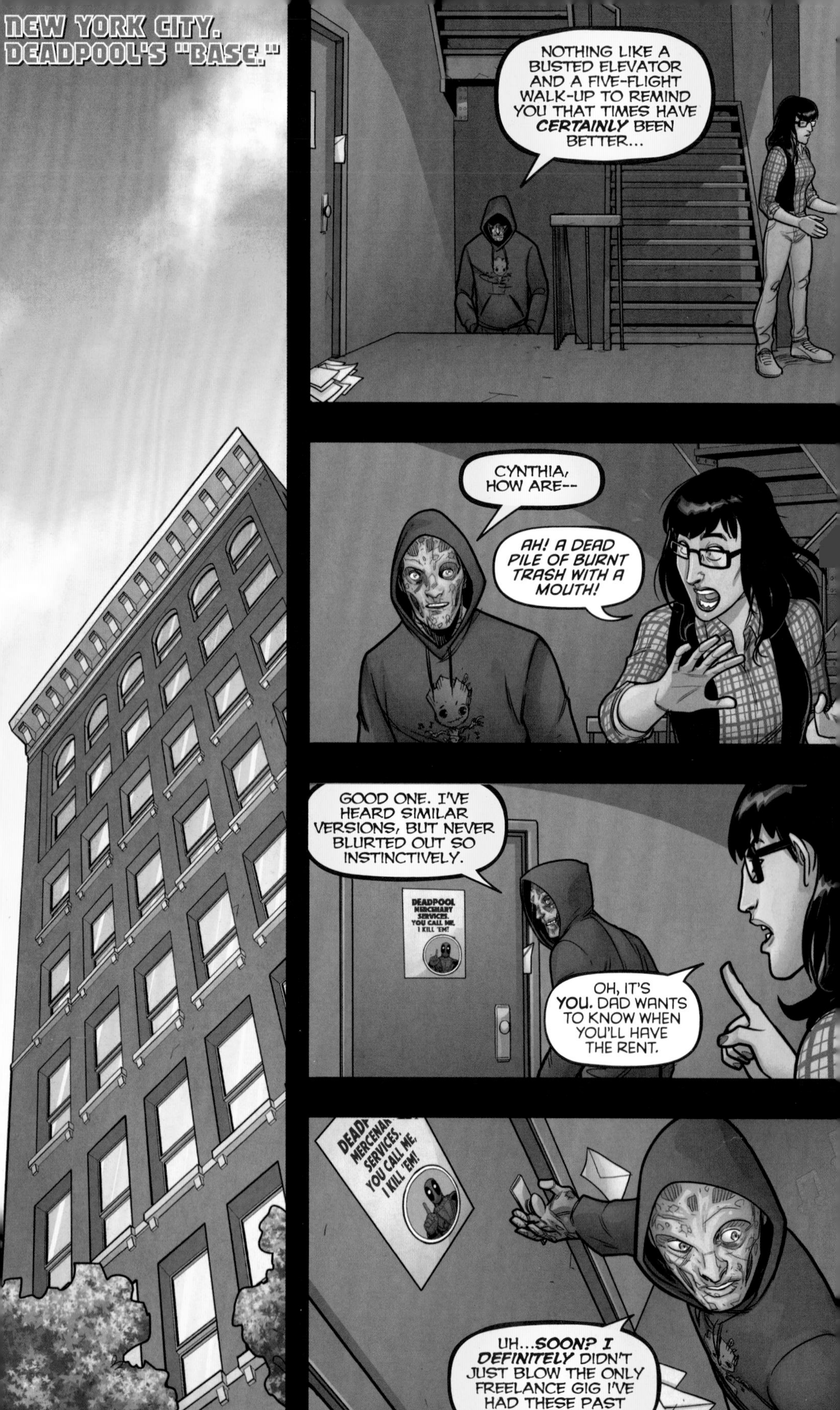
NEW YORK CITY. DEADPOOL'S "BASE."
NOTHING LIKE A BUSTED ELEVATOR AND A FIVE-FLIGHT WALK-UP TO REMIND YOU THAT TIMES HAVE CERTAINLY BEEN BETTER...
CYNTHIA, HOW ARE--
AH! A DEAD PILE OF BURNT TRASH WITH A MOUTH!
GOOD ONE. I'VE HEARD SIMILAR VERSIONS, BUT NEVER BLURTED OUT SO INSTINCTIVELY.
DEADPOOL MERCENARY SERVICES. YOU CALL ME. I KILL 'EM!
OH, IT'S YOU. DAD WANTS TO KNOW WHEN YOU'LL HAVE THE RENT.
UH...SOON? I DEFINITELY DIDN'T JUST BLOW THE ONLY FREELANCE GIG I'VE HAD THESE PAST FEW MONTHS.

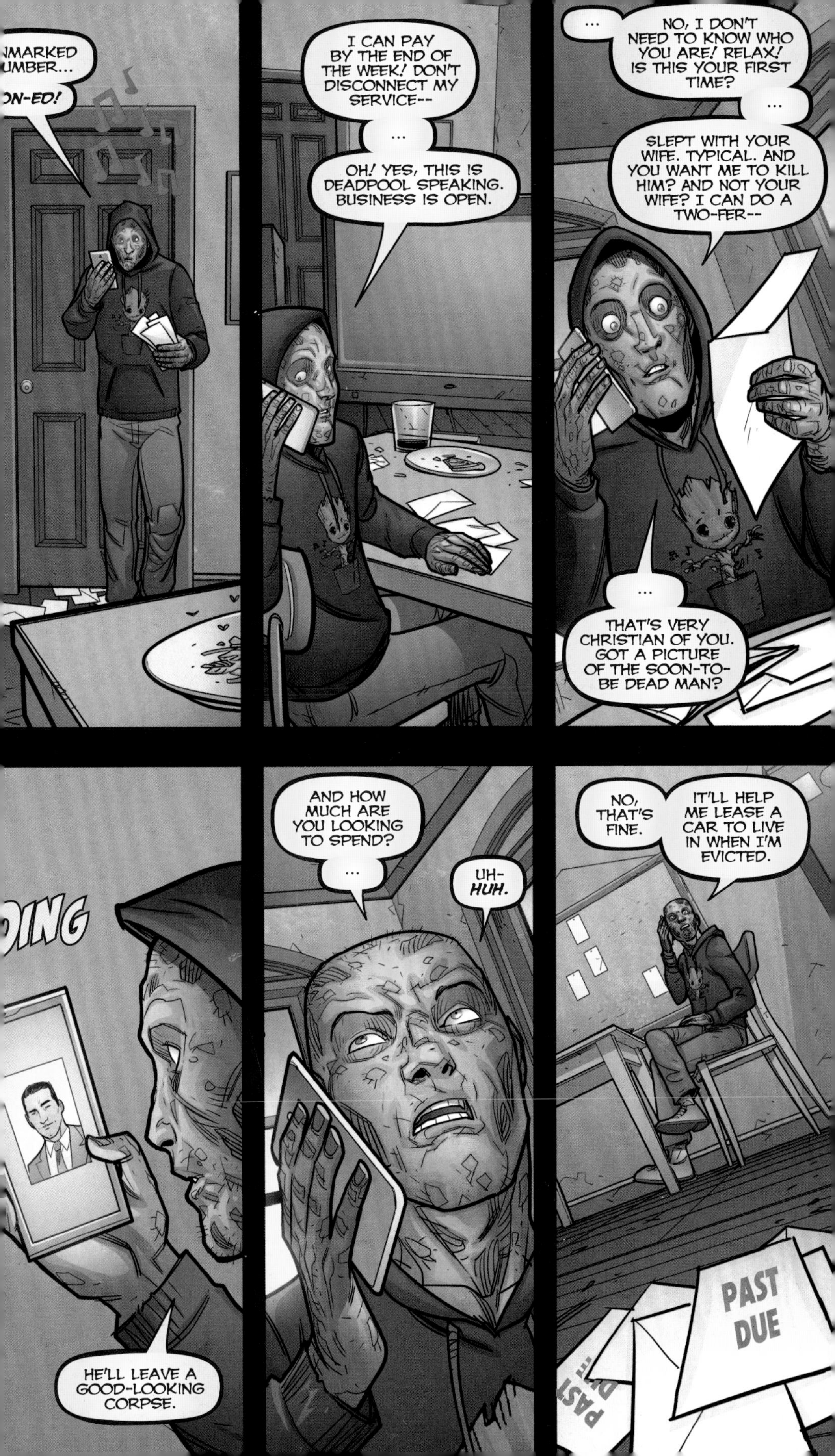

NMARKED
UMBER...
ON-ED!
I CAN PAY BY THE END OF THE WEEK! DON'T DISCONNECT MY SERVICE--
...
OH! YES, THIS IS DEADPOOL SPEAKING. BUSINESS IS OPEN.
...
NO, I DON'T NEED TO KNOW WHO YOU ARE! RELAX! IS THIS YOUR FIRST TIME?
...
SLEPT WITH YOUR WIFE. TYPICAL. AND YOU WANT ME TO KILL HIM? AND NOT YOUR WIFE? I CAN DO A TWO-FER--
...
THAT'S VERY CHRISTIAN OF YOU. GOT A PICTURE OF THE SOON-TO-BE DEAD MAN?
DING
HE'LL LEAVE A GOOD-LOOKING CORPSE.
AND HOW MUCH ARE YOU LOOKING TO SPEND?
...
UH-HUH.
NO, THAT'S FINE.
IT'LL HELP ME LEASE A CAR TO LIVE IN WHEN I'M EVICTED.
PAST DUE
PAST

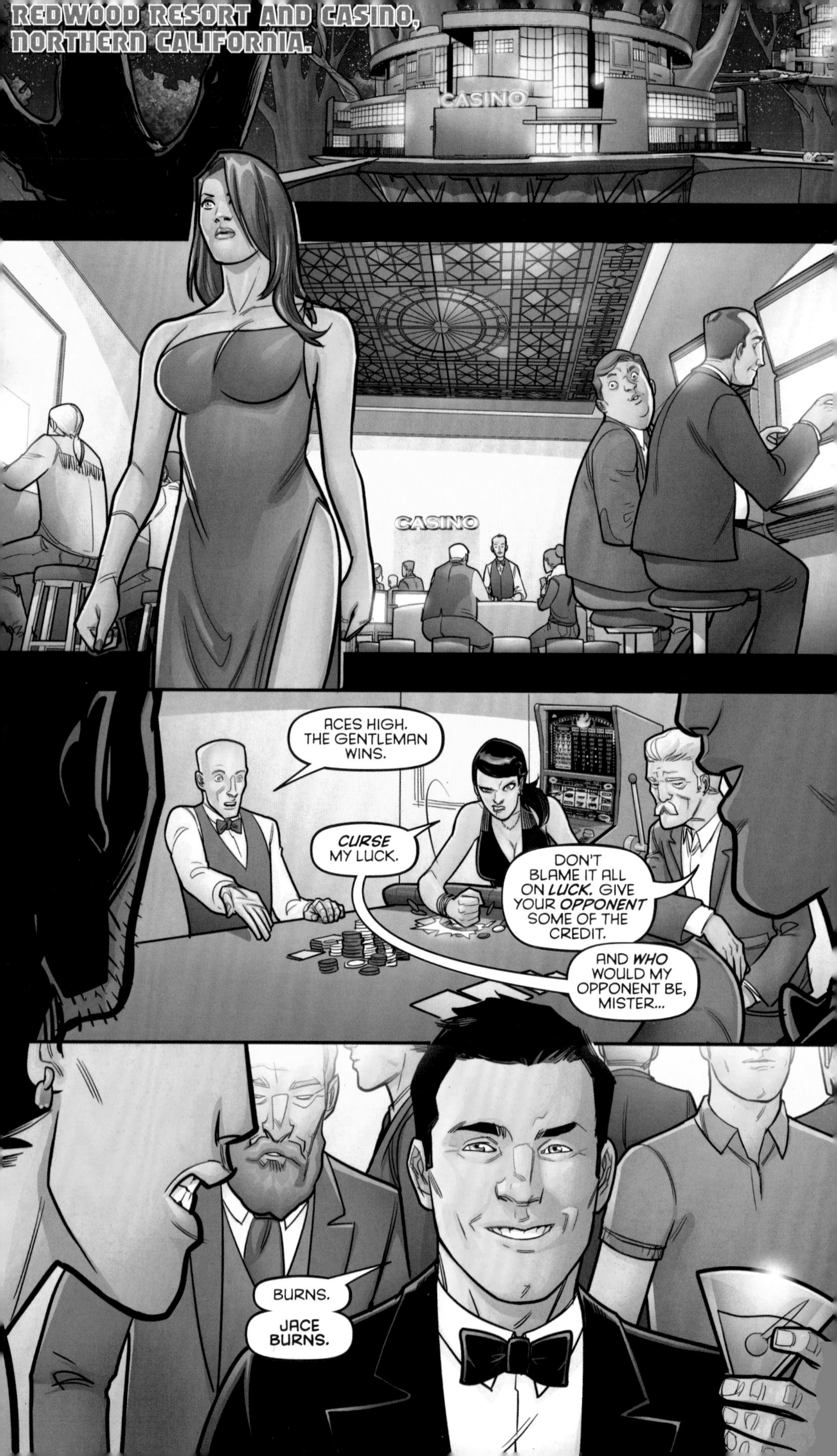
REDWOOD RESORT AND CASINO, NORTHERN CALIFORNIA.
CASINO
CASINO
ACES HIGH. THE GENTLEMAN WINS.
CURSE MY LUCK.
DON'T BLAME IT ALL ON LUCK. GIVE YOUR OPPONENT SOME OF THE CREDIT.
AND WHO WOULD MY OPPONENT BE, MISTER...
BURNS.
JACE BURNS.

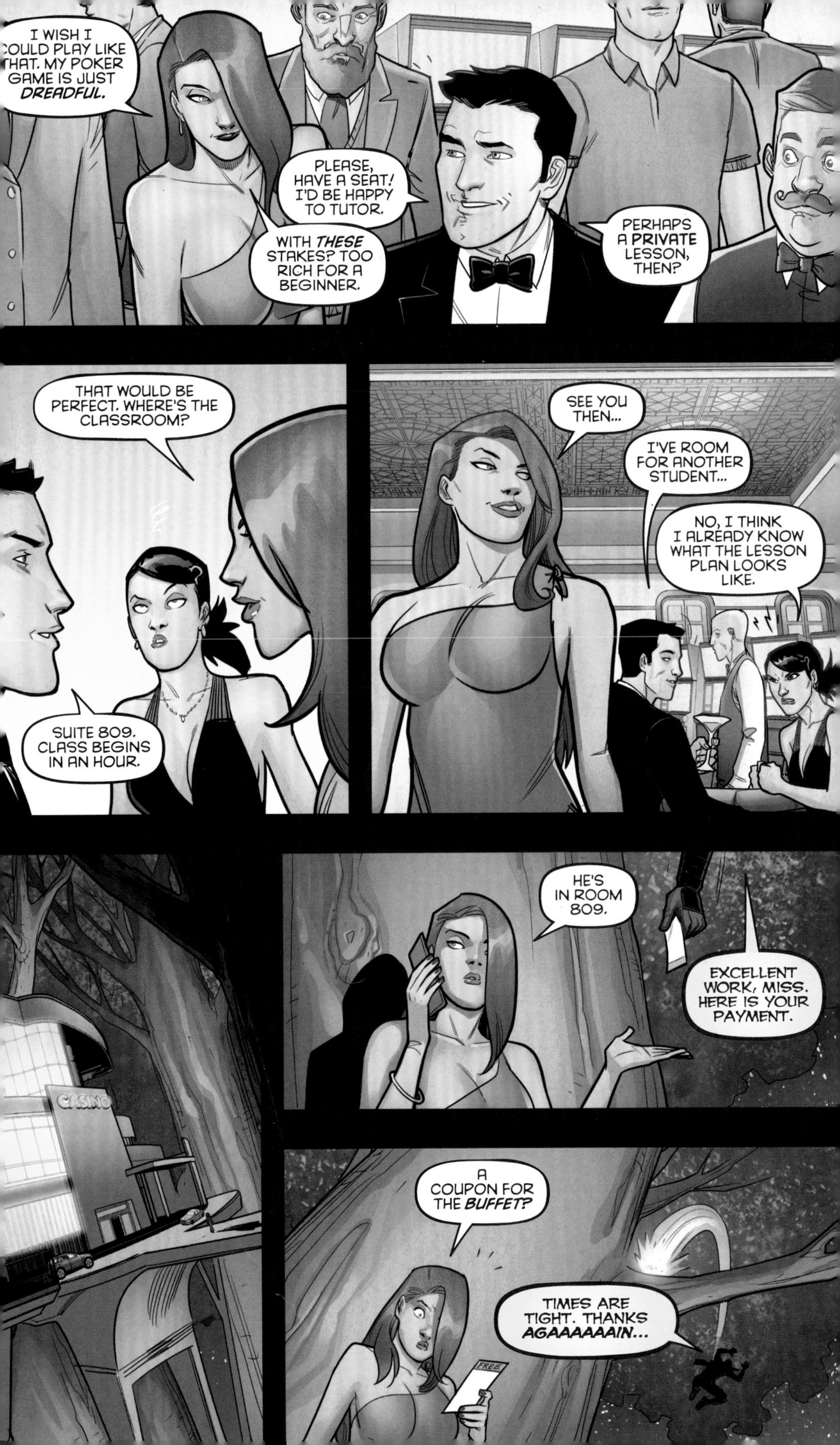

I WISH I COULD PLAY LIKE THAT. MY POKER GAME IS JUST *DREADFUL.*
PLEASE, HAVE A SEAT! I'D BE HAPPY TO TUTOR.
WITH *THESE* STAKES? TOO RICH FOR A BEGINNER.
PERHAPS A **PRIVATE** LESSON, THEN?
THAT WOULD BE PERFECT. WHERE'S THE CLASSROOM?
SUITE 809. CLASS BEGINS IN AN HOUR.
SEE YOU THEN...
I'VE ROOM FOR ANOTHER STUDENT...
NO, I THINK I ALREADY KNOW WHAT THE LESSON PLAN LOOKS LIKE.
CASINO
HE'S IN ROOM 809.
EXCELLENT WORK, MISS. HERE IS YOUR PAYMENT.
A COUPON FOR THE *BUFFET?*
FREE
TIMES ARE TIGHT. THANKS *AGAAAAAAIN...*

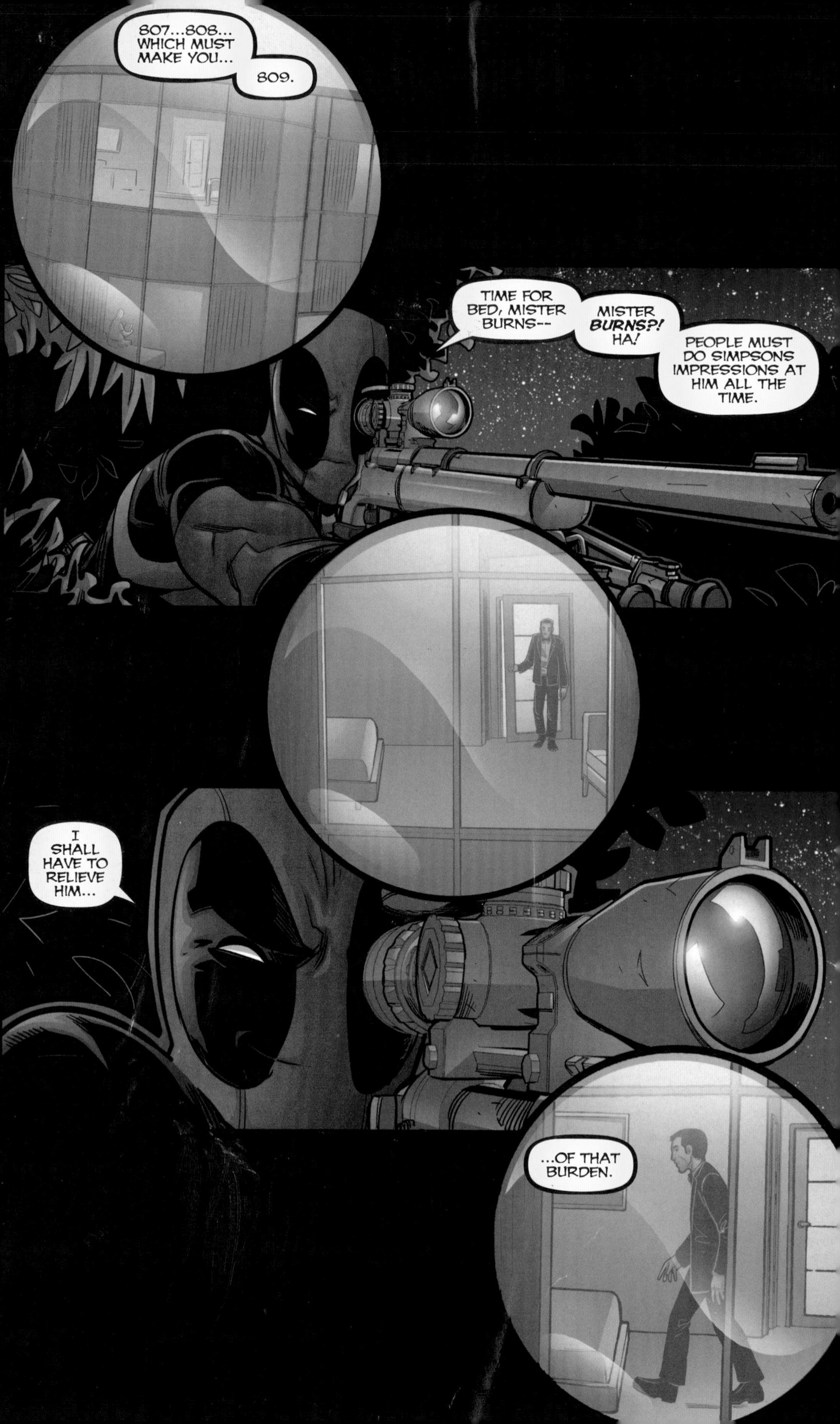
807...808...
WHICH MUST
MAKE YOU...
809.
TIME FOR
BED, MISTER
BURNS--
MISTER
BURNS?!
HA!
PEOPLE MUST
DO SIMPSONS
IMPRESSIONS AT
HIM ALL THE
TIME.
I
SHALL
HAVE TO
RELIEVE
HIM...
...OF THAT
BURDEN.

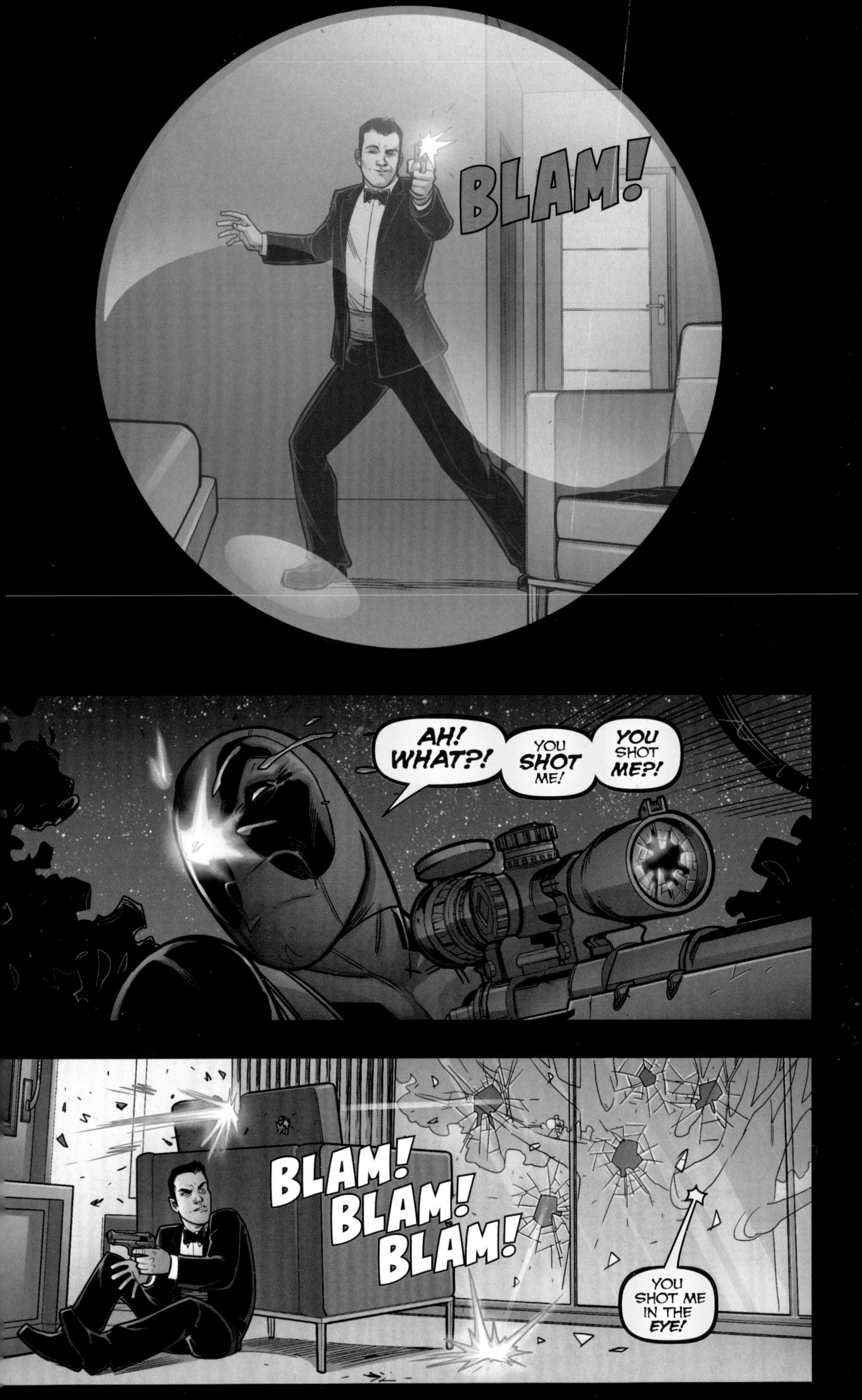
BLAM!
AH! WHAT?!
YOU SHOT ME!
YOU SHOT ME?!
BLAM! BLAM! BLAM!
YOU SHOT ME IN THE EYE!

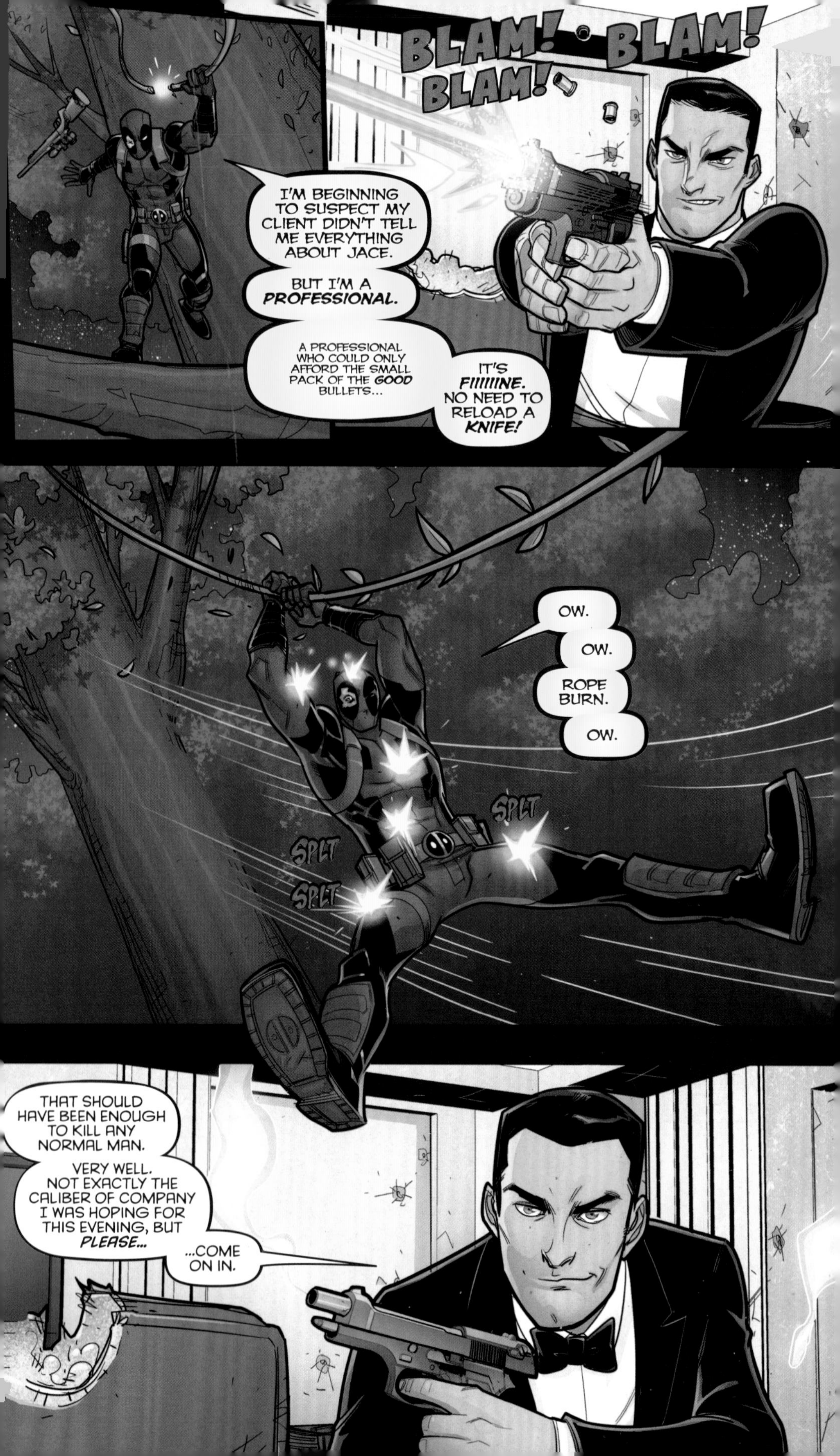
BLAM! BLAM! BLAM!
I'M BEGINNING TO SUSPECT MY CLIENT DIDN'T TELL ME EVERYTHING ABOUT JACE.
BUT I'M A *PROFESSIONAL.*
A PROFESSIONAL WHO COULD ONLY AFFORD THE SMALL PACK OF THE *GOOD* BULLETS...
IT'S *FIIIIIINE.* NO NEED TO RELOAD A *KNIFE!*
OW.
OW.
ROPE BURN.
OW.
SPLT
SPLT
SPLT
THAT SHOULD HAVE BEEN ENOUGH TO KILL ANY NORMAL MAN.
VERY WELL. NOT EXACTLY THE CALIBER OF COMPANY I WAS HOPING FOR THIS EVENING, BUT *PLEASE...*
...COME ON IN.

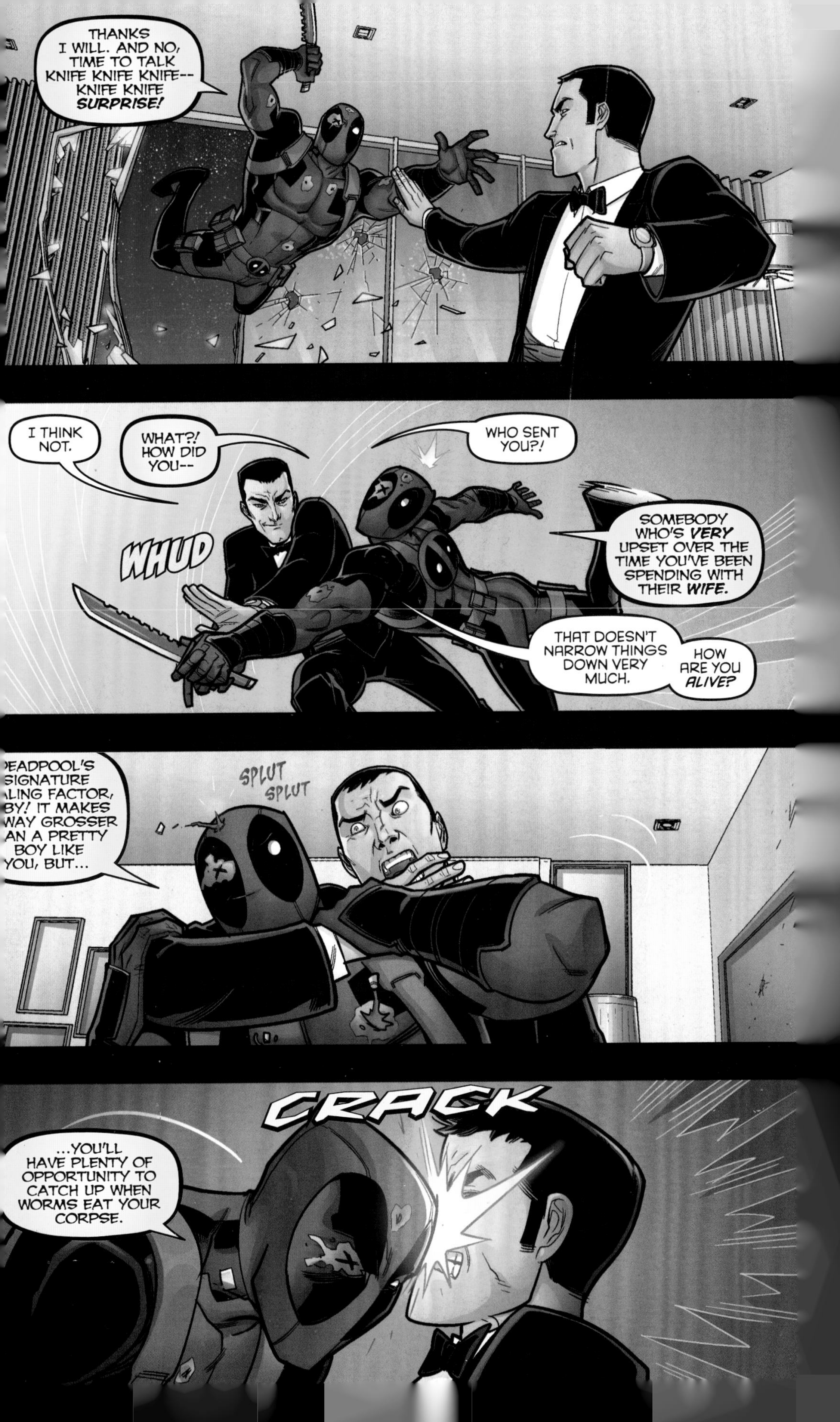
THANKS I WILL. AND NO, TIME TO TALK KNIFE KNIFE KNIFE-- KNIFE KNIFE SURPRISE!
I THINK NOT.
WHAT?! HOW DID YOU--
WHO SENT YOU?!
WHUD
SOMEBODY WHO'S VERY UPSET OVER THE TIME YOU'VE BEEN SPENDING WITH THEIR WIFE.
THAT DOESN'T NARROW THINGS DOWN VERY MUCH.
HOW ARE YOU ALIVE?
EADPOOL'S SIGNATURE LING FACTOR, BY! IT MAKES WAY GROSSER AN A PRETTY BOY LIKE YOU, BUT...
SPLUT SPLUT
CRACK
...YOU'LL HAVE PLENTY OF OPPORTUNITY TO CATCH UP WHEN WORMS EAT YOUR CORPSE.

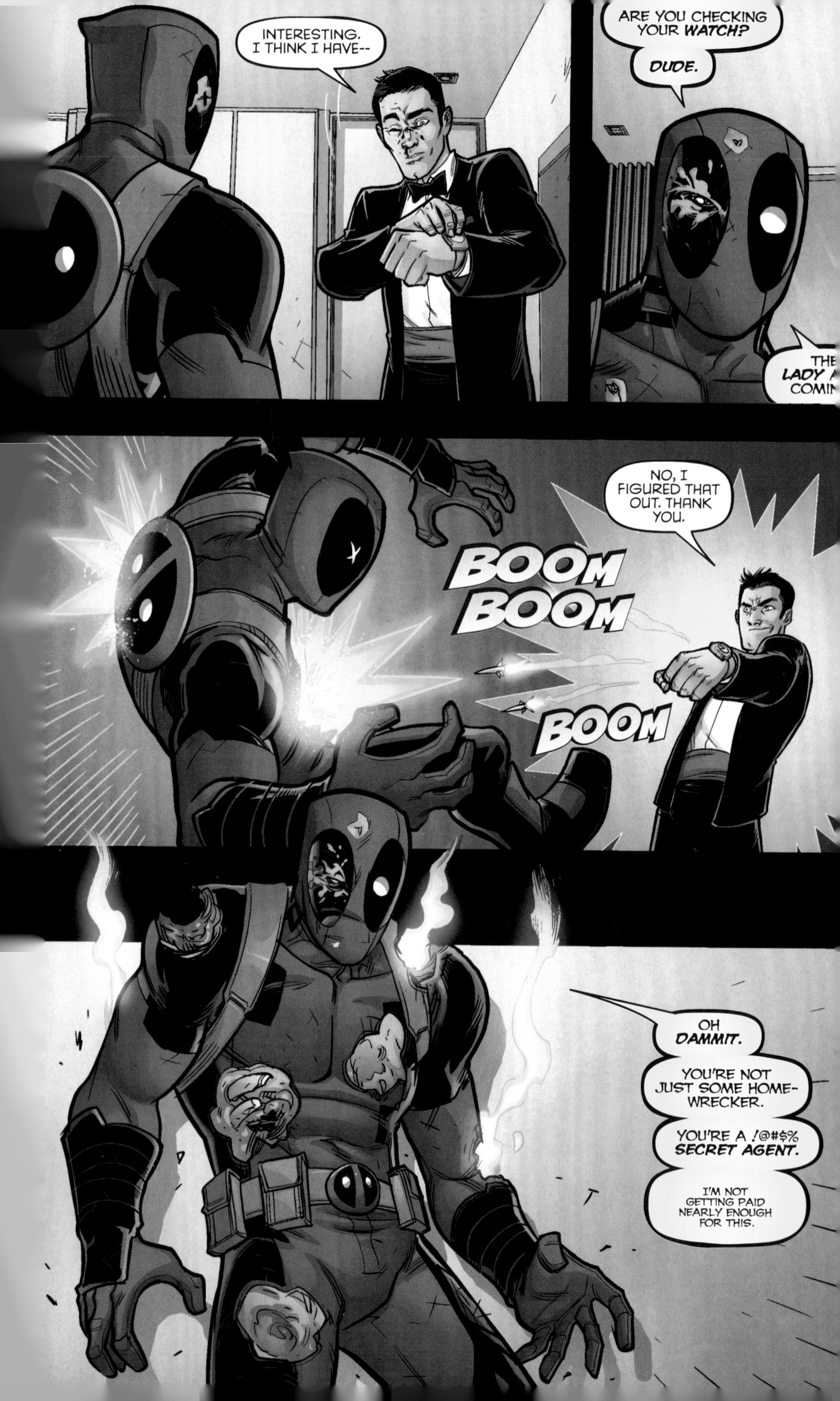
INTERESTING. I THINK I HAVE--
ARE YOU CHECKING YOUR WATCH?
DUDE.
THE LADY COMIN
NO, I FIGURED THAT OUT. THANK YOU.
BOOM
BOOM
BOOM
OH DAMMIT.
YOU'RE NOT JUST SOME HOME-WRECKER.
YOU'RE A !@#$% SECRET AGENT.
I'M NOT GETTING PAID NEARLY ENOUGH FOR THIS.

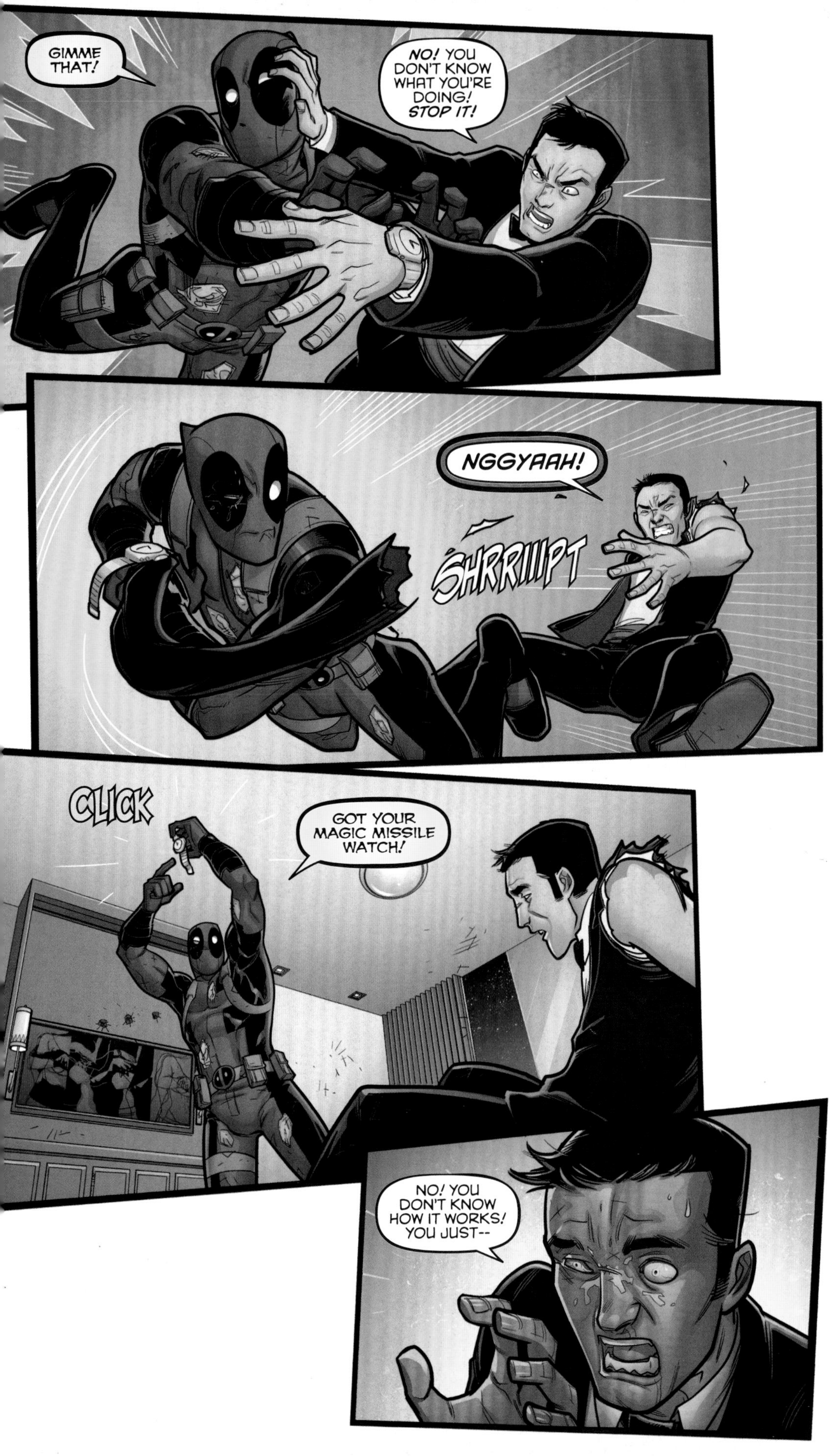
GIMME THAT!
NO! YOU DON'T KNOW WHAT YOU'RE DOING! STOP IT!
NGGYAAH!
SHRRIIIPT
CLICK
GOT YOUR MAGIC MISSILE WATCH!
NO! YOU DON'T KNOW HOW IT WORKS! YOU JUST--

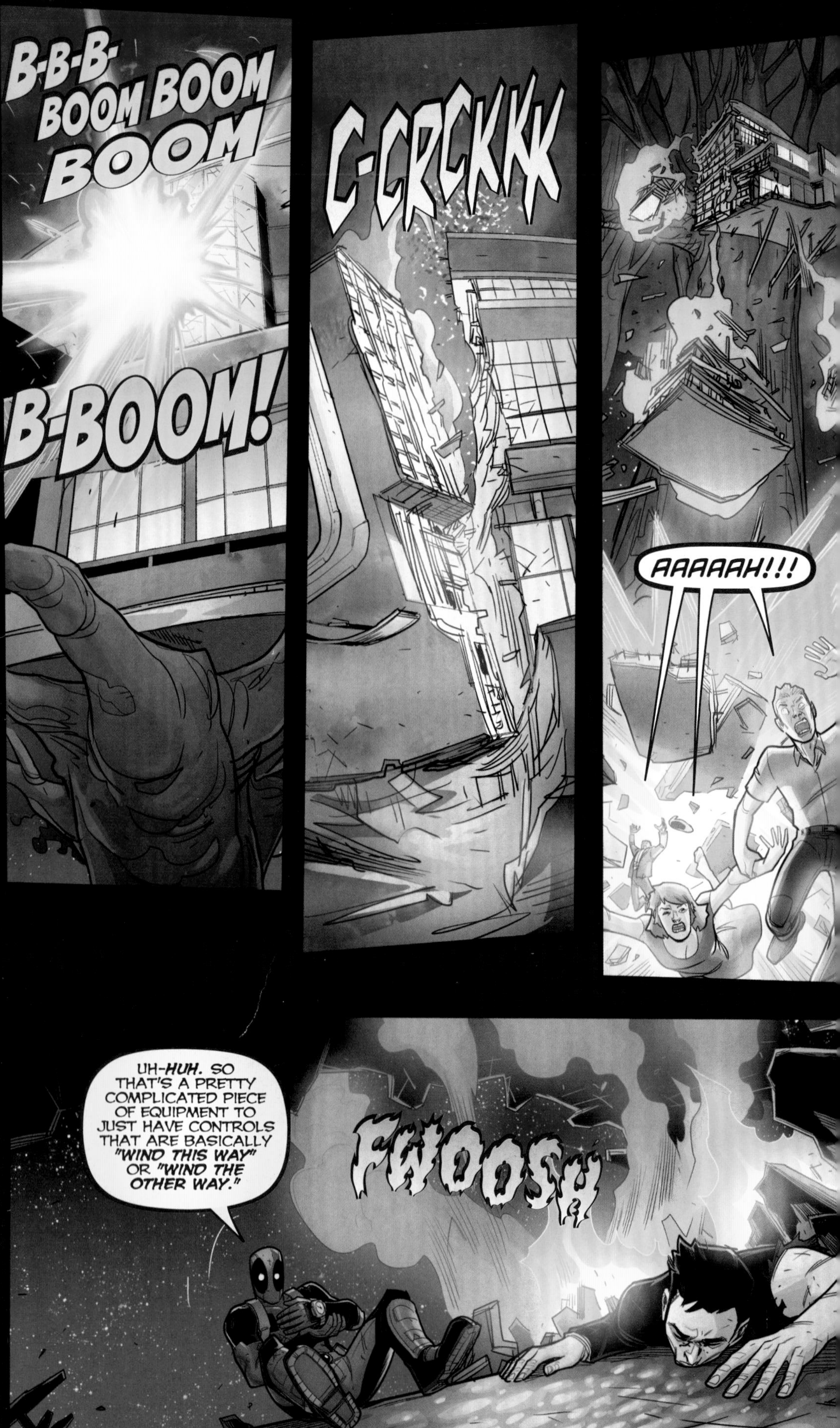
B-B-B-BOOM BOOM BOOM
B-BOOM!
C-CRCKKK
AAAAAH!!!
UH-HUH. SO THAT'S A PRETTY COMPLICATED PIECE OF EQUIPMENT TO JUST HAVE CONTROLS THAT ARE BASICALLY "WIND THIS WAY" OR "WIND THE OTHER WAY."
FWOOSH

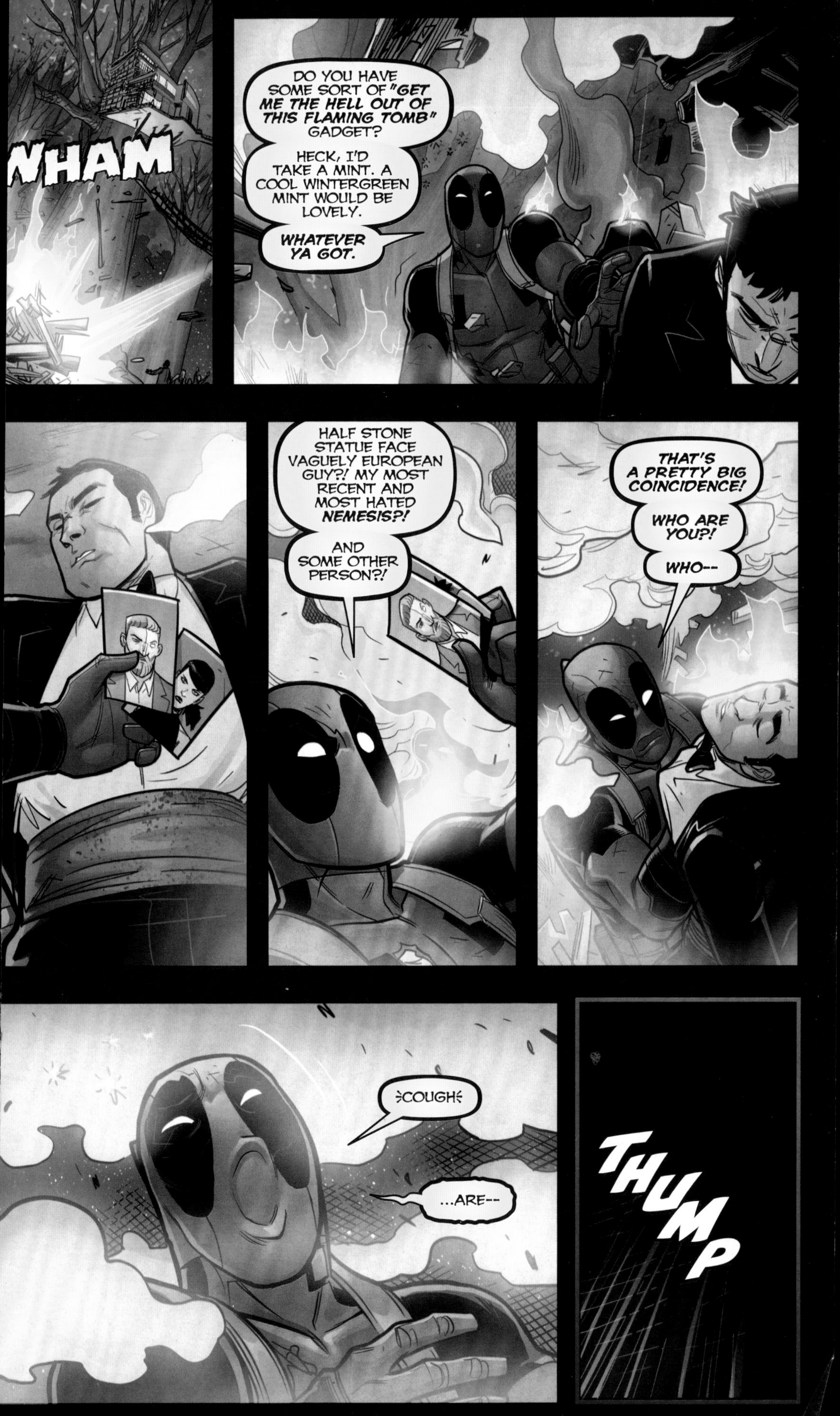
WHAM
DO YOU HAVE SOME SORT OF "GET ME THE HELL OUT OF THIS FLAMING TOMB" GADGET?
HECK, I'D TAKE A MINT. A COOL WINTERGREEN MINT WOULD BE LOVELY.
WHATEVER YA GOT.
HALF STONE STATUE FACE VAGUELY EUROPEAN GUY?! MY MOST RECENT AND MOST HATED NEMESIS?!
AND SOME OTHER PERSON?!
THAT'S A PRETTY BIG COINCIDENCE!
WHO ARE YOU?!
WHO--
COUGH
...ARE--
THUMP

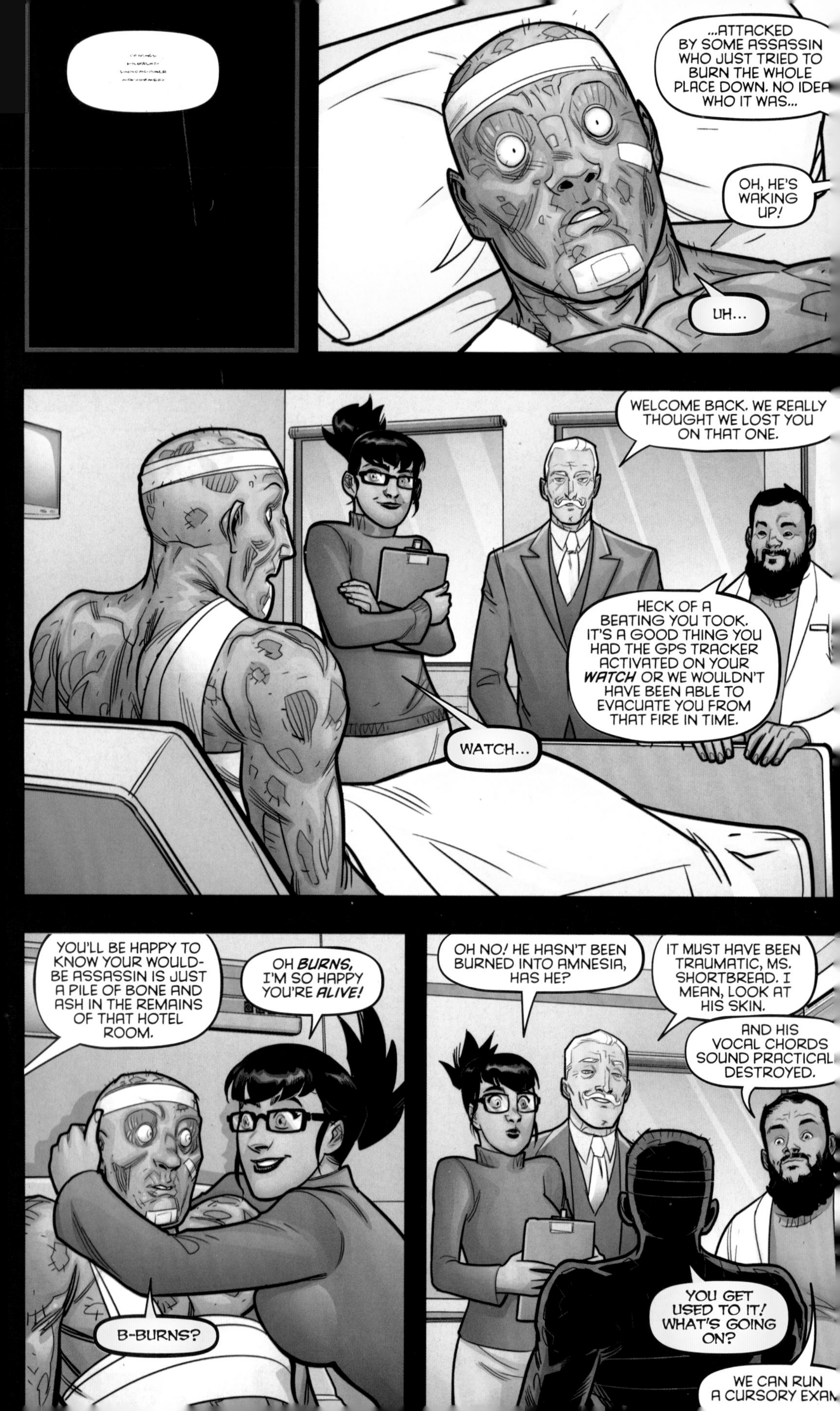

...ATTACKED BY SOME ASSASSIN WHO JUST TRIED TO BURN THE WHOLE PLACE DOWN. NO IDEA WHO IT WAS...
OH, HE'S WAKING UP!
UH...
WELCOME BACK. WE REALLY THOUGHT WE LOST YOU ON THAT ONE.
HECK OF A BEATING YOU TOOK. IT'S A GOOD THING YOU HAD THE GPS TRACKER ACTIVATED ON YOUR *WATCH* OR WE WOULDN'T HAVE BEEN ABLE TO EVACUATE YOU FROM THAT FIRE IN TIME.
WATCH...
YOU'LL BE HAPPY TO KNOW YOUR WOULD-BE ASSASSIN IS JUST A PILE OF BONE AND ASH IN THE REMAINS OF THAT HOTEL ROOM.
OH *BURNS,* I'M SO HAPPY YOU'RE *ALIVE!*
B-BURNS?
OH NO! HE HASN'T BEEN BURNED INTO AMNESIA, HAS HE?
IT MUST HAVE BEEN TRAUMATIC, MS. SHORTBREAD. I MEAN, LOOK AT HIS SKIN.
AND HIS VOCAL CHORDS SOUND PRACTICAL DESTROYED.
YOU GET USED TO IT! WHAT'S GOING ON?
WE CAN RUN A CURSORY EXAM

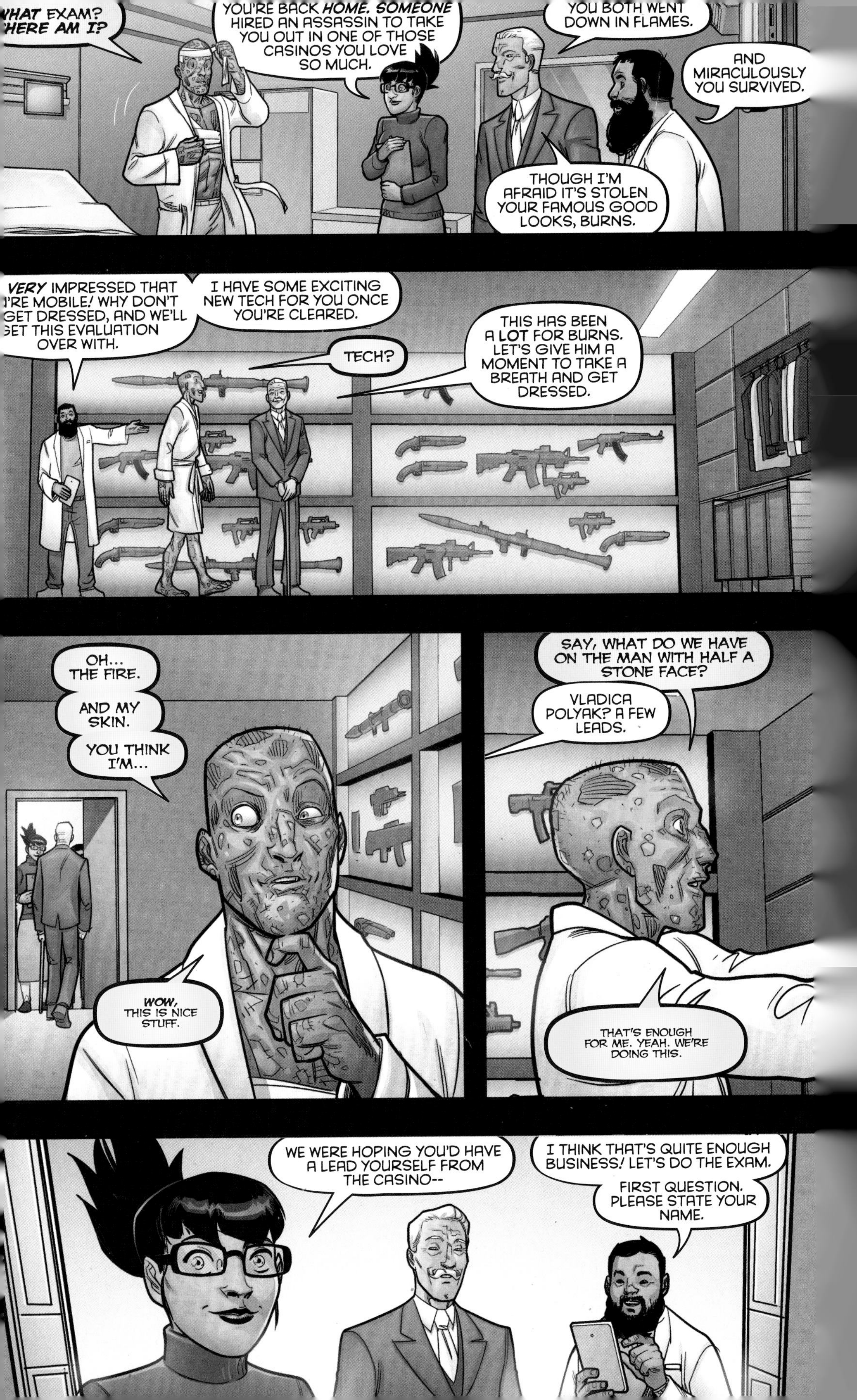
HAT EXAM? HERE AM I?
YOU'RE BACK *HOME. SOMEONE* HIRED AN ASSASSIN TO TAKE YOU OUT IN ONE OF THOSE CASINOS YOU LOVE SO MUCH.
YOU BOTH WENT DOWN IN FLAMES.
AND MIRACULOUSLY YOU SURVIVED.
THOUGH I'M AFRAID IT'S STOLEN YOUR FAMOUS GOOD LOOKS, BURNS.
VERY IMPRESSED THAT 'RE MOBILE! WHY DON'T GET DRESSED, AND WE'LL GET THIS EVALUATION OVER WITH.
I HAVE SOME EXCITING NEW TECH FOR YOU ONCE YOU'RE CLEARED.
TECH?
THIS HAS BEEN A **LOT** FOR BURNS. LET'S GIVE HIM A MOMENT TO TAKE A BREATH AND GET DRESSED.
OH... THE FIRE.
AND MY SKIN.
YOU THINK I'M...
WOW, THIS IS NICE STUFF.
SAY, WHAT DO WE HAVE ON THE MAN WITH HALF A STONE FACE?
VLADICA POLYAK? A FEW LEADS.
THAT'S ENOUGH FOR ME. YEAH. WE'RE DOING THIS.
WE WERE HOPING YOU'D HAVE A LEAD YOURSELF FROM THE CASINO--
I THINK THAT'S QUITE ENOUGH BUSINESS! LET'S DO THE EXAM.
FIRST QUESTION. PLEASE STATE YOUR NAME.

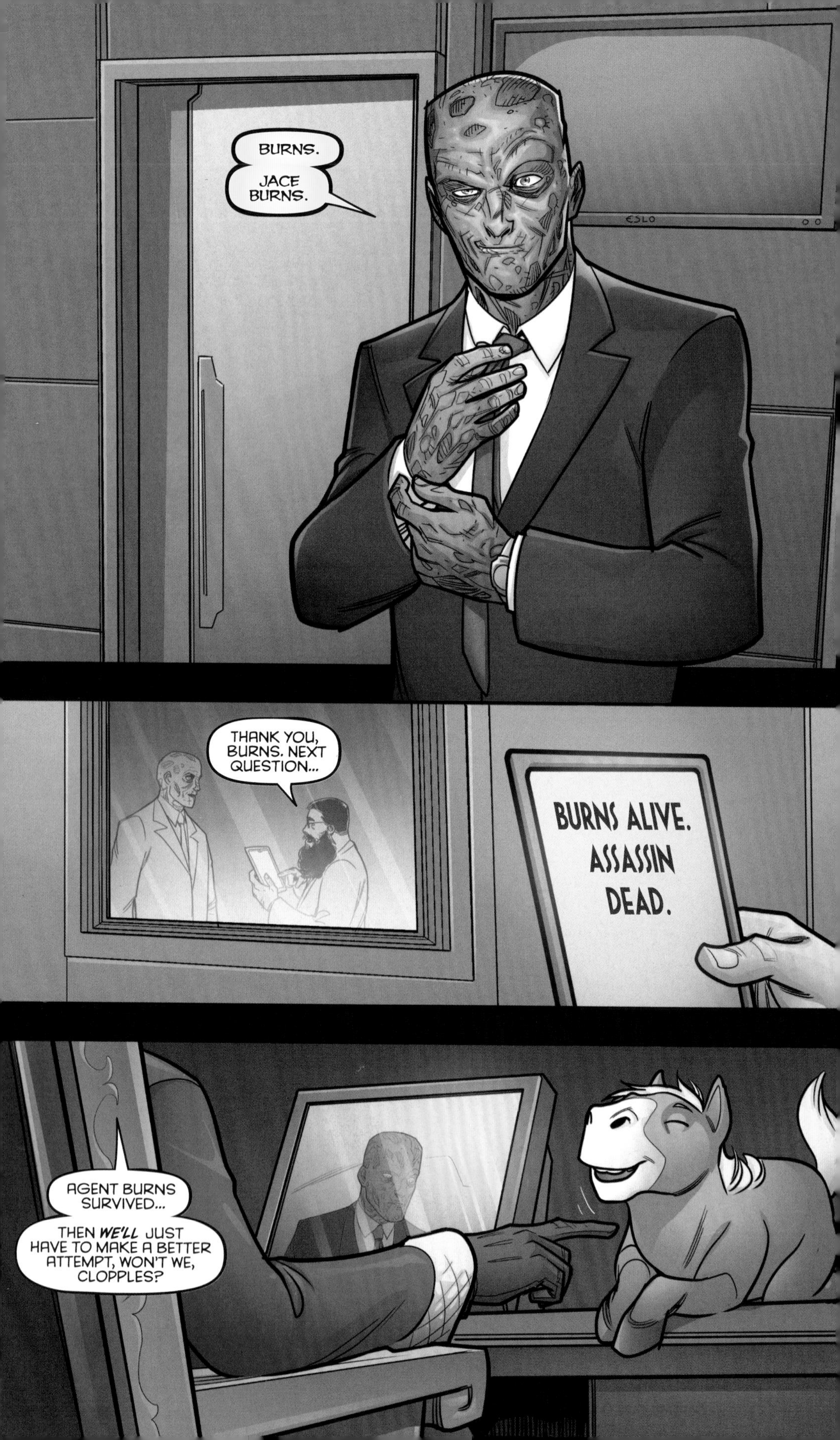
BURNS.
JACE BURNS.
THANK YOU, BURNS. NEXT QUESTION...
BURNS ALIVE. ASSASSIN DEAD.
AGENT BURNS SURVIVED...
THEN WE'LL JUST HAVE TO MAKE A BETTER ATTEMPT, WON'T WE, CLOPPLES?

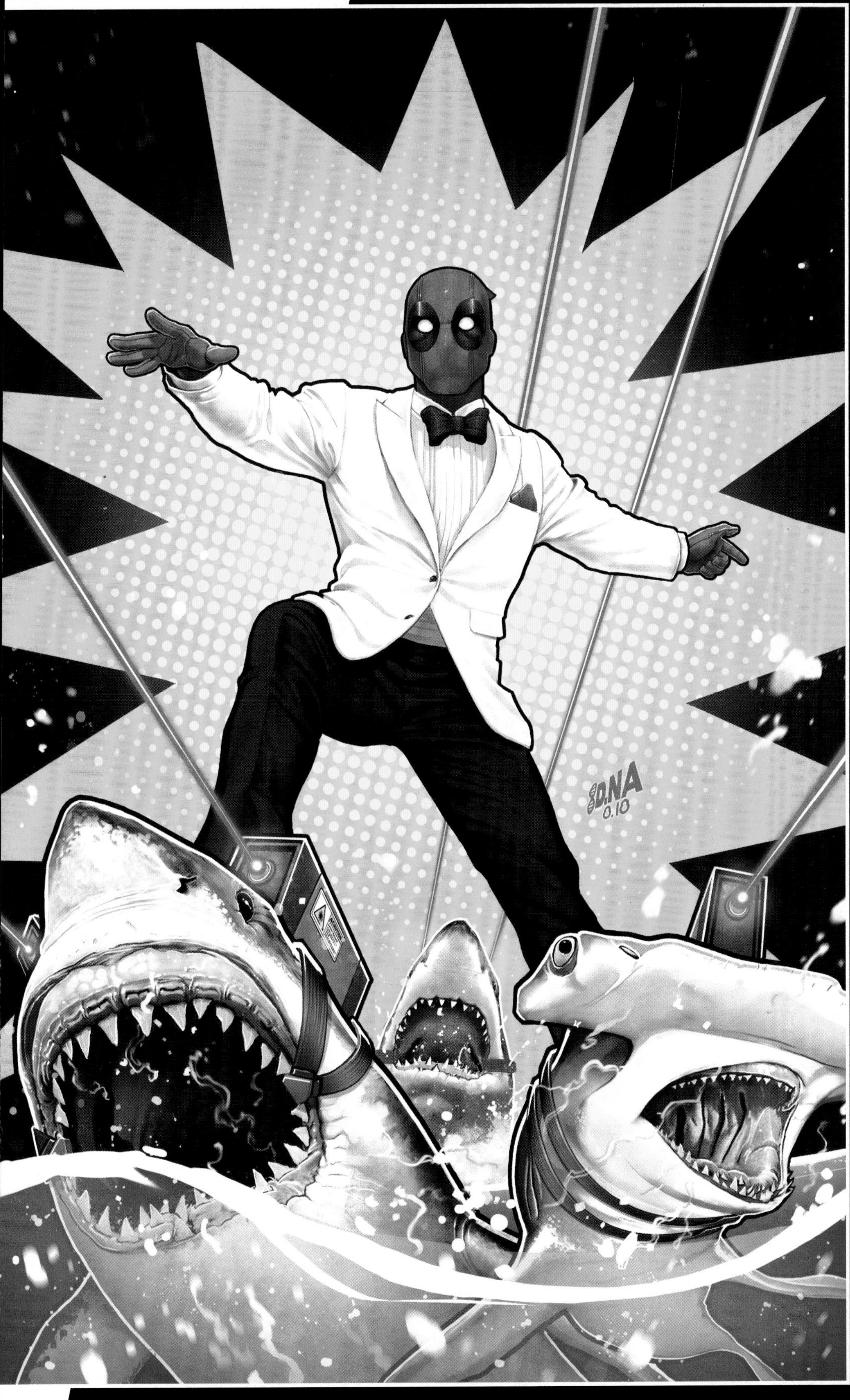
D.NA
8.18

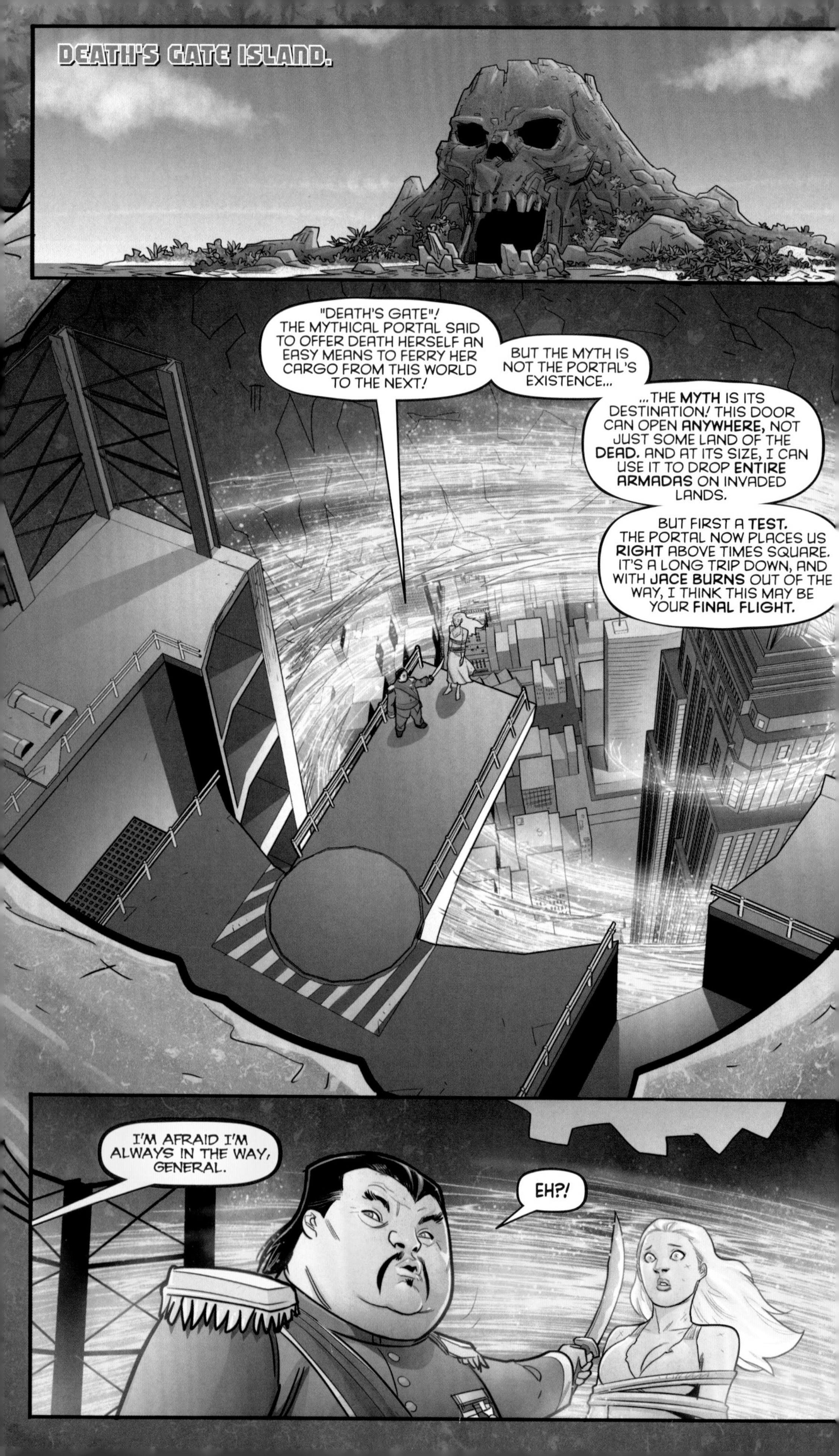
DEATH'S GATE ISLAND.
"DEATH'S GATE"! THE MYTHICAL PORTAL SAID TO OFFER DEATH HERSELF AN EASY MEANS TO FERRY HER CARGO FROM THIS WORLD TO THE NEXT!
BUT THE MYTH IS NOT THE PORTAL'S EXISTENCE...
...THE MYTH IS ITS DESTINATION! THIS DOOR CAN OPEN ANYWHERE, NOT JUST SOME LAND OF THE DEAD. AND AT ITS SIZE, I CAN USE IT TO DROP ENTIRE ARMADAS ON INVADED LANDS.
BUT FIRST A TEST. THE PORTAL NOW PLACES US RIGHT ABOVE TIMES SQUARE. IT'S A LONG TRIP DOWN, AND WITH JACE BURNS OUT OF THE WAY, I THINK THIS MAY BE YOUR FINAL FLIGHT.
I'M AFRAID I'M ALWAYS IN THE WAY, GENERAL.
EH?!

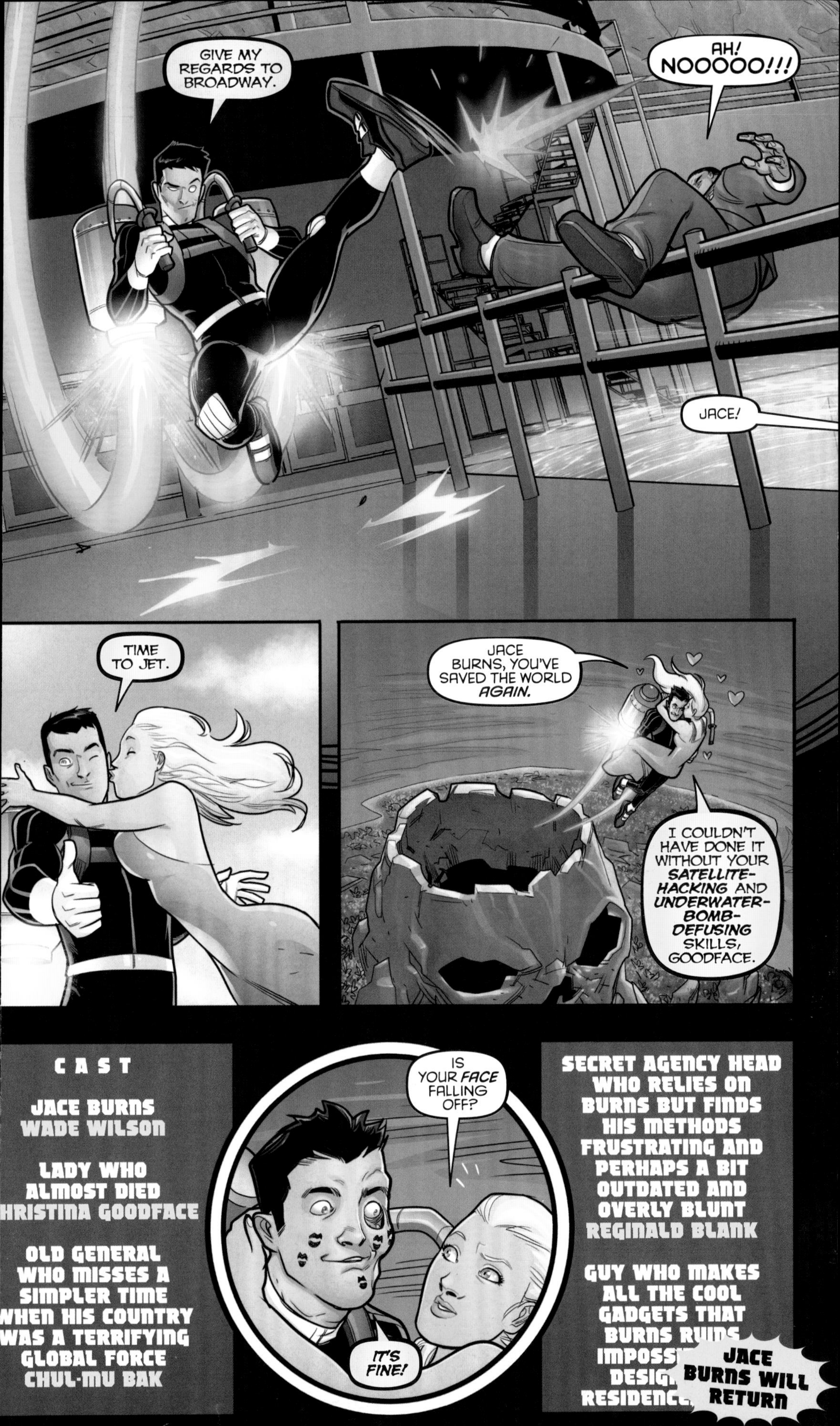

GIVE MY REGARDS TO BROADWAY.
AH! NOOOOO!!!
JACE!
TIME TO JET.
JACE BURNS, YOU'VE SAVED THE WORLD *AGAIN.*
I COULDN'T HAVE DONE IT WITHOUT YOUR ***SATELLITE-HACKING*** AND ***UNDERWATER-BOMB-DEFUSING*** SKILLS, GOODFACE.
CAST
JACE BURNS
WADE WILSON
LADY WHO ALMOST DIED
HRISTINA GOODFACE
OLD GENERAL WHO MISSES A SIMPLER TIME
HEN HIS COUNTRY
AS A TERRIFYING GLOBAL FORCE
CHUL-MU BAK
IS YOUR *FACE* FALLING OFF?
IT'S FINE!
SECRET AGENCY HEAD WHO RELIES ON BURNS BUT FINDS HIS METHODS FRUSTRATING AND PERHAPS A BIT OUTDATED AND OVERLY BLUNT
REGINALD BLANK
GUY WHO MAKES ALL THE COOL GADGETS THAT BURNS RUI
IMPOSS
DESIG
RESIDENCE
JACE BURNS WILL RETURN

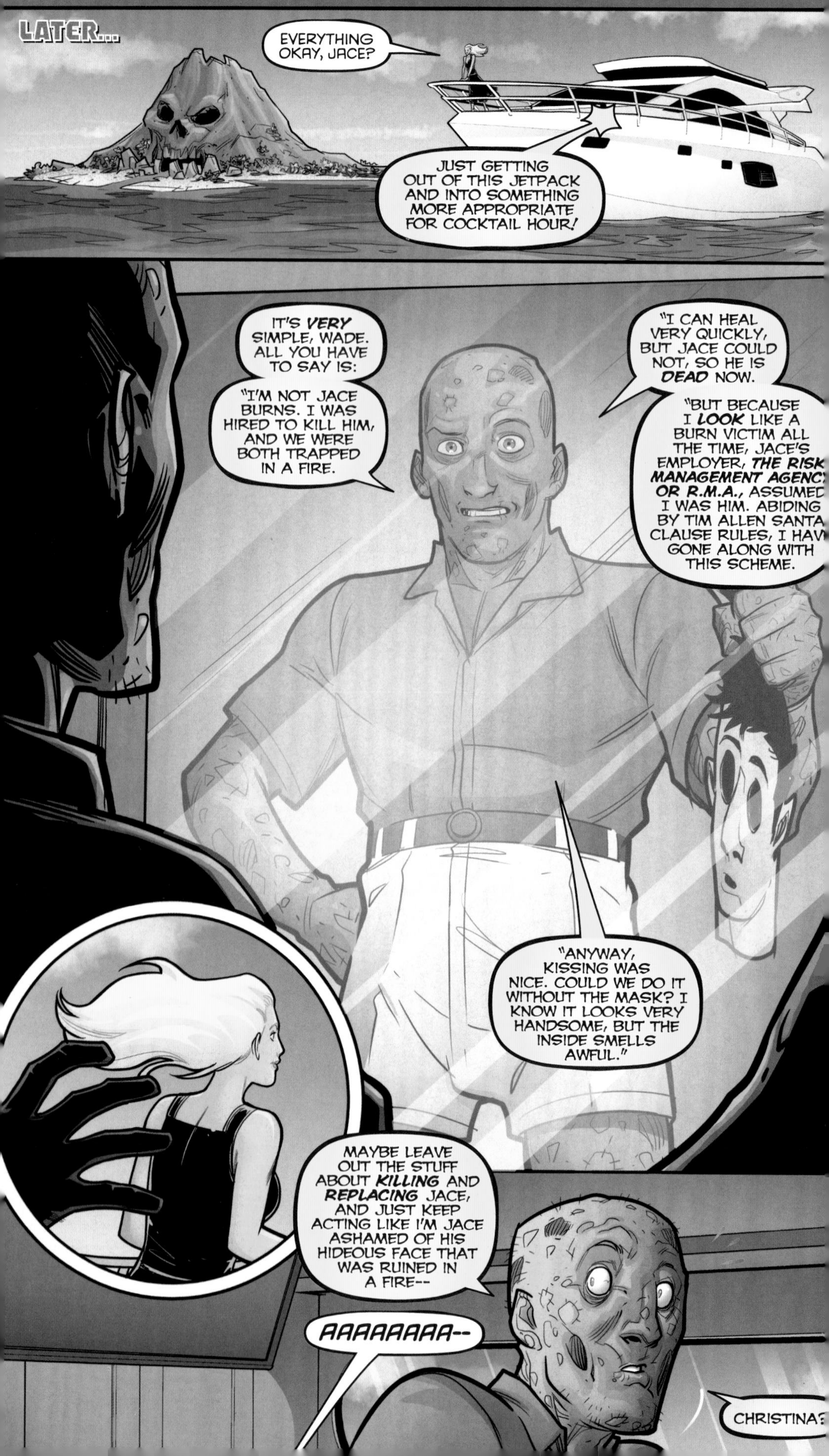
LATER...
EVERYTHING OKAY, JACE?
JUST GETTING OUT OF THIS JETPACK AND INTO SOMETHING MORE APPROPRIATE FOR COCKTAIL HOUR!
IT'S VERY SIMPLE, WADE. ALL YOU HAVE TO SAY IS:
"I'M NOT JACE BURNS. I WAS HIRED TO KILL HIM, AND WE WERE BOTH TRAPPED IN A FIRE.
"I CAN HEAL VERY QUICKLY, BUT JACE COULD NOT, SO HE IS DEAD NOW.
"BUT BECAUSE I LOOK LIKE A BURN VICTIM ALL THE TIME, JACE'S EMPLOYER, THE RISK MANAGEMENT AGENCY OR R.M.A., ASSUMED I WAS HIM. ABIDING BY TIM ALLEN SANTA CLAUSE RULES, I HAVE GONE ALONG WITH THIS SCHEME.
"ANYWAY, KISSING WAS NICE. COULD WE DO IT WITHOUT THE MASK? I KNOW IT LOOKS VERY HANDSOME, BUT THE INSIDE SMELLS AWFUL."
MAYBE LEAVE OUT THE STUFF ABOUT KILLING AND REPLACING JACE, AND JUST KEEP ACTING LIKE I'M JACE ASHAMED OF HIS HIDEOUS FACE THAT WAS RUINED IN A FIRE--
AAAAAAAA--
CHRISTINA?

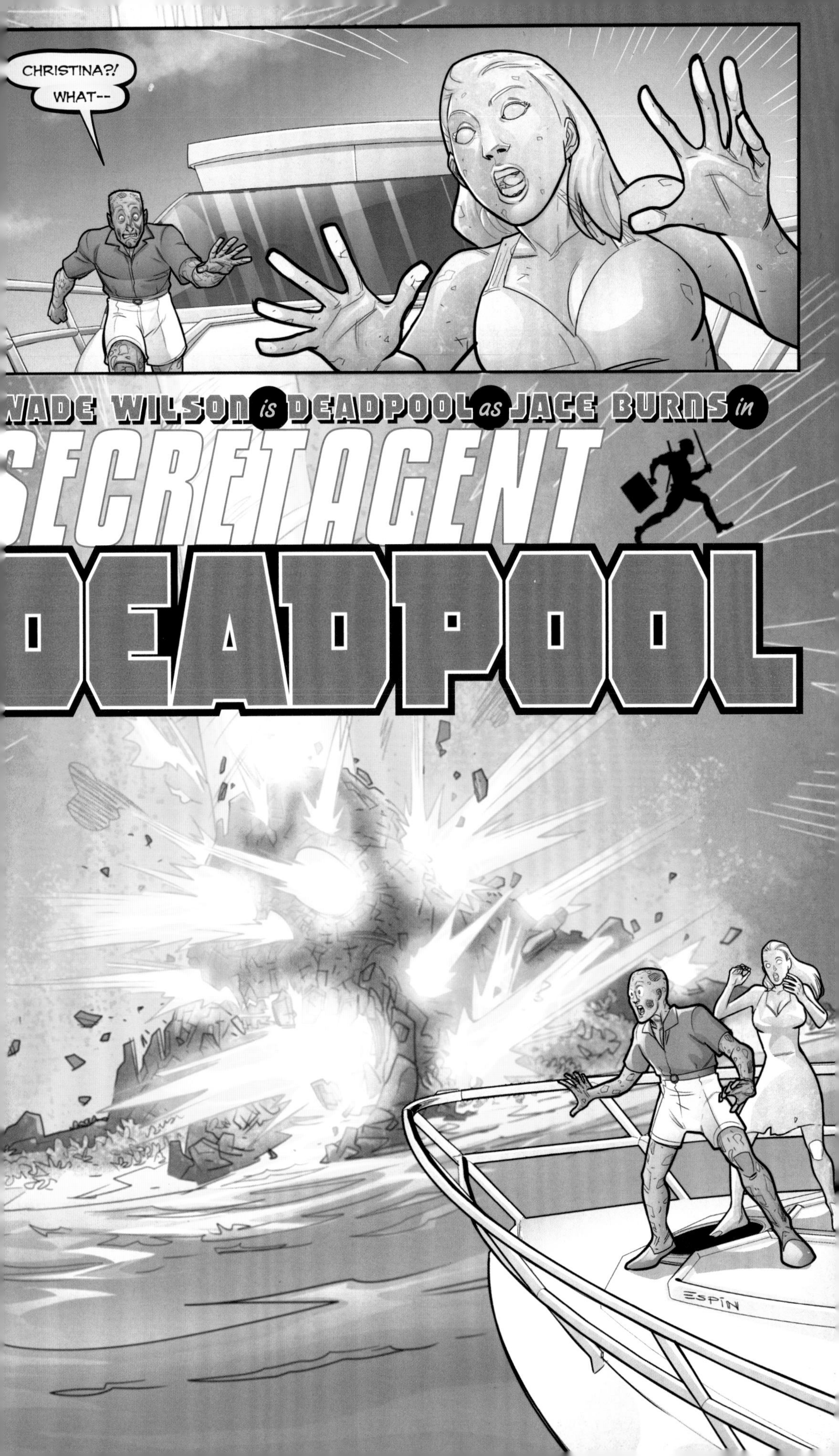
CHRISTINA?! WHAT--
WADE WILSON is DEADPOOL as JACE BURNS in
SECRET AGENT
DEADPOOL
ESPIN

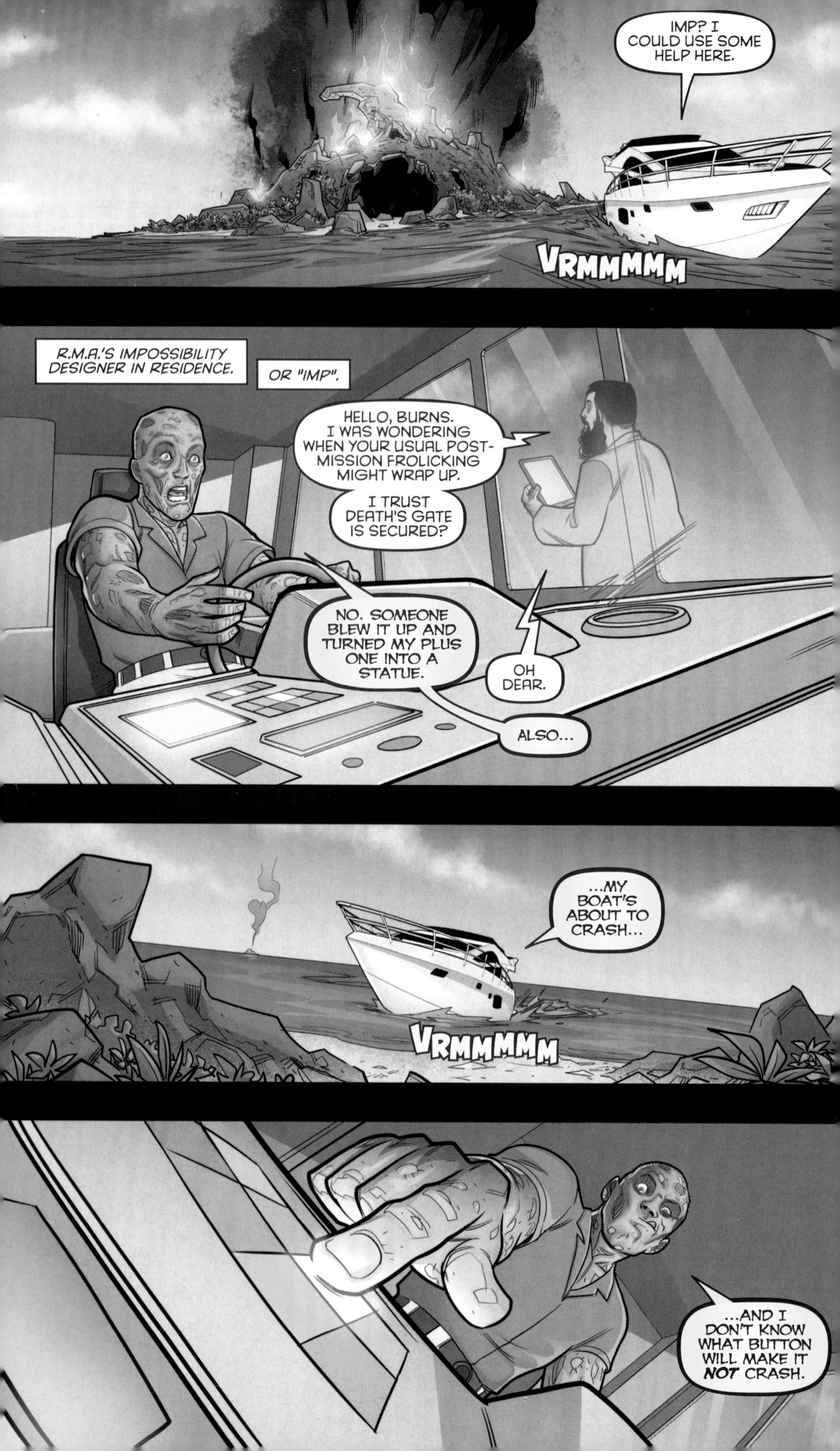
IMP? I COULD USE SOME HELP HERE.
VRMMMMM
R.M.A.'S IMPOSSIBILITY DESIGNER IN RESIDENCE.
OR "IMP".
HELLO, BURNS. I WAS WONDERING WHEN YOUR USUAL POST-MISSION FROLICKING MIGHT WRAP UP.
I TRUST DEATH'S GATE IS SECURED?
NO. SOMEONE BLEW IT UP AND TURNED MY PLUS ONE INTO A STATUE.
OH DEAR.
ALSO...
...MY BOAT'S ABOUT TO CRASH...
VRMMMMM
...AND I DON'T KNOW WHAT BUTTON WILL MAKE IT ***NOT*** CRASH.

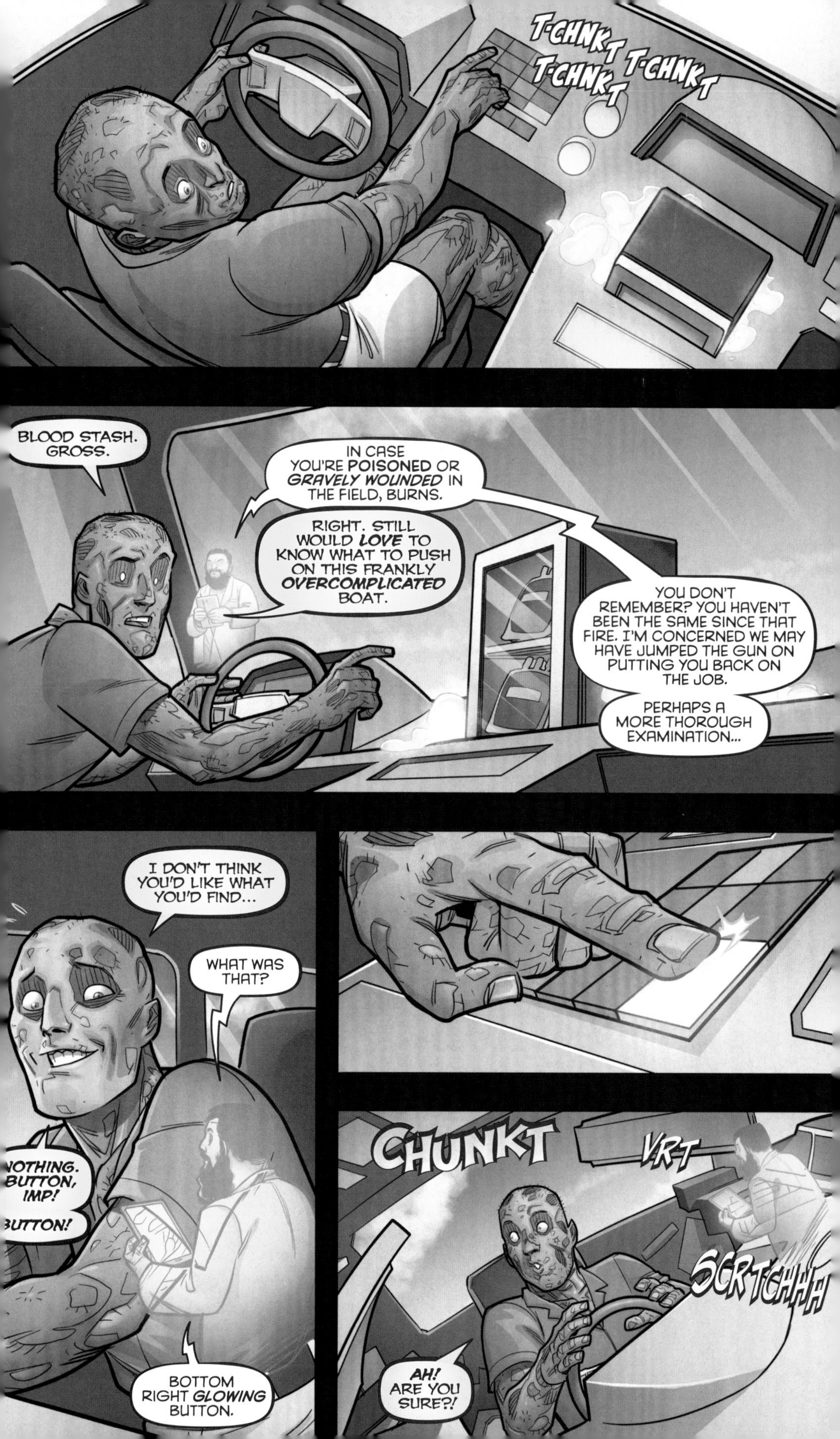
T-CHNKT T-CHNKT T-CHNKT
BLOOD STASH. GROSS.
IN CASE YOU'RE **POISONED** OR ***GRAVELY WOUNDED*** IN THE FIELD, BURNS.
RIGHT. STILL WOULD ***LOVE*** TO KNOW WHAT TO PUSH ON THIS FRANKLY ***OVERCOMPLICATED*** BOAT.
YOU DON'T REMEMBER? YOU HAVEN'T BEEN THE SAME SINCE THAT FIRE. I'M CONCERNED WE MAY HAVE JUMPED THE GUN ON PUTTING YOU BACK ON THE JOB.
PERHAPS A MORE THOROUGH EXAMINATION...
I DON'T THINK YOU'D LIKE WHAT YOU'D FIND...
WHAT WAS THAT?
NOTHING. BUTTON, IMP!
BUTTON!
BOTTOM RIGHT ***GLOWING*** BUTTON.
CHUNKT
VRT
SCRTCHHH
AH! ARE YOU SURE?!

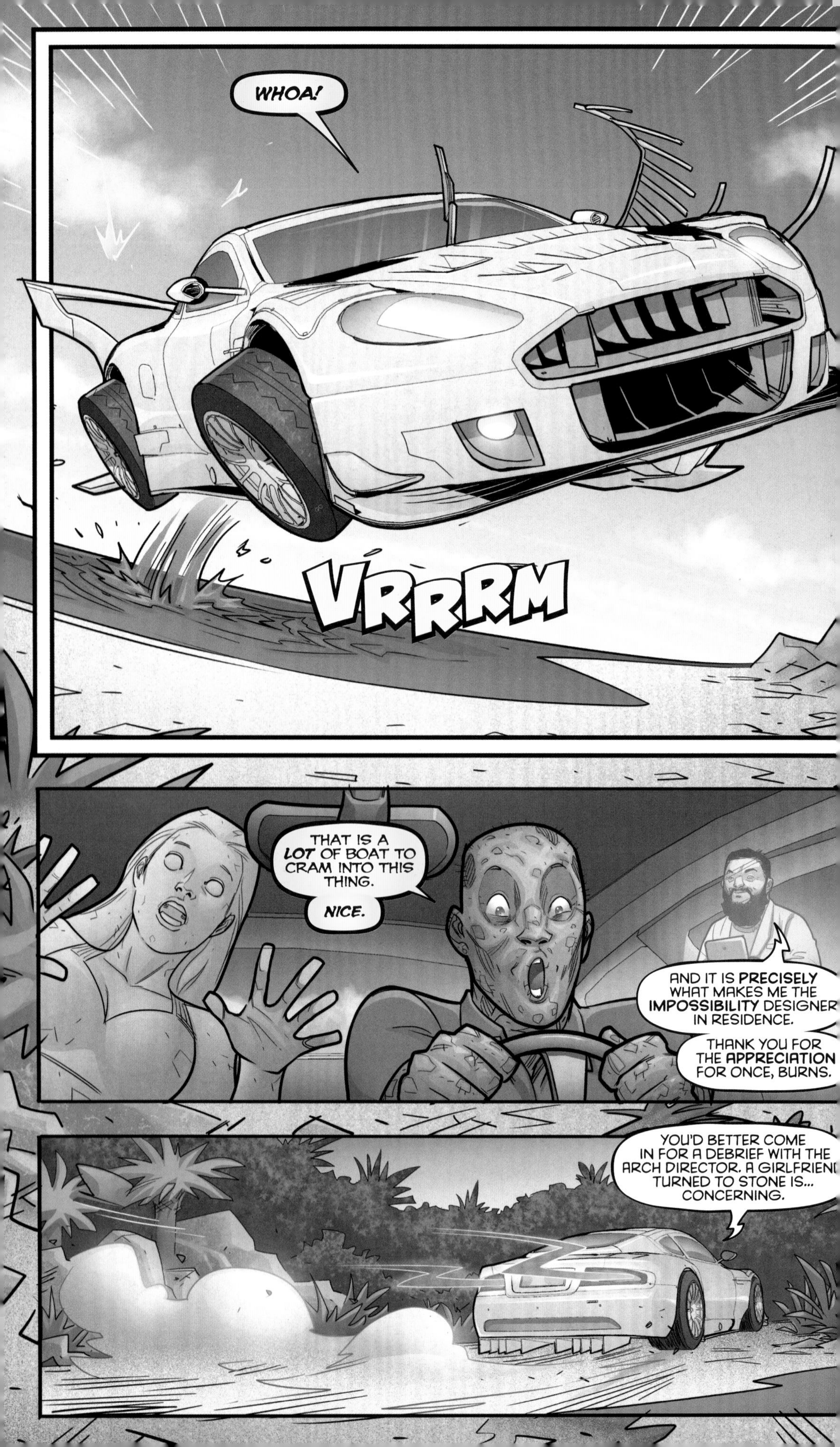
WHOA!
VRRRM
THAT IS A LOT OF BOAT TO CRAM INTO THIS THING.
NICE.
AND IT IS PRECISELY WHAT MAKES ME THE IMPOSSIBILITY DESIGNER IN RESIDENCE.
THANK YOU FOR THE APPRECIATION FOR ONCE, BURNS.
YOU'D BETTER COME IN FOR A DEBRIEF WITH THE ARCH DIRECTOR. A GIRLFRIEND TURNED TO STONE IS... CONCERNING.

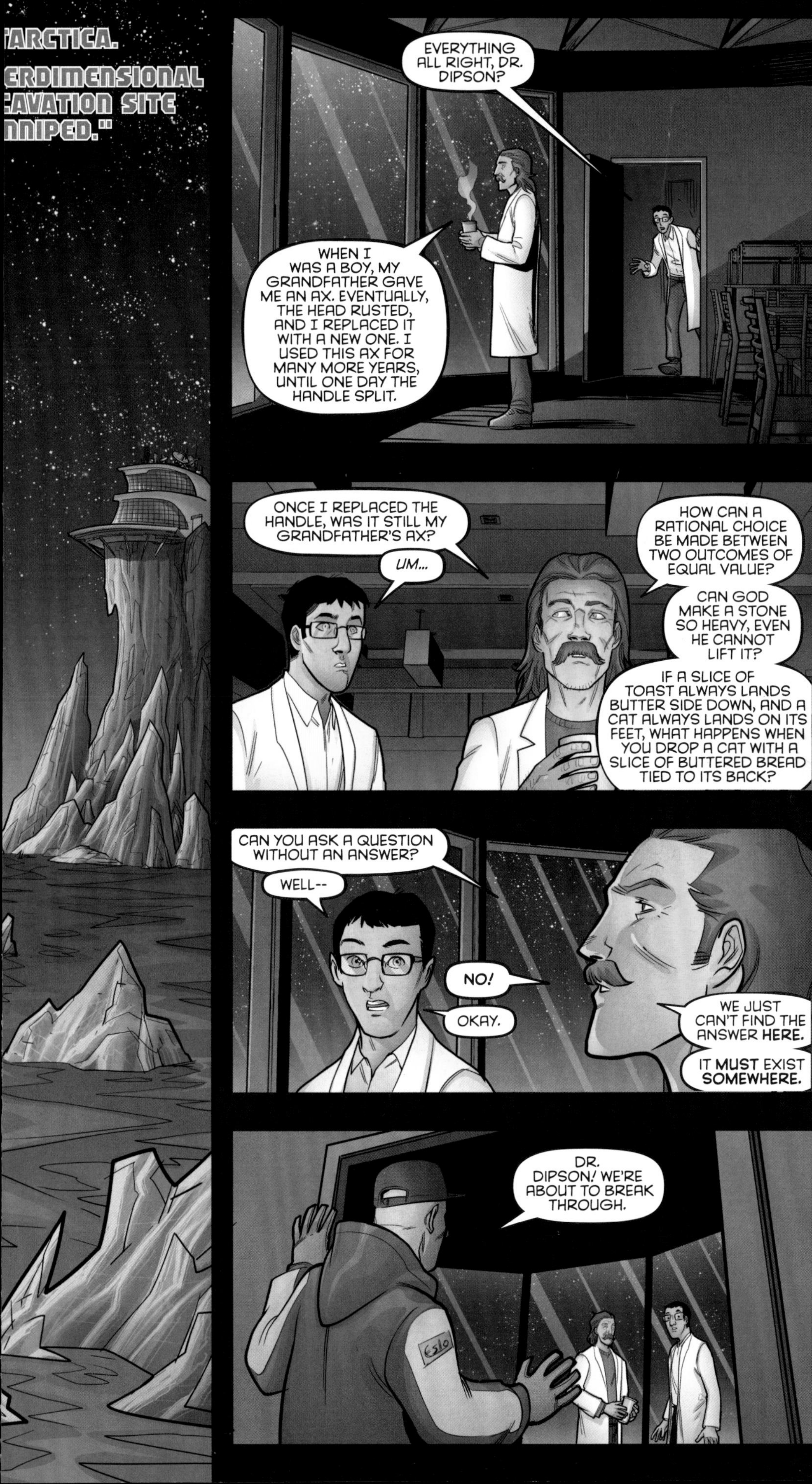

:ARCTICA.
:ERDIMENSIONAL
:CAVATION SITE
:NNIPED."
EVERYTHING ALL RIGHT, DR. DIPSON?
WHEN I WAS A BOY, MY GRANDFATHER GAVE ME AN AX. EVENTUALLY, THE HEAD RUSTED, AND I REPLACED IT WITH A NEW ONE. I USED THIS AX FOR MANY MORE YEARS, UNTIL ONE DAY THE HANDLE SPLIT.
ONCE I REPLACED THE HANDLE, WAS IT STILL MY GRANDFATHER'S AX?
UM...
HOW CAN A RATIONAL CHOICE BE MADE BETWEEN TWO OUTCOMES OF EQUAL VALUE?
CAN GOD MAKE A STONE SO HEAVY, EVEN HE CANNOT LIFT IT?
IF A SLICE OF TOAST ALWAYS LANDS BUTTER SIDE DOWN, AND A CAT ALWAYS LANDS ON ITS FEET, WHAT HAPPENS WHEN YOU DROP A CAT WITH A SLICE OF BUTTERED BREAD TIED TO ITS BACK?
CAN YOU ASK A QUESTION WITHOUT AN ANSWER?
WELL--
NO!
OKAY.
WE JUST CAN'T FIND THE ANSWER **HERE.**
IT **MUST** EXIST **SOMEWHERE.**
DR. DIPSON! WE'RE ABOUT TO BREAK THROUGH.

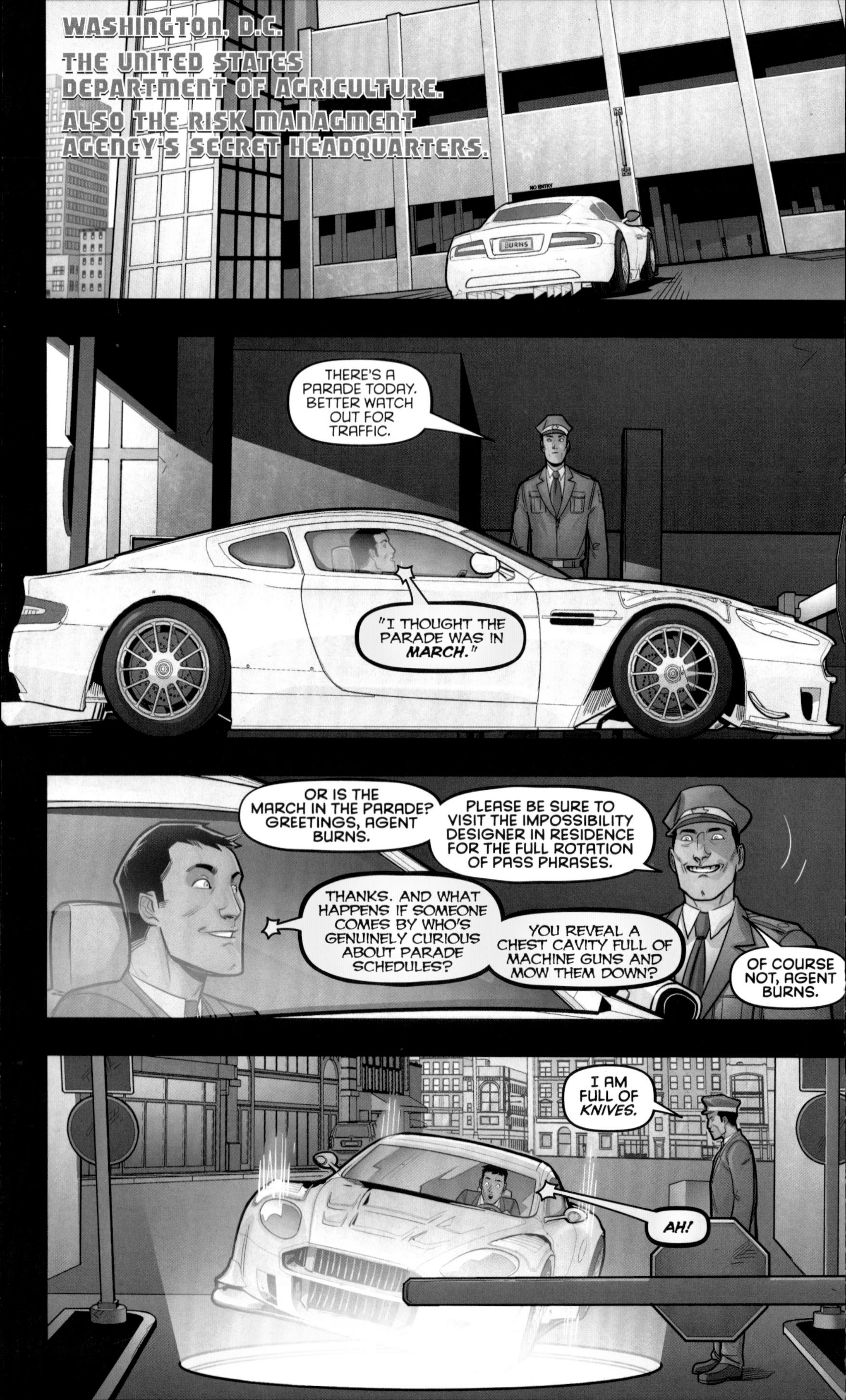
WASHINGTON, D.C.
THE UNITED STATES DEPARTMENT OF AGRICULTURE.
ALSO THE RISK MANAGMENT AGENCY'S SECRET HEADQUARTERS.
NO ENTRY
BURNS
THERE'S A PARADE TODAY. BETTER WATCH OUT FOR TRAFFIC.
"I THOUGHT THE PARADE WAS IN *MARCH*."
OR IS THE MARCH IN THE PARADE? GREETINGS, AGENT BURNS.
PLEASE BE SURE TO VISIT THE IMPOSSIBILITY DESIGNER IN RESIDENCE FOR THE FULL ROTATION OF PASS PHRASES.
THANKS. AND WHAT HAPPENS IF SOMEONE COMES BY WHO'S GENUINELY CURIOUS ABOUT PARADE SCHEDULES?
YOU REVEAL A CHEST CAVITY FULL OF MACHINE GUNS AND MOW THEM DOWN?
OF COURSE NOT, AGENT BURNS.
I AM FULL OF *KNIVES.*
AH!

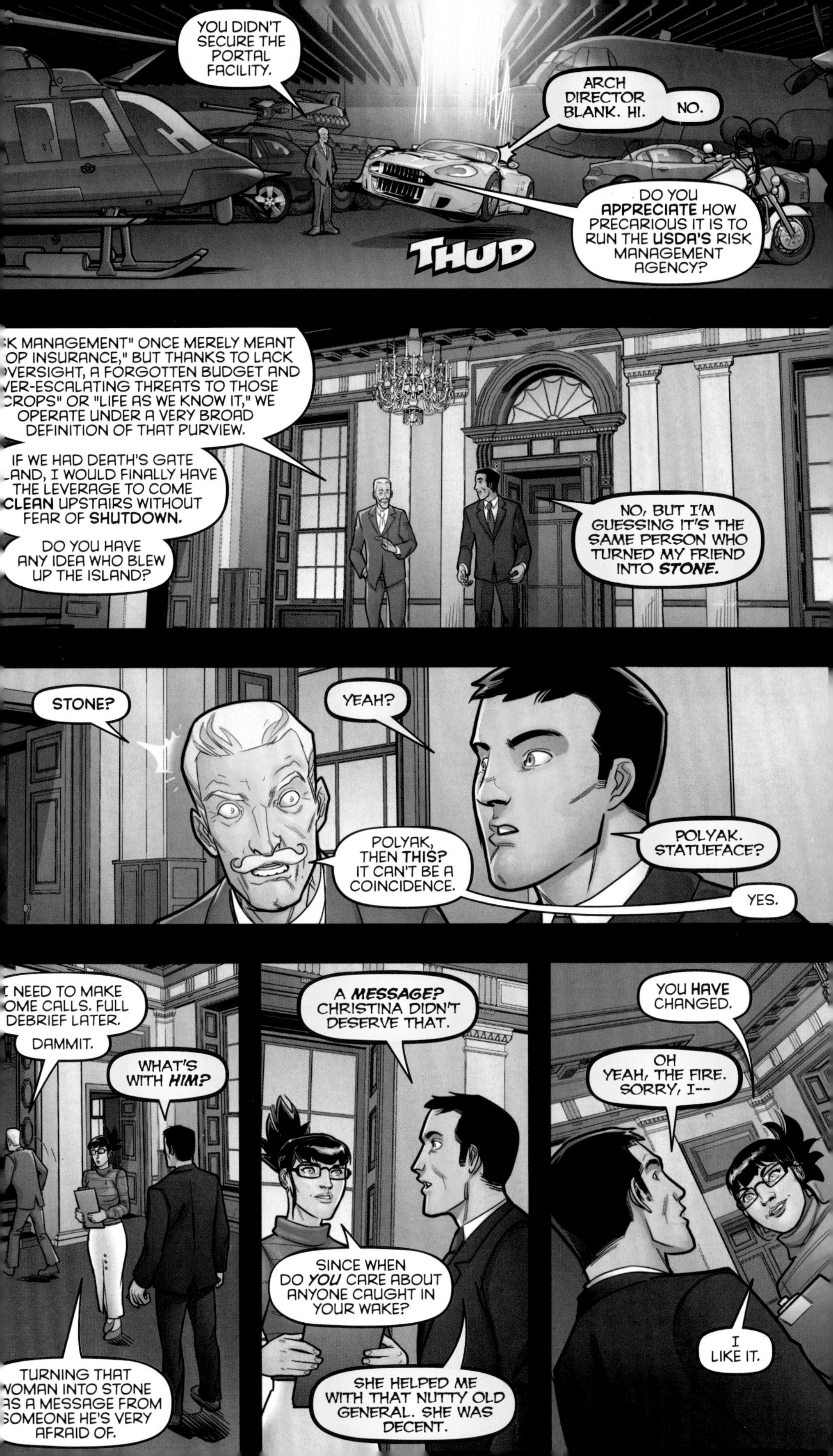

YOU DIDN'T SECURE THE PORTAL FACILITY.
ARCH DIRECTOR BLANK. HI.
NO.
DO YOU **APPRECIATE** HOW PRECARIOUS IT IS TO RUN THE **USDA'S** RISK MANAGEMENT AGENCY?
THUD
K MANAGEMENT" ONCE MERELY MEANT OP INSURANCE," BUT THANKS TO LACK OVERSIGHT, A FORGOTTEN BUDGET AND VER-ESCALATING THREATS TO THOSE CROPS" OR "LIFE AS WE KNOW IT," WE OPERATE UNDER A VERY BROAD DEFINITION OF THAT PURVIEW.
IF WE HAD DEATH'S GATE LAND, I WOULD FINALLY HAVE THE LEVERAGE TO COME **CLEAN** UPSTAIRS WITHOUT FEAR OF **SHUTDOWN.**
DO YOU HAVE ANY IDEA WHO BLEW UP THE ISLAND?
NO, BUT I'M GUESSING IT'S THE SAME PERSON WHO TURNED MY FRIEND INTO ***STONE.***
STONE?
YEAH?
POLYAK. STATUEFACE?
POLYAK, THEN **THIS?** IT CAN'T BE A COINCIDENCE.
YES.
I NEED TO MAKE OME CALLS. FULL DEBRIEF LATER.
DAMMIT.
WHAT'S WITH ***HIM?***
TURNING THAT VOMAN INTO STONE AS A MESSAGE FROM SOMEONE HE'S VERY AFRAID OF.
A ***MESSAGE?*** CHRISTINA DIDN'T DESERVE THAT.
SINCE WHEN DO ***YOU*** CARE ABOUT ANYONE CAUGHT IN YOUR WAKE?
SHE HELPED ME WITH THAT NUTTY OLD GENERAL. SHE WAS DECENT.
YOU **HAVE** CHANGED.
OH YEAH, THE FIRE. SORRY, I--
I LIKE IT.

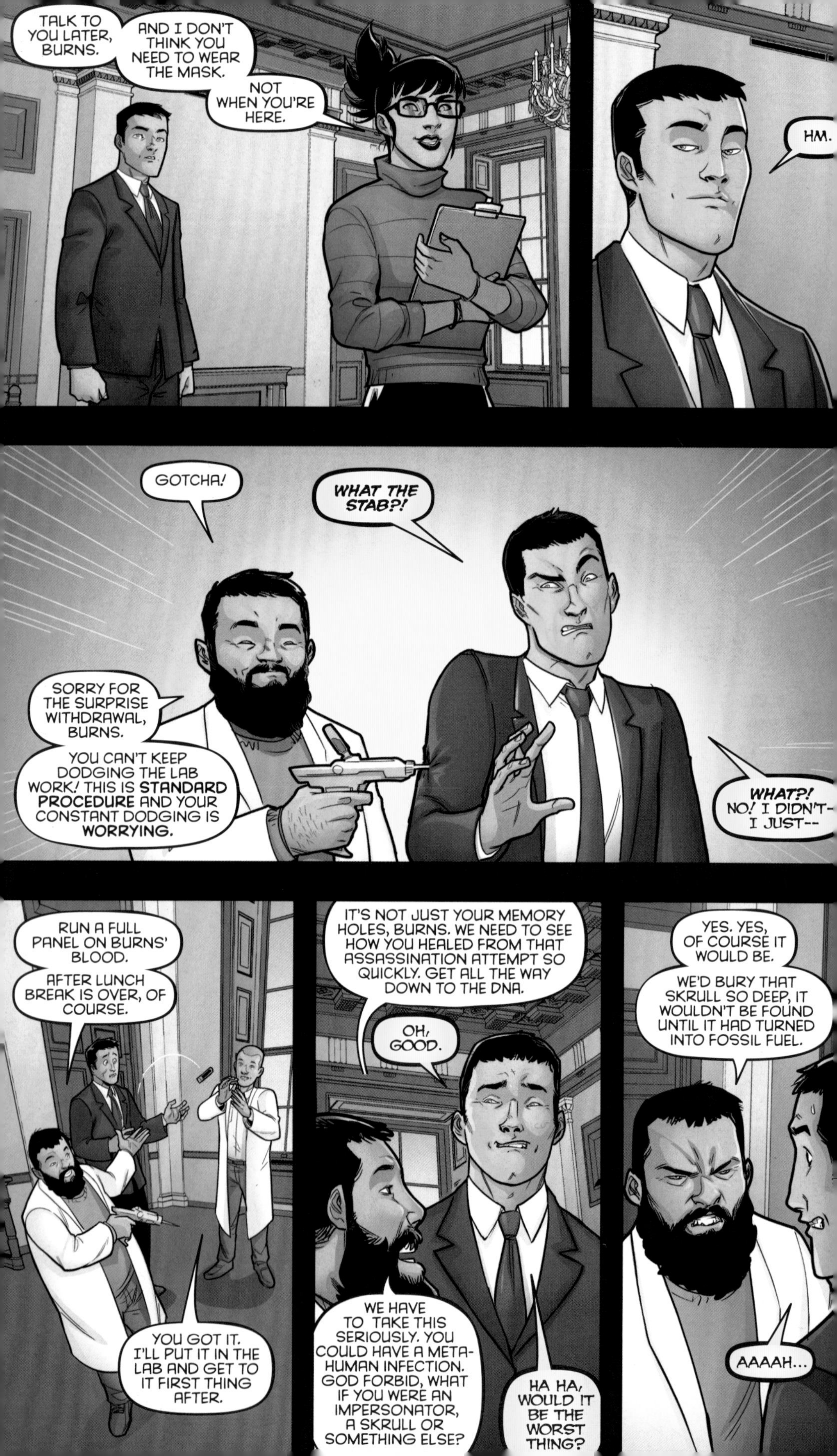
TALK TO YOU LATER, BURNS.
AND I DON'T THINK YOU NEED TO WEAR THE MASK.
NOT WHEN YOU'RE HERE.
HM.
GOTCHA!
WHAT THE STAB?!
SORRY FOR THE SURPRISE WITHDRAWAL, BURNS.
YOU CAN'T KEEP DODGING THE LAB WORK! THIS IS STANDARD PROCEDURE AND YOUR CONSTANT DODGING IS WORRYING.
WHAT?! NO! I DIDN'T- I JUST--
RUN A FULL PANEL ON BURNS' BLOOD.
AFTER LUNCH BREAK IS OVER, OF COURSE.
YOU GOT IT. I'LL PUT IT IN THE LAB AND GET TO IT FIRST THING AFTER.
IT'S NOT JUST YOUR MEMORY HOLES, BURNS. WE NEED TO SEE HOW YOU HEALED FROM THAT ASSASSINATION ATTEMPT SO QUICKLY. GET ALL THE WAY DOWN TO THE DNA.
OH, GOOD.
WE HAVE TO TAKE THIS SERIOUSLY. YOU COULD HAVE A META-HUMAN INFECTION. GOD FORBID, WHAT IF YOU WERE AN IMPERSONATOR, A SKRULL OR SOMETHING ELSE?
HA HA, WOULD IT BE THE WORST THING?
YES. YES, OF COURSE IT WOULD BE.
WE'D BURY THAT SKRULL SO DEEP, IT WOULDN'T BE FOUND UNTIL IT HAD TURNED INTO FOSSIL FUEL.
AAAAH...

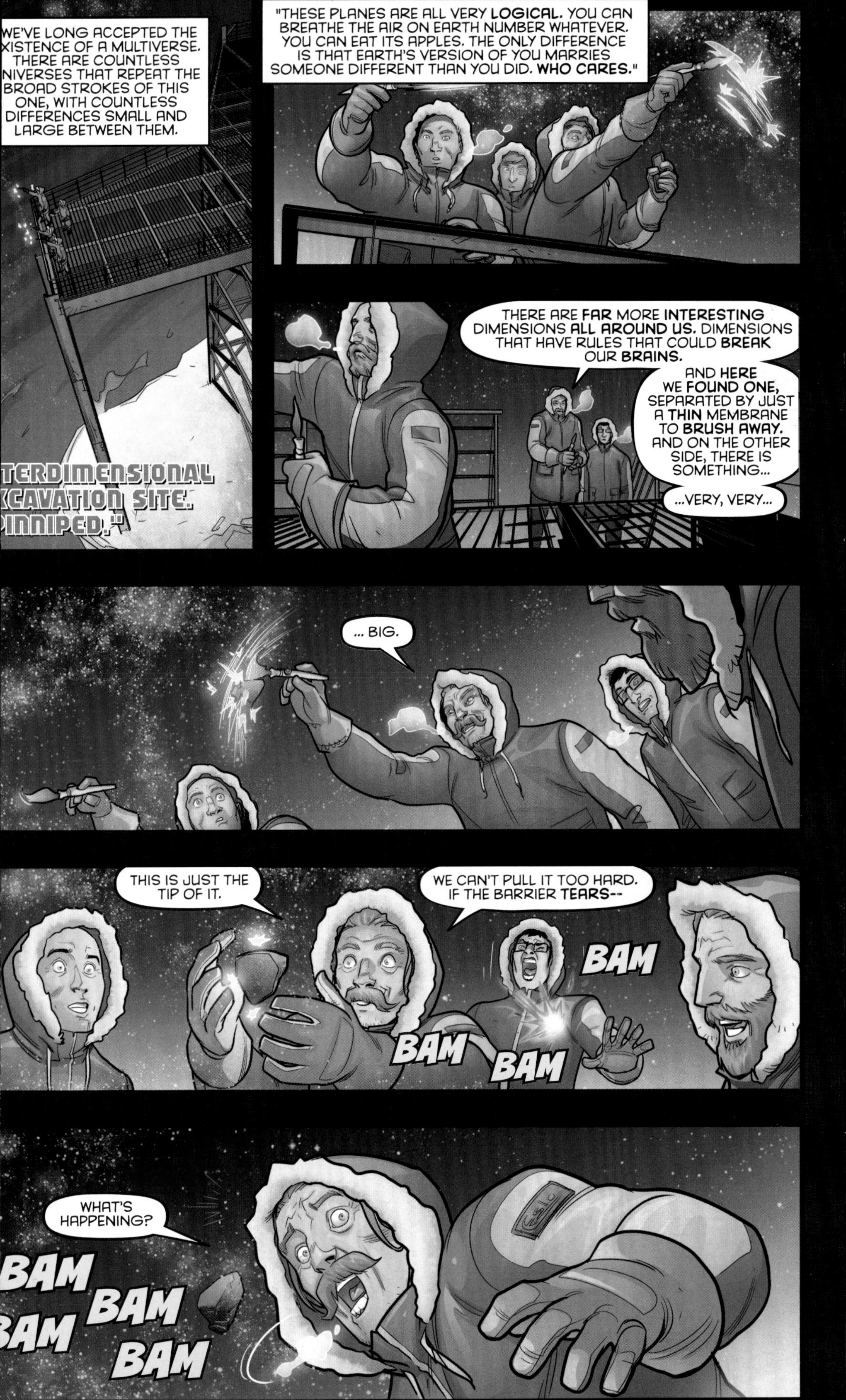

WE'VE LONG ACCEPTED THE XISTENCE OF A MULTIVERSE. THERE ARE COUNTLESS NIVERSES THAT REPEAT THE BROAD STROKES OF THIS ONE, WITH COUNTLESS DIFFERENCES SMALL AND LARGE BETWEEN THEM.
TERDIMENSIONAL XCAVATION SITE. INNIPED."
"THESE PLANES ARE ALL VERY LOGICAL. YOU CAN BREATHE THE AIR ON EARTH NUMBER WHATEVER. YOU CAN EAT ITS APPLES. THE ONLY DIFFERENCE IS THAT EARTH'S VERSION OF YOU MARRIES SOMEONE DIFFERENT THAN YOU DID. WHO CARES."
THERE ARE FAR MORE INTERESTING DIMENSIONS ALL AROUND US. DIMENSIONS THAT HAVE RULES THAT COULD BREAK OUR BRAINS.
AND HERE WE FOUND ONE, SEPARATED BY JUST A THIN MEMBRANE TO BRUSH AWAY. AND ON THE OTHER SIDE, THERE IS SOMETHING...
...VERY, VERY...
... BIG.
THIS IS JUST THE TIP OF IT.
WE CAN'T PULL IT TOO HARD. IF THE BARRIER TEARS--
BAM
BAM
BAM
WHAT'S HAPPENING?
BAM
BAM
BAM
BAM

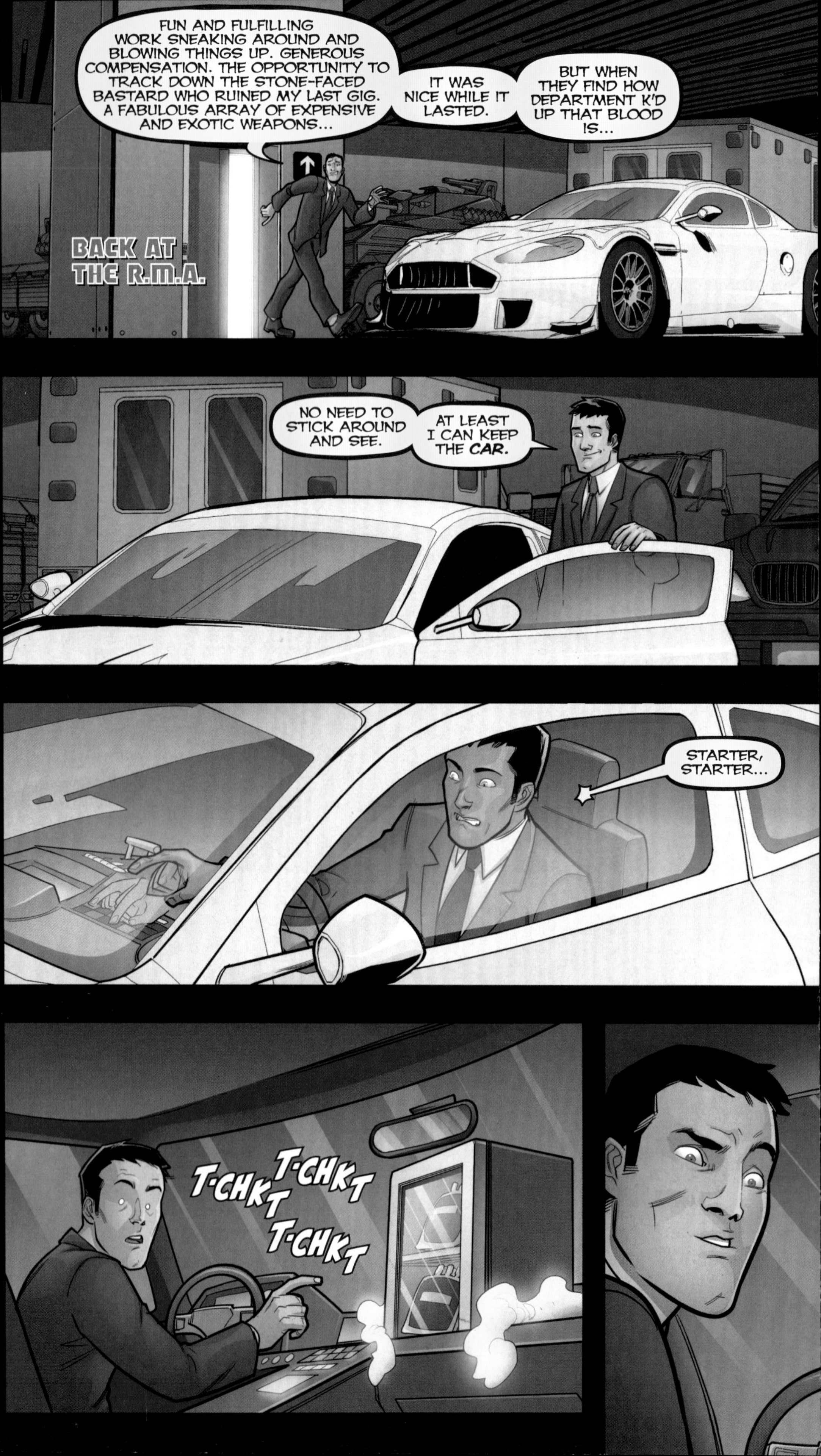
FUN AND FULFILLING WORK SNEAKING AROUND AND BLOWING THINGS UP. GENEROUS COMPENSATION. THE OPPORTUNITY TO TRACK DOWN THE STONE-FACED BASTARD WHO RUINED MY LAST GIG. A FABULOUS ARRAY OF EXPENSIVE AND EXOTIC WEAPONS...
IT WAS NICE WHILE IT LASTED.
BUT WHEN THEY FIND HOW DEPARTMENT K'D UP THAT BLOOD IS...
BACK AT THE R.M.A.
NO NEED TO STICK AROUND AND SEE.
AT LEAST I CAN KEEP THE CAR.
STARTER, STARTER...
T-CHKT T-CHKT T-CHKT

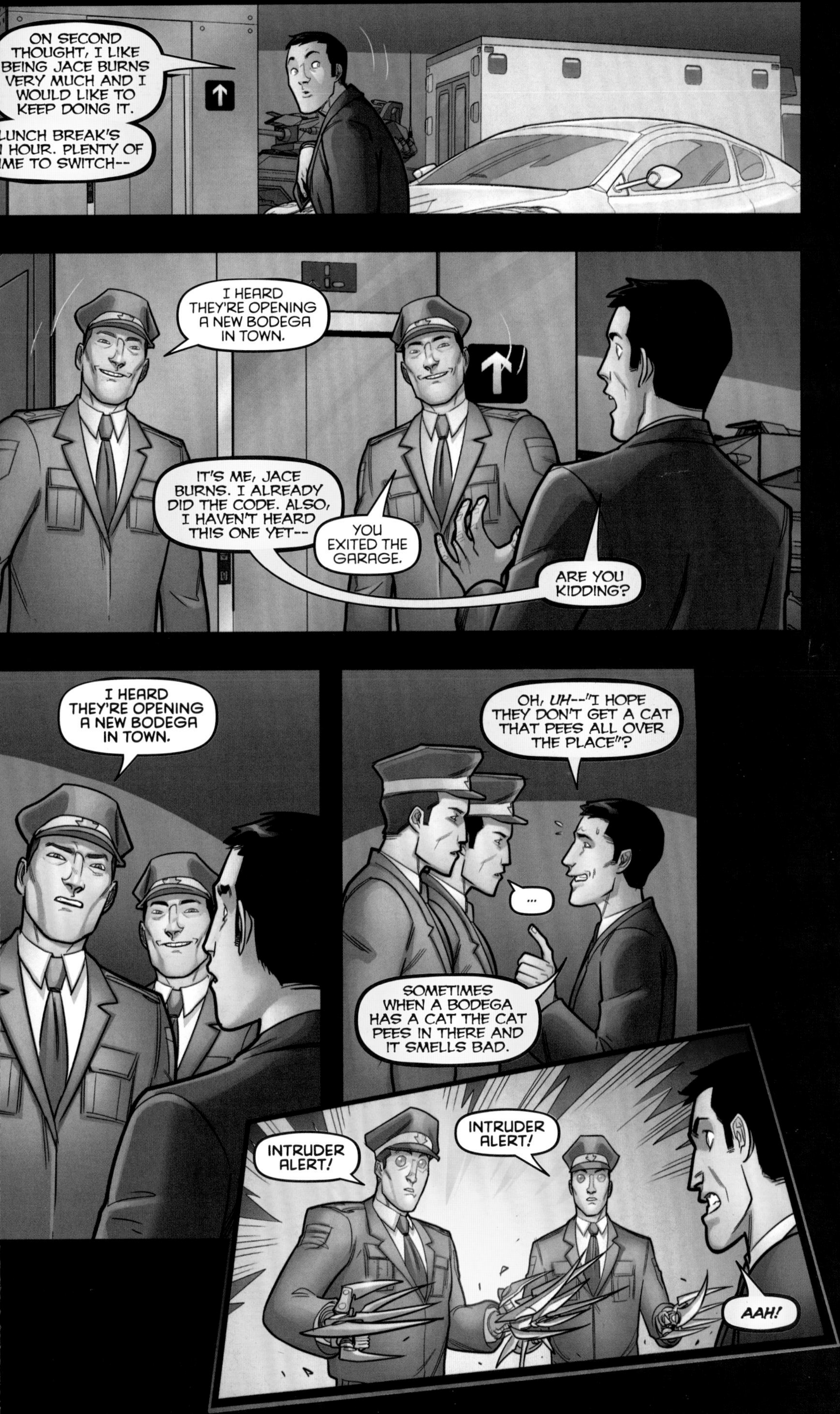
ON SECOND THOUGHT, I LIKE BEING JACE BURNS VERY MUCH AND I WOULD LIKE TO KEEP DOING IT.
LUNCH BREAK'S HOUR. PLENTY OF ME TO SWITCH--
I HEARD THEY'RE OPENING A NEW BODEGA IN TOWN.
IT'S ME, JACE BURNS. I ALREADY DID THE CODE. ALSO, I HAVEN'T HEARD THIS ONE YET--
YOU EXITED THE GARAGE.
ARE YOU KIDDING?
I HEARD THEY'RE OPENING A NEW BODEGA IN TOWN.
OH, UH--"I HOPE THEY DON'T GET A CAT THAT PEES ALL OVER THE PLACE"?
...
SOMETIMES WHEN A BODEGA HAS A CAT THE CAT PEES IN THERE AND IT SMELLS BAD.
INTRUDER ALERT!
INTRUDER ALERT!
AAH!

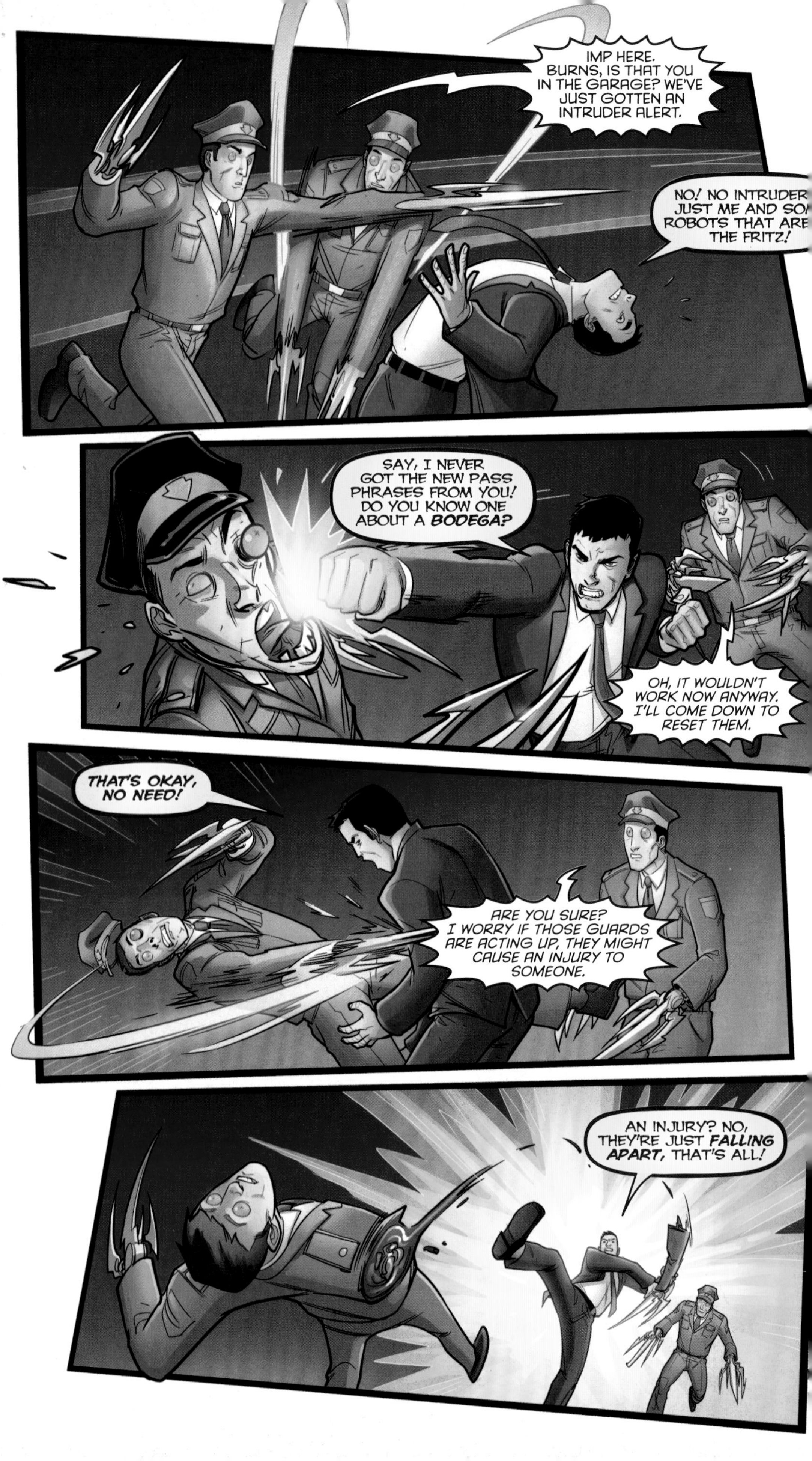
IMP HERE. BURNS, IS THAT YOU IN THE GARAGE? WE'VE JUST GOTTEN AN INTRUDER ALERT.
NO! NO INTRUDER JUST ME AND SO ROBOTS THAT ARE THE FRITZ!
SAY, I NEVER GOT THE NEW PASS PHRASES FROM YOU! DO YOU KNOW ONE ABOUT A BODEGA?
OH, IT WOULDN'T WORK NOW ANYWAY. I'LL COME DOWN TO RESET THEM.
THAT'S OKAY, NO NEED!
ARE YOU SURE? I WORRY IF THOSE GUARDS ARE ACTING UP, THEY MIGHT CAUSE AN INJURY TO SOMEONE.
AN INJURY? NO, THEY'RE JUST FALLING APART, THAT'S ALL!

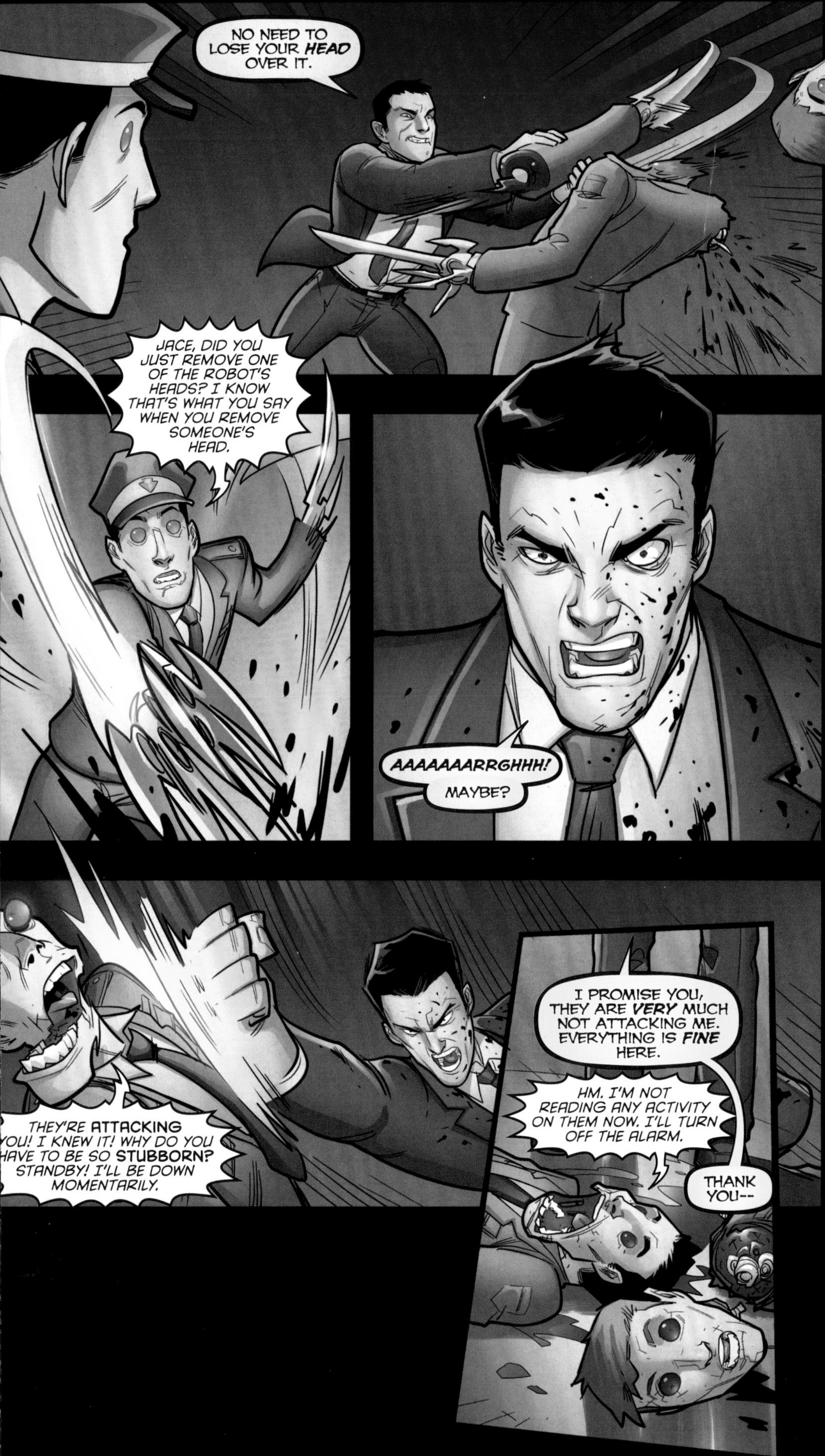
NO NEED TO LOSE YOUR **HEAD** OVER IT.
JACE, DID YOU JUST REMOVE ONE OF THE ROBOT'S HEADS? I KNOW THAT'S WHAT YOU SAY WHEN YOU REMOVE SOMEONE'S HEAD.
AAAAAAARRGHHH!
MAYBE?
THEY'RE **ATTACKING** YOU! I KNEW IT! WHY DO YOU HAVE TO BE SO **STUBBORN?** STANDBY! I'LL BE DOWN MOMENTARILY.
I PROMISE YOU, THEY ARE ***VERY*** MUCH NOT ATTACKING ME. EVERYTHING IS ***FINE*** HERE.
HM. I'M NOT READING ANY ACTIVITY ON THEM NOW. I'LL TURN OFF THE ALARM.
THANK YOU--

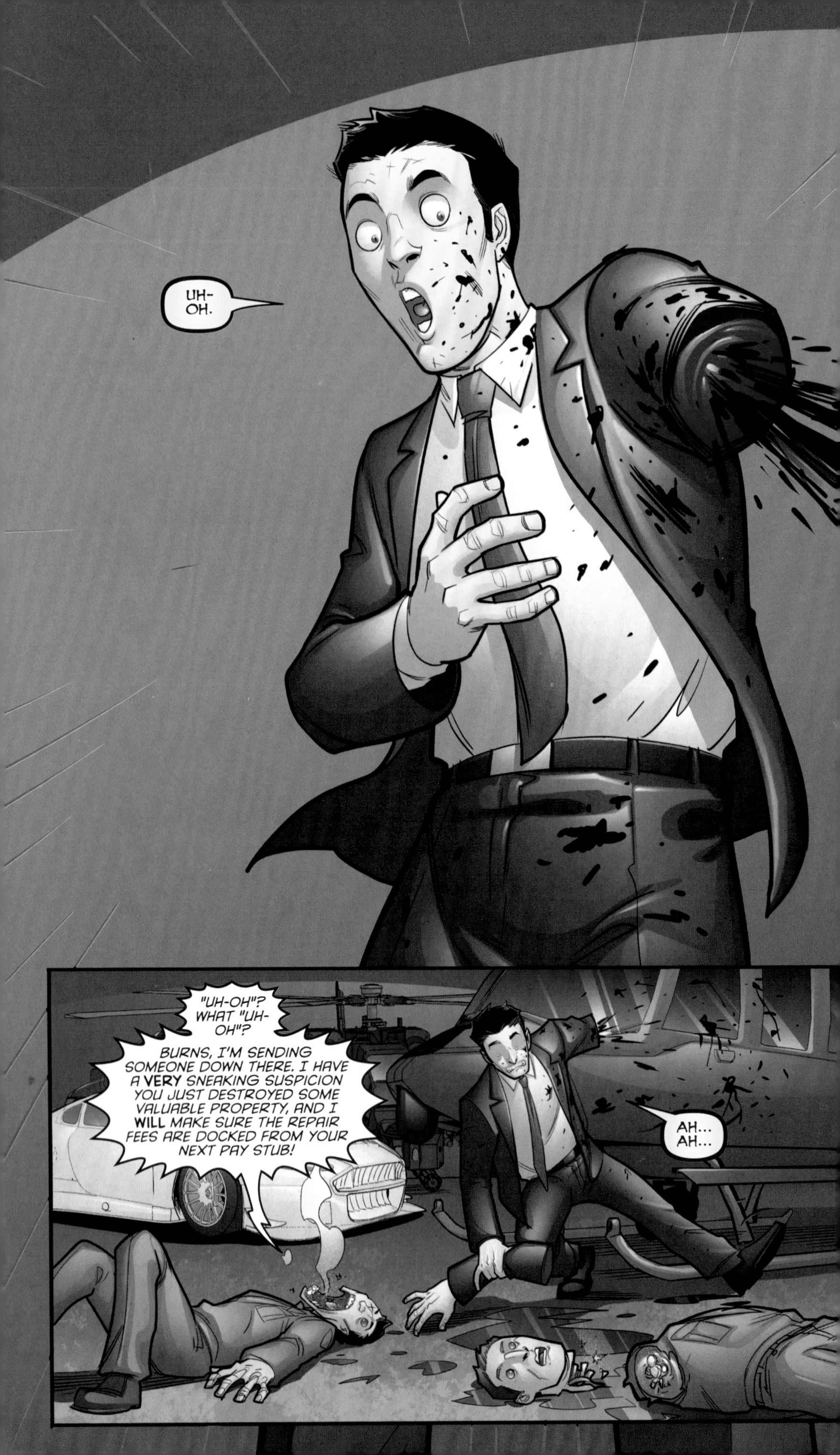
UH-
OH.
"UH-OH"? WHAT "UH-OH"?
BURNS, I'M SENDING SOMEONE DOWN THERE. I HAVE A **VERY** SNEAKING SUSPICION YOU JUST DESTROYED SOME VALUABLE PROPERTY, AND I **WILL** MAKE SURE THE REPAIR FEES ARE DOCKED FROM YOUR NEXT PAY STUB!
AH... AH...

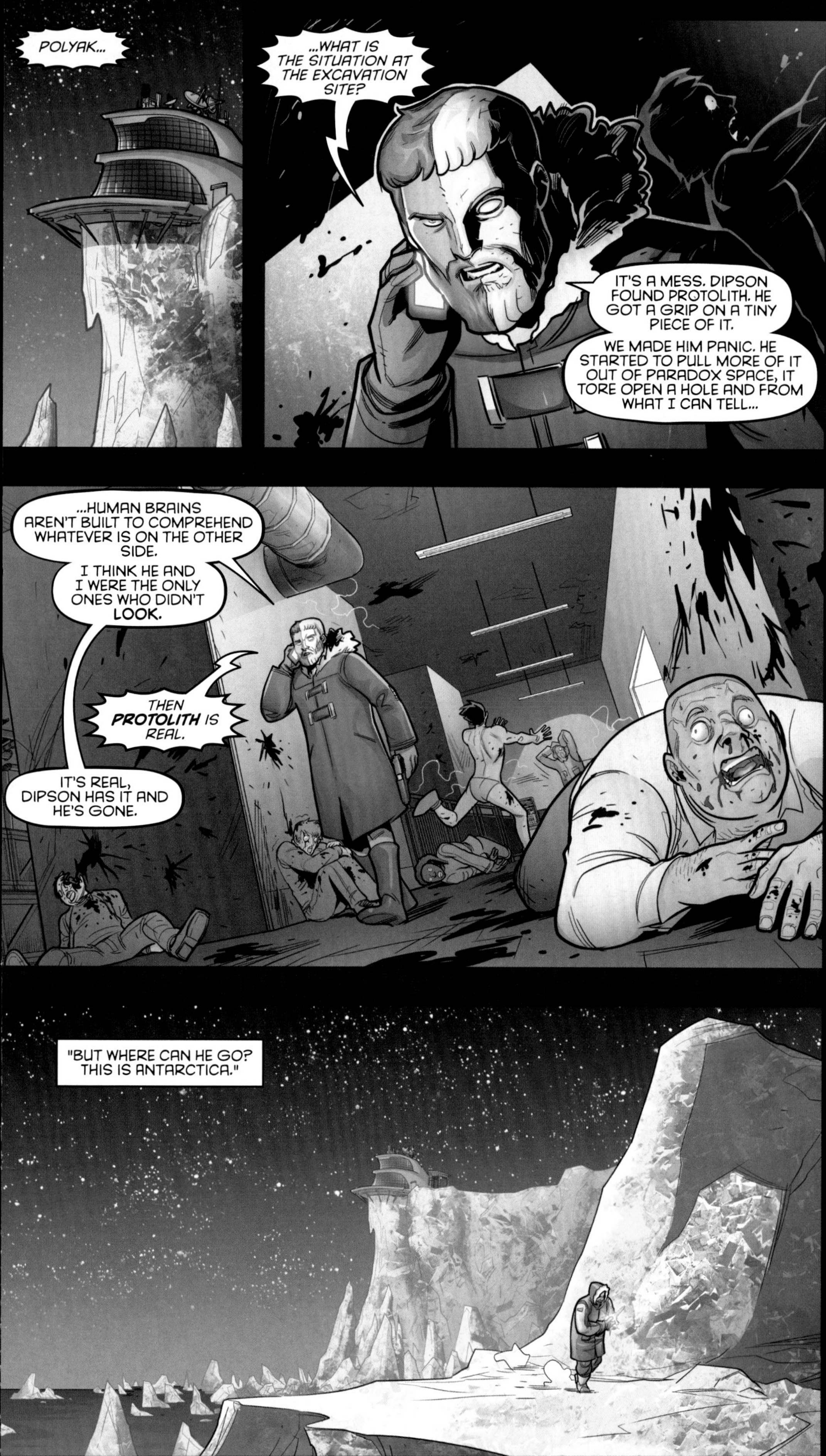

POLYAK...
...WHAT IS THE SITUATION AT THE EXCAVATION SITE?
IT'S A MESS. DIPSON FOUND PROTOLITH. HE GOT A GRIP ON A TINY PIECE OF IT.
WE MADE HIM PANIC. HE STARTED TO PULL MORE OF IT OUT OF PARADOX SPACE, IT TORE OPEN A HOLE AND FROM WHAT I CAN TELL...
...HUMAN BRAINS AREN'T BUILT TO COMPREHEND WHATEVER IS ON THE OTHER SIDE.
I THINK HE AND I WERE THE ONLY ONES WHO DIDN'T LOOK.
THEN PROTOLITH IS REAL.
IT'S REAL, DIPSON HAS IT AND HE'S GONE.
"BUT WHERE CAN HE GO? THIS IS ANTARCTICA."

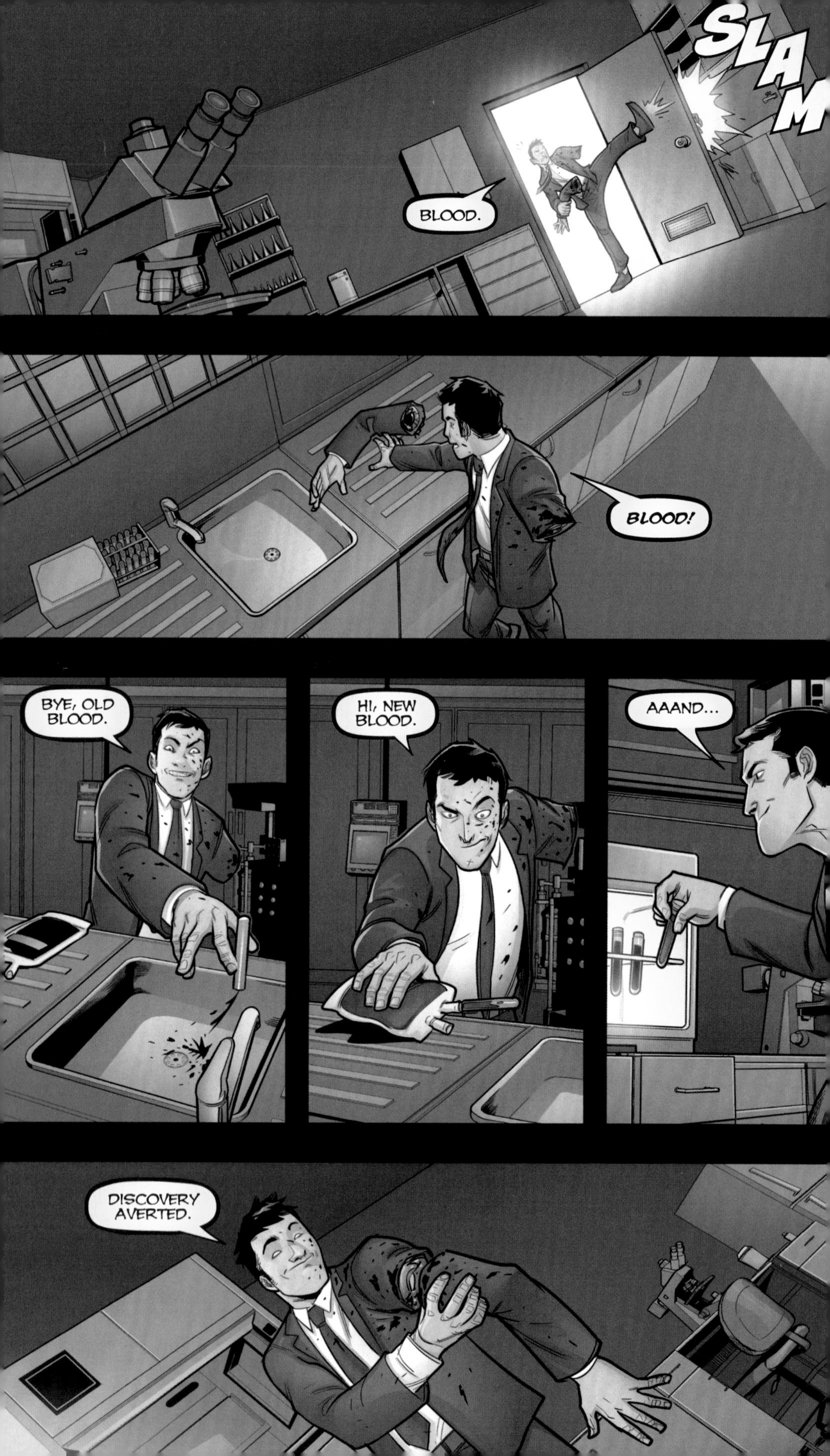
SLAM
BLOOD.
BLOOD!
BYE, OLD BLOOD.
HI, NEW BLOOD.
AAAND...
DISCOVERY AVERTED.

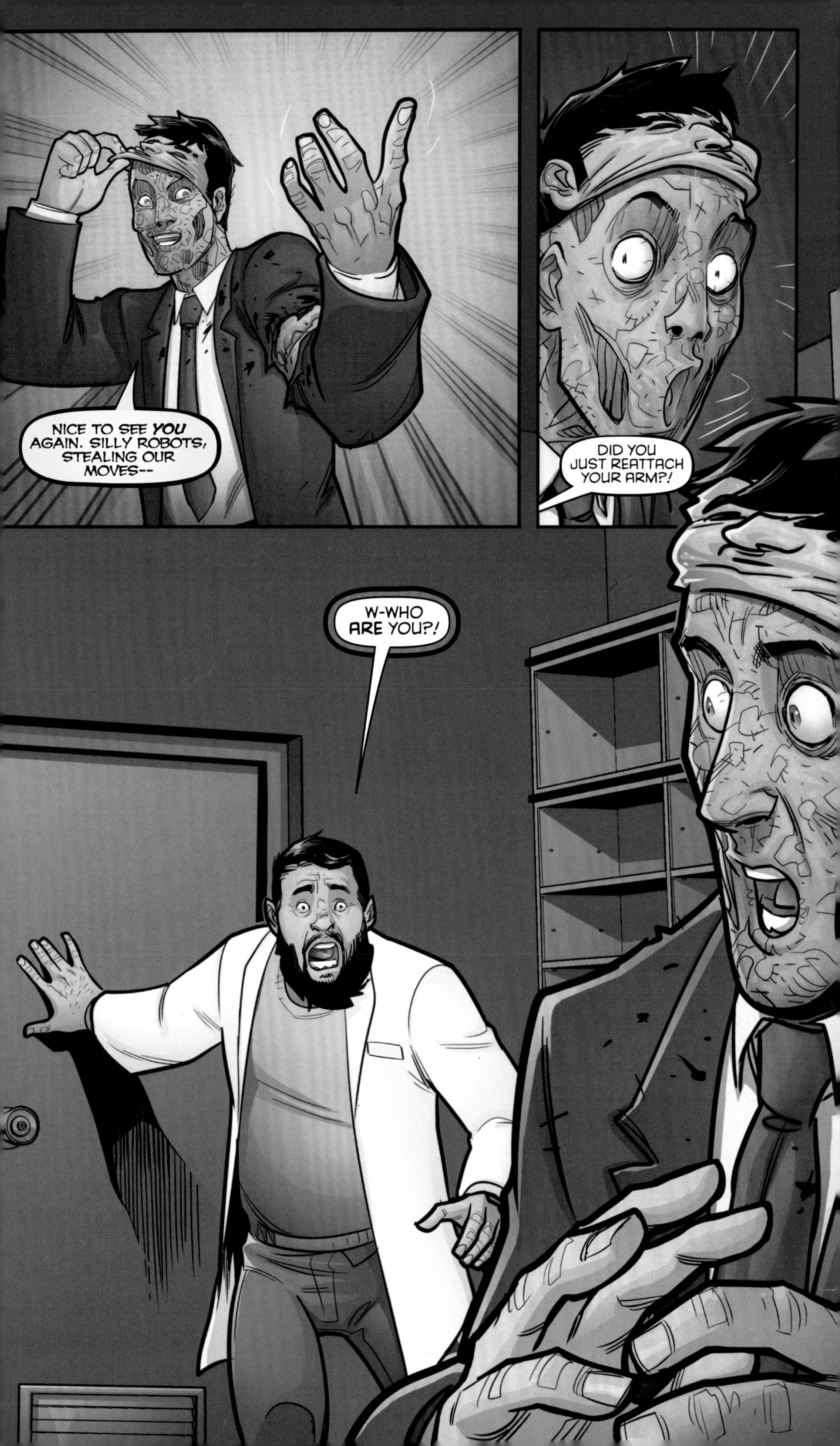
NICE TO SEE YOU AGAIN. SILLY ROBOTS, STEALING OUR MOVES--
DID YOU JUST REATTACH YOUR ARM?!
W-WHO ARE YOU?!

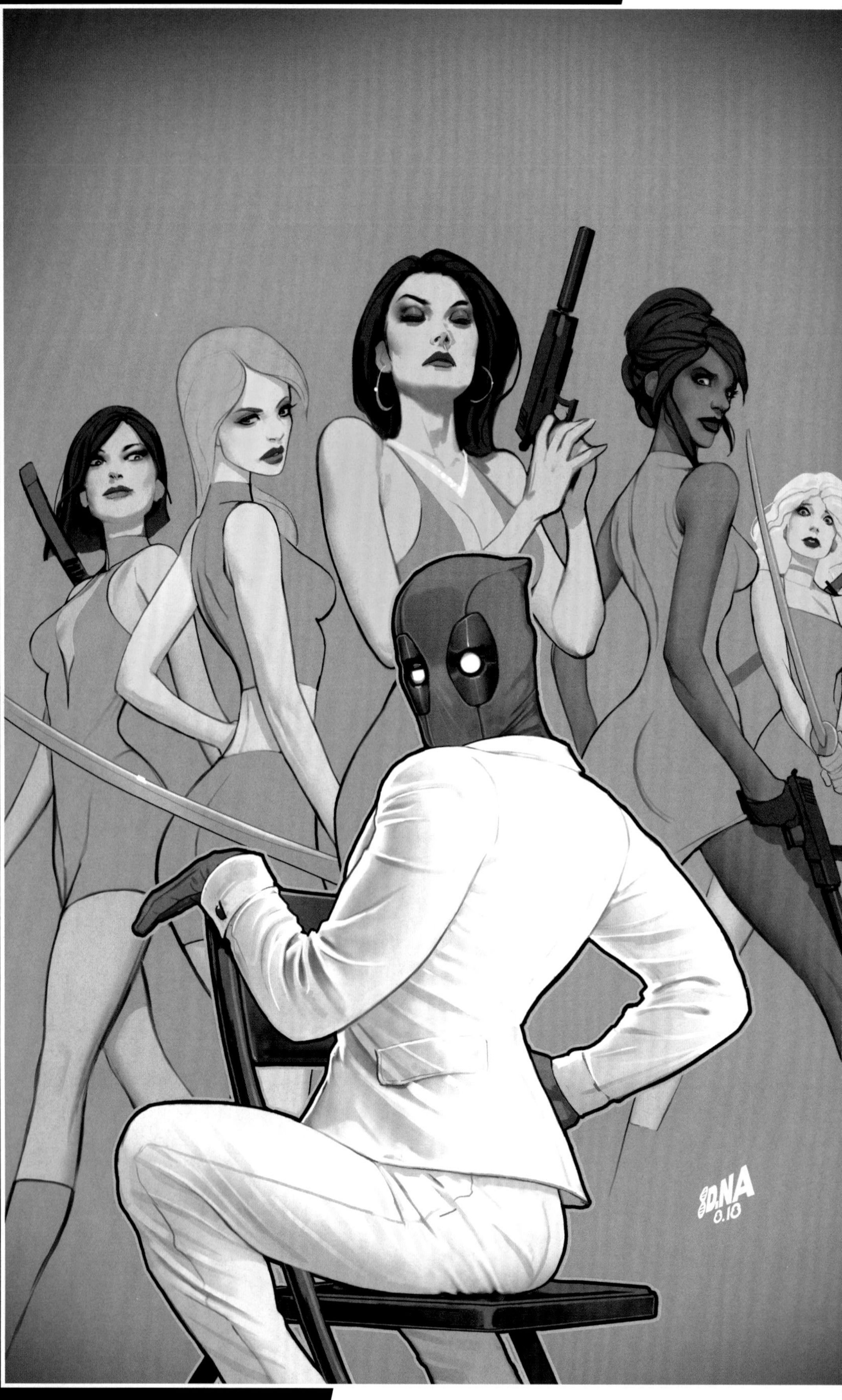

3

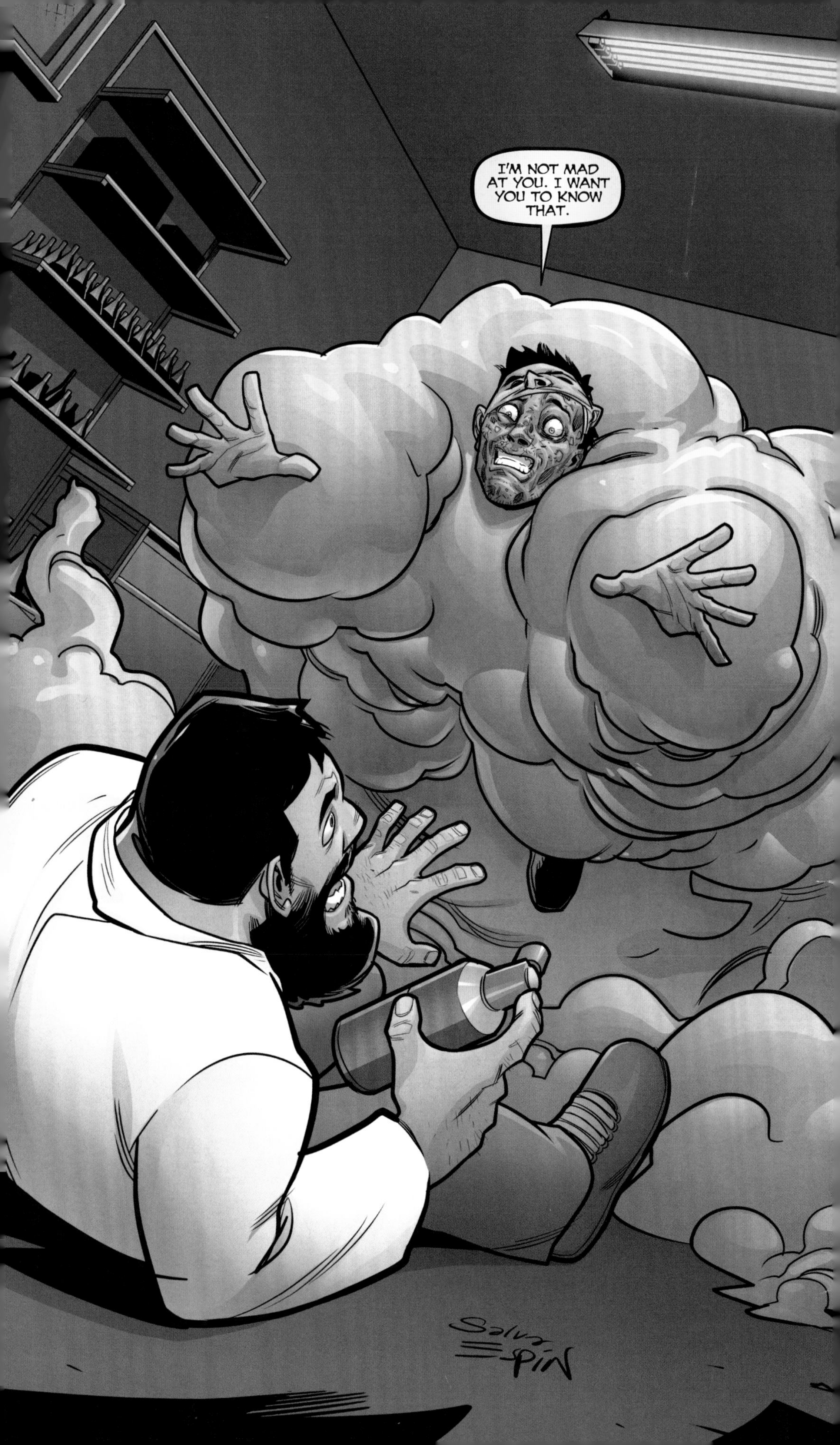
I'M NOT MAD AT YOU. I WANT YOU TO KNOW THAT.
Salva Espin

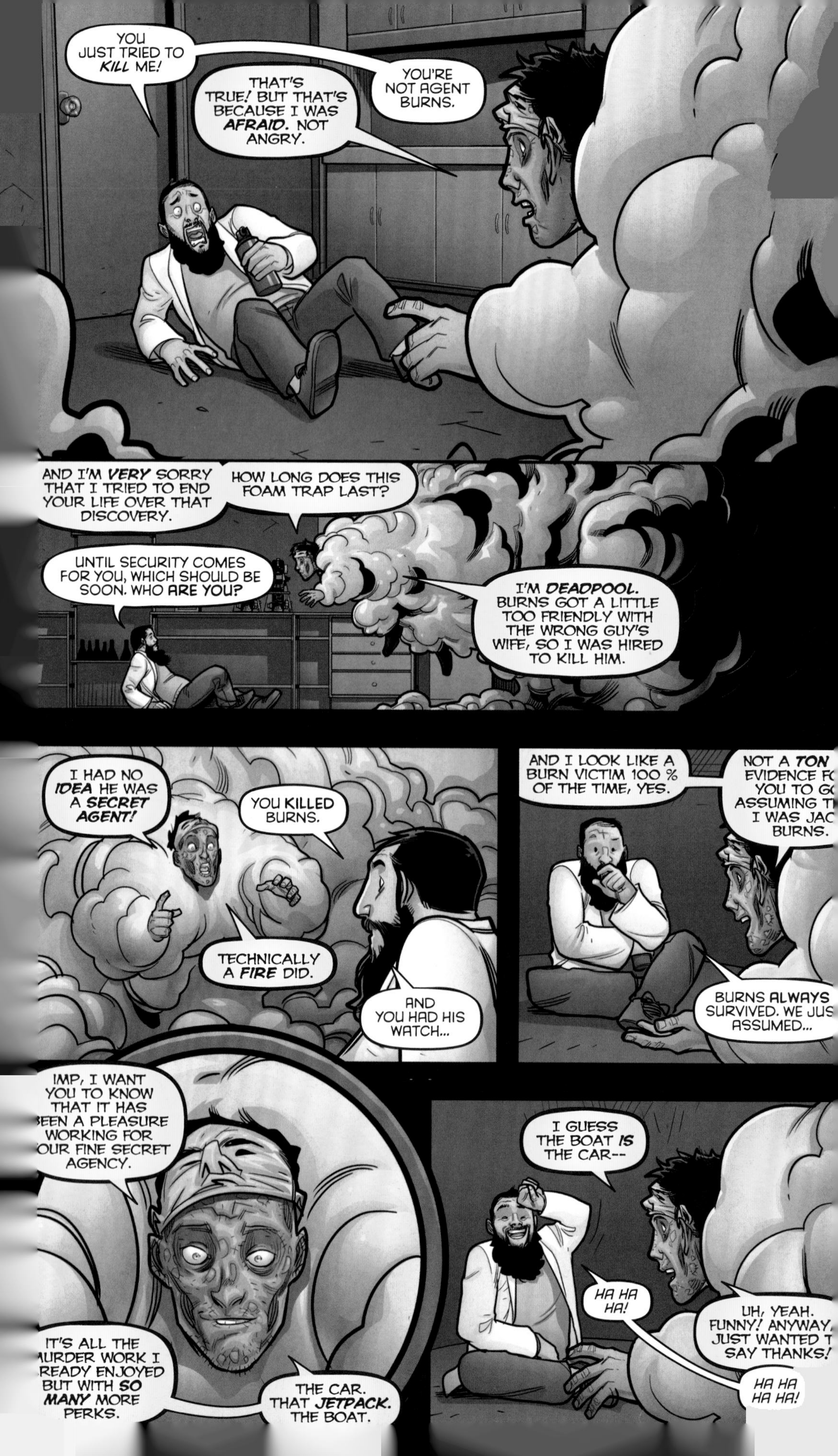
YOU JUST TRIED TO KILL ME!
YOU'RE NOT AGENT BURNS.
THAT'S TRUE! BUT THAT'S BECAUSE I WAS AFRAID. NOT ANGRY.
AND I'M VERY SORRY THAT I TRIED TO END YOUR LIFE OVER THAT DISCOVERY.
HOW LONG DOES THIS FOAM TRAP LAST?
UNTIL SECURITY COMES FOR YOU, WHICH SHOULD BE SOON. WHO ARE YOU?
I'M DEADPOOL. BURNS GOT A LITTLE TOO FRIENDLY WITH THE WRONG GUY'S WIFE, SO I WAS HIRED TO KILL HIM.
I HAD NO IDEA HE WAS A SECRET AGENT!
YOU KILLED BURNS.
TECHNICALLY A FIRE DID.
AND YOU HAD HIS WATCH...
AND I LOOK LIKE A BURN VICTIM 100 % OF THE TIME, YES.
NOT A TON EVIDENCE F YOU TO G ASSUMING T I WAS JAC BURNS.
BURNS ALWAYS SURVIVED. WE JUS ASSUMED...
IMP, I WANT YOU TO KNOW THAT IT HAS EEN A PLEASURE WORKING FOR OUR FINE SECRET AGENCY.
IT'S ALL THE URDER WORK I READY ENJOYED BUT WITH SO MANY MORE PERKS.
THE CAR. THAT JETPACK. THE BOAT.
I GUESS THE BOAT IS THE CAR--
HA HA HA!
UH, YEAH. FUNNY! ANYWAY JUST WANTED T SAY THANKS!
HA HA HA HA!

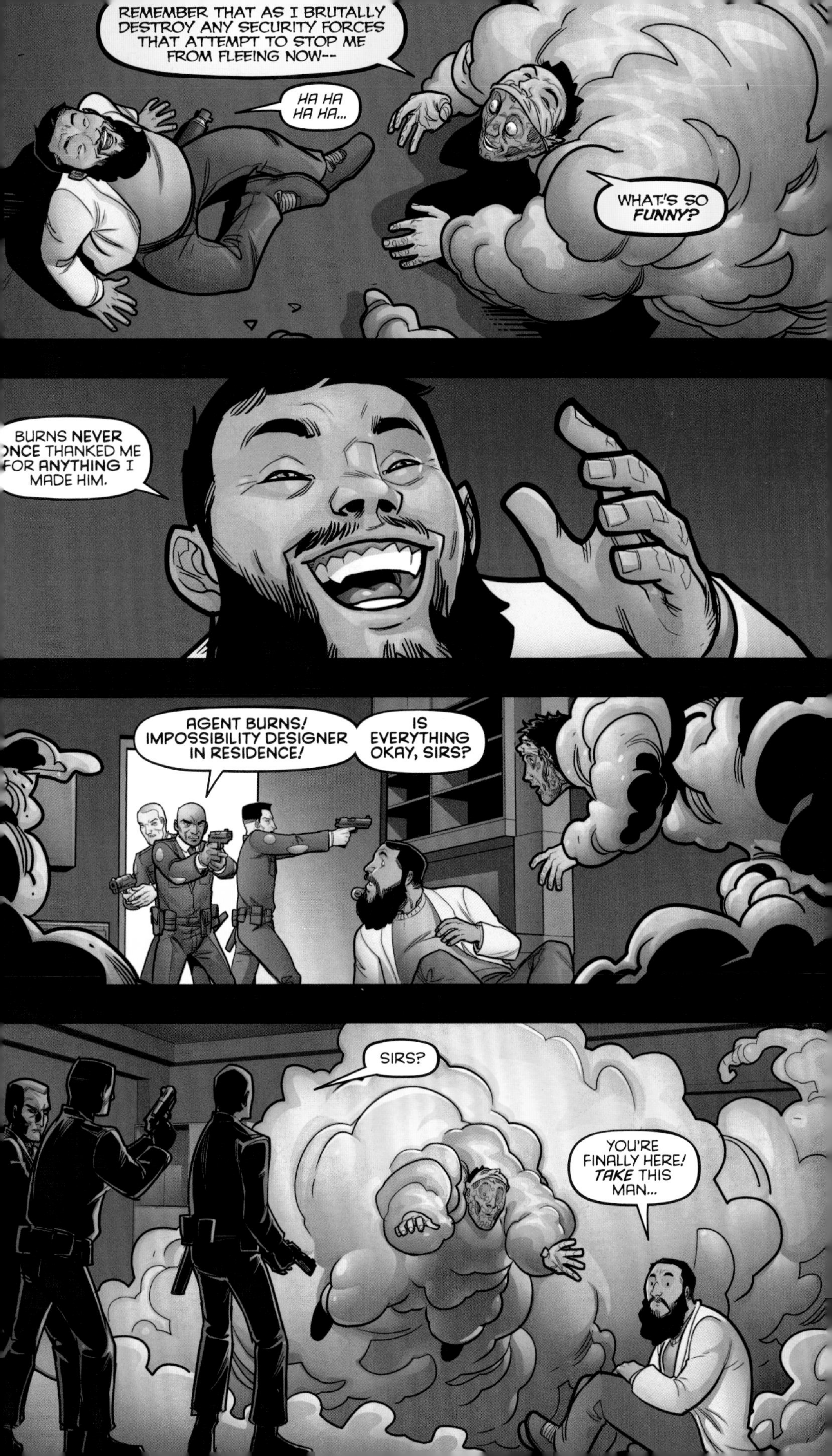
REMEMBER THAT AS I BRUTALLY DESTROY ANY SECURITY FORCES THAT ATTEMPT TO STOP ME FROM FLEEING NOW--
HA HA HA HA...
WHAT'S SO FUNNY?
BURNS NEVER ONCE THANKED ME FOR ANYTHING I MADE HIM.
AGENT BURNS! IMPOSSIBILITY DESIGNER IN RESIDENCE!
IS EVERYTHING OKAY, SIRS?
SIRS?
YOU'RE FINALLY HERE! TAKE THIS MAN...

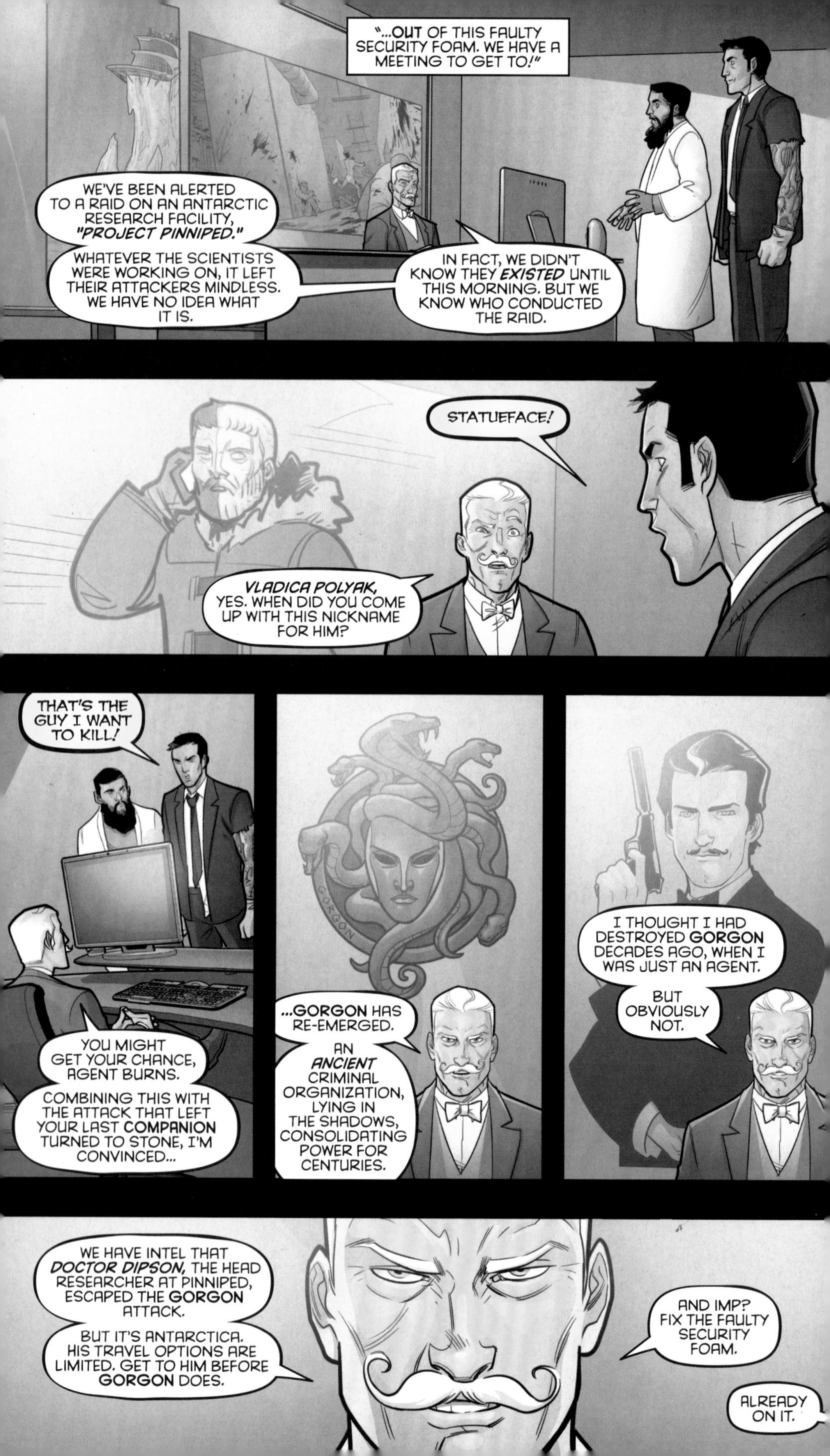
"...OUT OF THIS FAULTY SECURITY FOAM. WE HAVE A MEETING TO GET TO!"
WE'VE BEEN ALERTED TO A RAID ON AN ANTARCTIC RESEARCH FACILITY, "PROJECT PINNIPED."
WHATEVER THE SCIENTISTS WERE WORKING ON, IT LEFT THEIR ATTACKERS MINDLESS. WE HAVE NO IDEA WHAT IT IS.
IN FACT, WE DIDN'T KNOW THEY EXISTED UNTIL THIS MORNING. BUT WE KNOW WHO CONDUCTED THE RAID.
STATUEFACE!
VLADICA POLYAK, YES. WHEN DID YOU COME UP WITH THIS NICKNAME FOR HIM?
THAT'S THE GUY I WANT TO KILL!
YOU MIGHT GET YOUR CHANCE, AGENT BURNS.
COMBINING THIS WITH THE ATTACK THAT LEFT YOUR LAST COMPANION TURNED TO STONE, I'M CONVINCED...
GORGON
...GORGON HAS RE-EMERGED.
AN ANCIENT CRIMINAL ORGANIZATION, LYING IN THE SHADOWS, CONSOLIDATING POWER FOR CENTURIES.
I THOUGHT I HAD DESTROYED GORGON DECADES AGO, WHEN I WAS JUST AN AGENT.
BUT OBVIOUSLY NOT.
WE HAVE INTEL THAT DOCTOR DIPSON, THE HEAD RESEARCHER AT PINNIPED, ESCAPED THE GORGON ATTACK.
BUT IT'S ANTARCTICA. HIS TRAVEL OPTIONS ARE LIMITED. GET TO HIM BEFORE GORGON DOES.
AND IMP? FIX THE FAULTY SECURITY FOAM.
ALREADY ON IT.

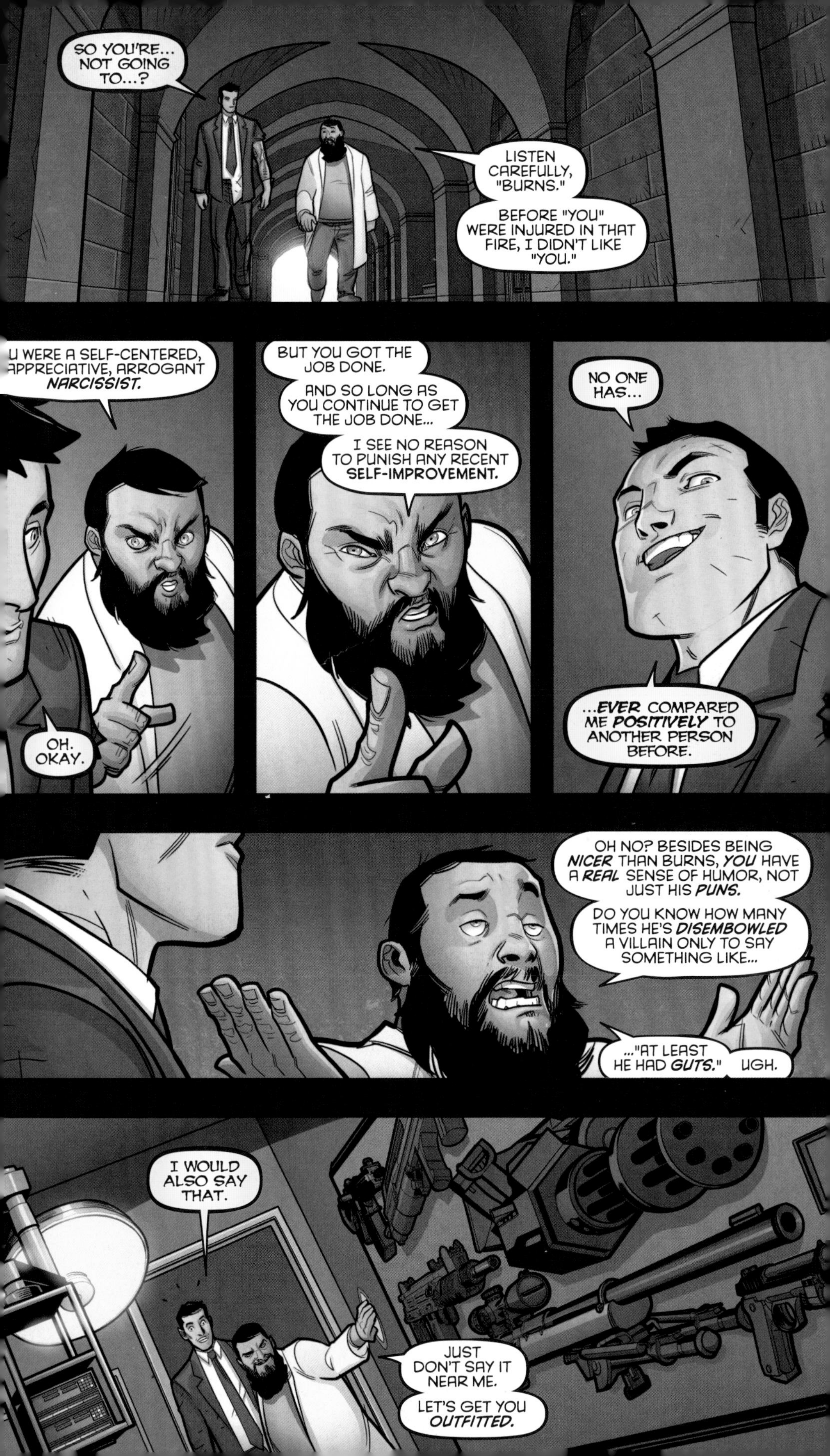
SO YOU'RE... NOT GOING TO...?
LISTEN CAREFULLY, "BURNS."
BEFORE "YOU" WERE INJURED IN THAT FIRE, I DIDN'T LIKE "YOU."
U WERE A SELF-CENTERED, APPRECIATIVE, ARROGANT NARCISSIST.
OH. OKAY.
BUT YOU GOT THE JOB DONE.
AND SO LONG AS YOU CONTINUE TO GET THE JOB DONE...
I SEE NO REASON TO PUNISH ANY RECENT SELF-IMPROVEMENT.
NO ONE HAS...
...EVER COMPARED ME POSITIVELY TO ANOTHER PERSON BEFORE.
OH NO? BESIDES BEING NICER THAN BURNS, YOU HAVE A REAL SENSE OF HUMOR, NOT JUST HIS PUNS.
DO YOU KNOW HOW MANY TIMES HE'S DISEMBOWLED A VILLAIN ONLY TO SAY SOMETHING LIKE...
..."AT LEAST HE HAD GUTS."
UGH.
I WOULD ALSO SAY THAT.
JUST DON'T SAY IT NEAR ME.
LET'S GET YOU OUTFITTED.

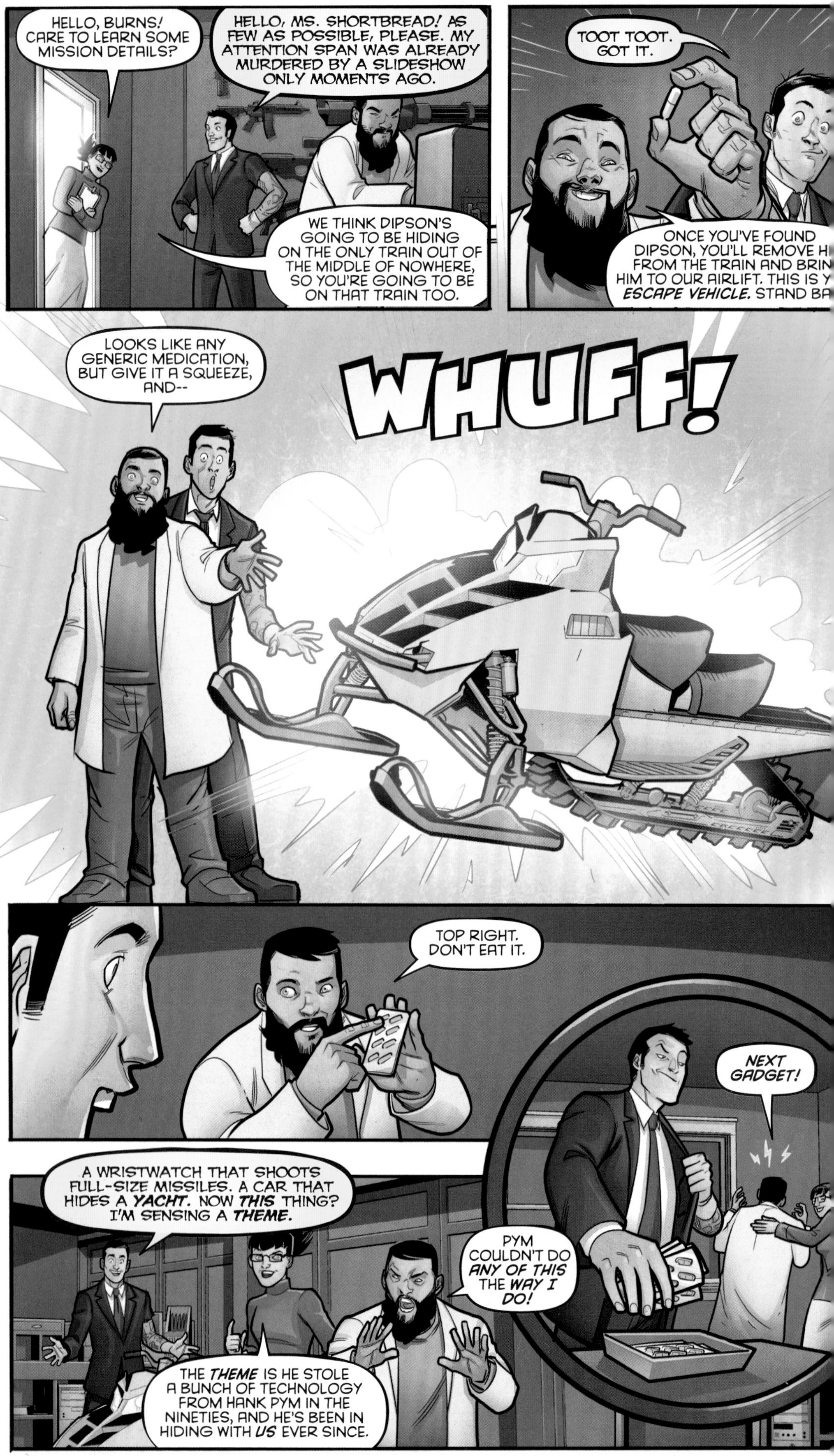
HELLO, BURNS! CARE TO LEARN SOME MISSION DETAILS?
HELLO, MS. SHORTBREAD! AS FEW AS POSSIBLE, PLEASE. MY ATTENTION SPAN WAS ALREADY MURDERED BY A SLIDESHOW ONLY MOMENTS AGO.
WE THINK DIPSON'S GOING TO BE HIDING ON THE ONLY TRAIN OUT OF THE MIDDLE OF NOWHERE, SO YOU'RE GOING TO BE ON THAT TRAIN TOO.
TOOT TOOT. GOT IT.
ONCE YOU'VE FOUND DIPSON, YOU'LL REMOVE H
FROM THE TRAIN AND BRIN
HIM TO OUR AIRLIFT. THIS IS Y
ESCAPE VEHICLE. STAND BA
LOOKS LIKE ANY GENERIC MEDICATION, BUT GIVE IT A SQUEEZE, AND--
WHUFF!
TOP RIGHT. DON'T EAT IT.
NEXT GADGET!
A WRISTWATCH THAT SHOOTS FULL-SIZE MISSILES. A CAR THAT HIDES A YACHT. NOW THIS THING? I'M SENSING A THEME.
THE THEME IS HE STOLE A BUNCH OF TECHNOLOGY FROM HANK PYM IN THE NINETIES, AND HE'S BEEN IN HIDING WITH US EVER SINCE.
PYM COULDN'T DO ANY OF THIS THE WAY I DO!

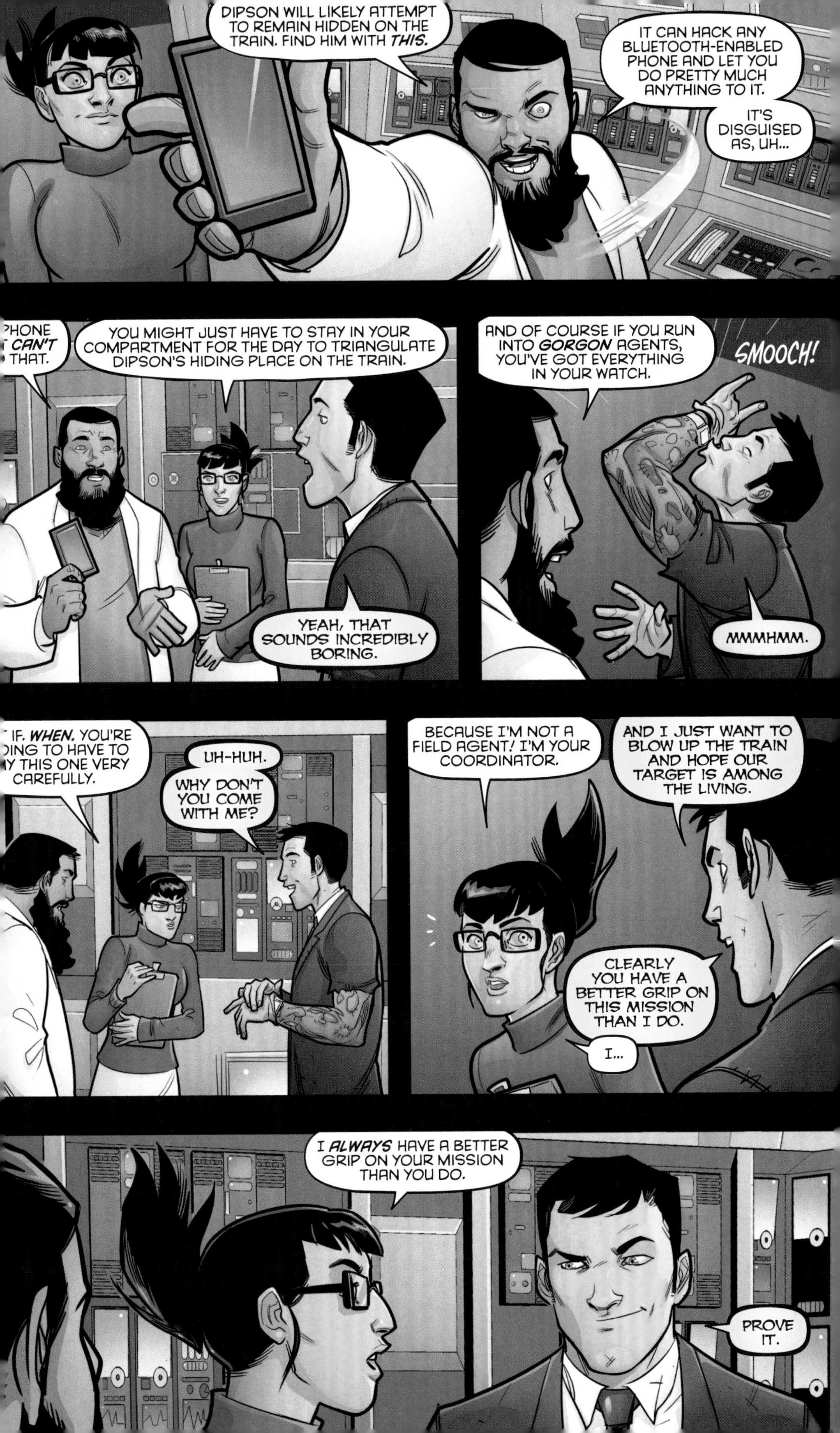
DIPSON WILL LIKELY ATTEMPT TO REMAIN HIDDEN ON THE TRAIN. FIND HIM WITH *THIS.*
IT CAN HACK ANY BLUETOOTH-ENABLED PHONE AND LET YOU DO PRETTY MUCH ANYTHING TO IT.
IT'S DISGUISED AS, UH...
CAN'T THAT.
YOU MIGHT JUST HAVE TO STAY IN YOUR COMPARTMENT FOR THE DAY TO TRIANGULATE DIPSON'S HIDING PLACE ON THE TRAIN.
YEAH, THAT SOUNDS INCREDIBLY BORING.
AND OF COURSE IF YOU RUN INTO *GORGON* AGENTS, YOU'VE GOT EVERYTHING IN YOUR WATCH.
SMOOCH!
MMMHMM.
IF. *WHEN.* YOU'RE TO HAVE TO THIS ONE VERY CAREFULLY.
UH-HUH.
WHY DON'T YOU COME WITH ME?
BECAUSE I'M NOT A FIELD AGENT! I'M YOUR COORDINATOR.
AND I JUST WANT TO BLOW UP THE TRAIN AND HOPE OUR TARGET IS AMONG THE LIVING.
CLEARLY YOU HAVE A BETTER GRIP ON THIS MISSION THAN I DO.
I...
I *ALWAYS* HAVE A BETTER GRIP ON YOUR MISSION THAN YOU DO.
PROVE IT.

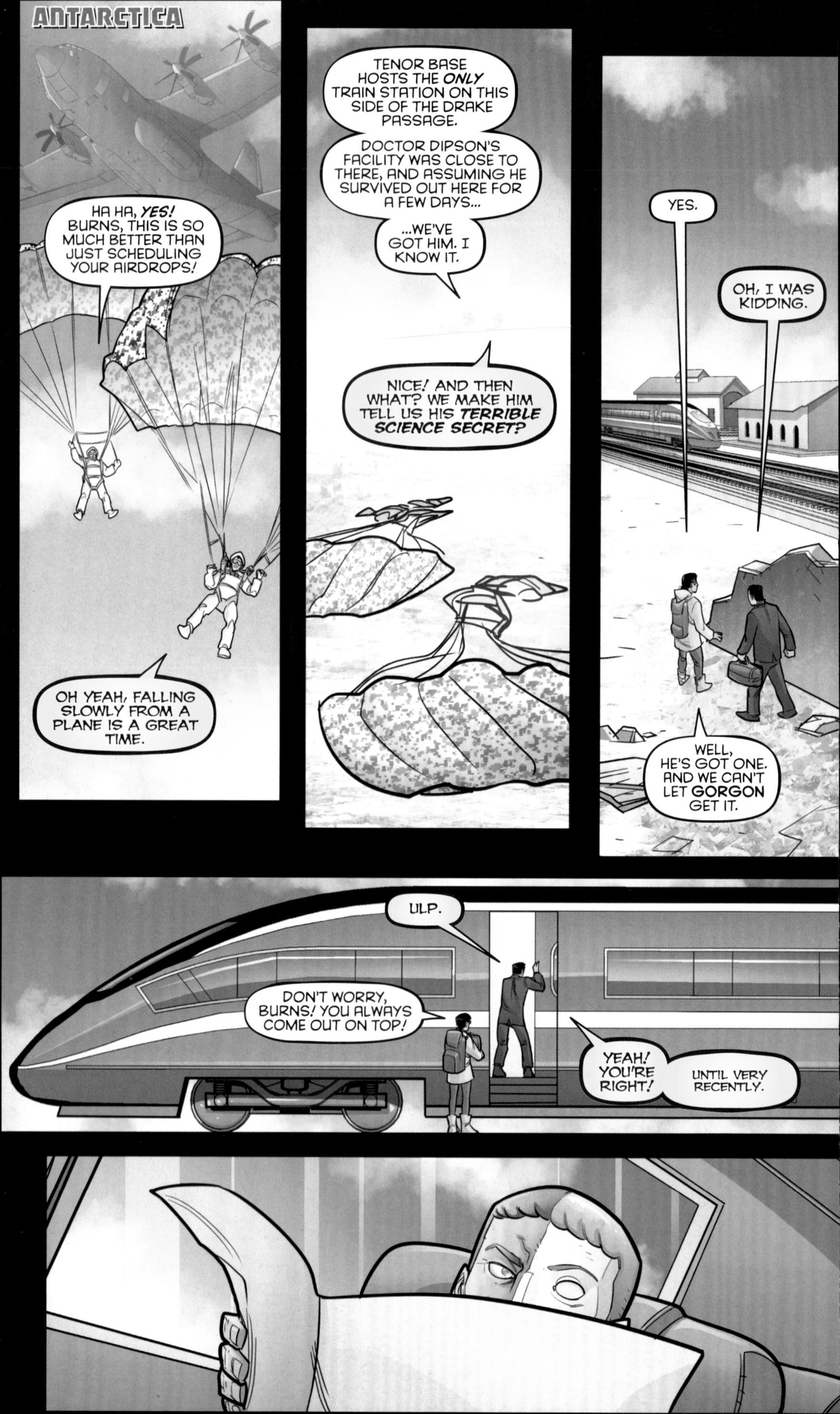
ANTARCTICA
HA HA, YES! BURNS, THIS IS SO MUCH BETTER THAN JUST SCHEDULING YOUR AIRDROPS!
OH YEAH, FALLING SLOWLY FROM A PLANE IS A GREAT TIME.
TENOR BASE HOSTS THE ONLY TRAIN STATION ON THIS SIDE OF THE DRAKE PASSAGE.
DOCTOR DIPSON'S FACILITY WAS CLOSE TO THERE, AND ASSUMING HE SURVIVED OUT HERE FOR A FEW DAYS...
...WE'VE GOT HIM. I KNOW IT.
NICE! AND THEN WHAT? WE MAKE HIM TELL US HIS TERRIBLE SCIENCE SECRET?
YES.
OH, I WAS KIDDING.
WELL, HE'S GOT ONE. AND WE CAN'T LET GORGON GET IT.
ULP.
DON'T WORRY, BURNS! YOU ALWAYS COME OUT ON TOP!
YEAH! YOU'RE RIGHT!
UNTIL VERY RECENTLY.

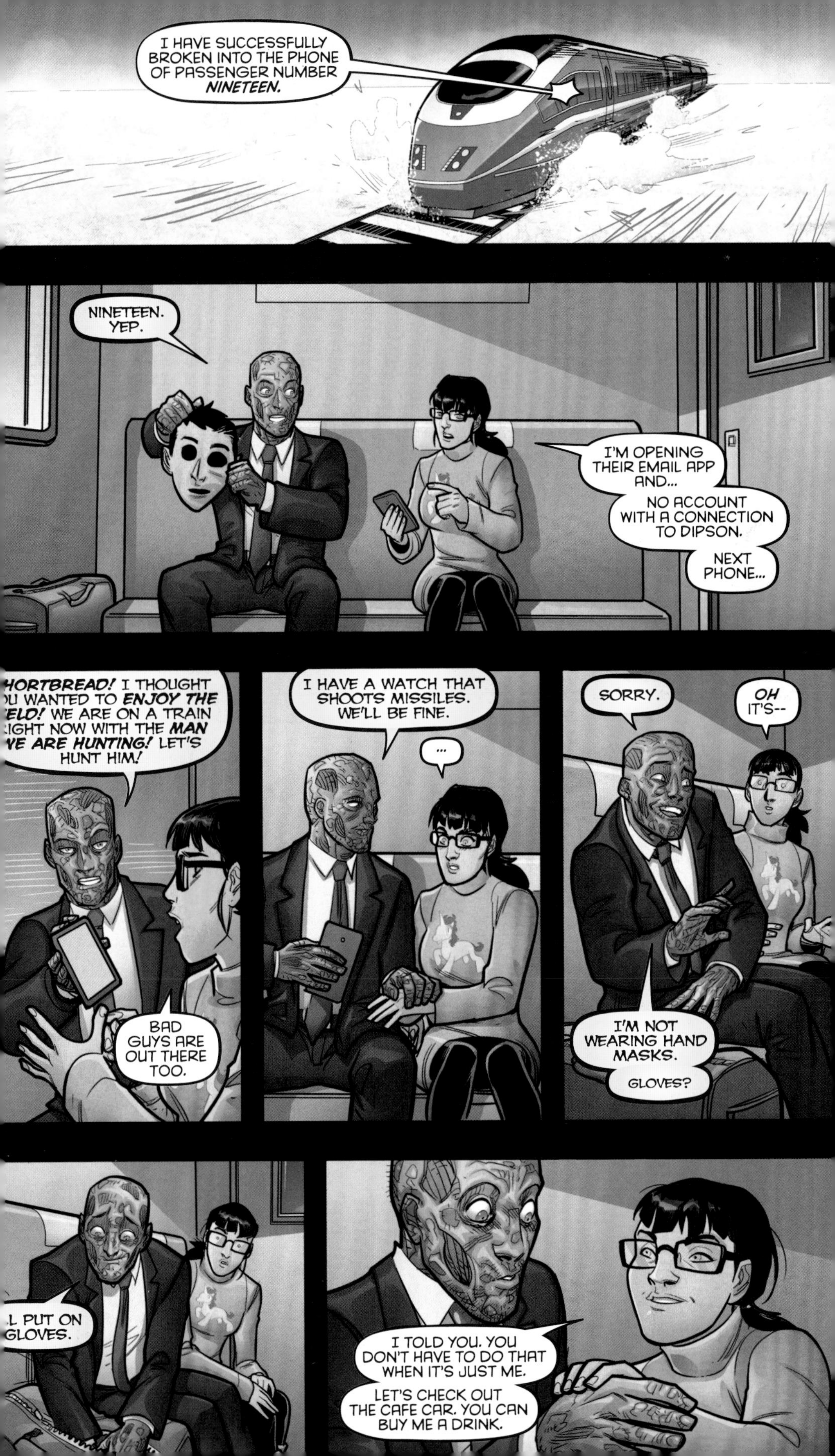
I HAVE SUCCESSFULLY BROKEN INTO THE PHONE OF PASSENGER NUMBER *NINETEEN.*
NINETEEN. YEP.
I'M OPENING THEIR EMAIL APP AND...
NO ACCOUNT WITH A CONNECTION TO DIPSON.
NEXT PHONE...
HORTBREAD! I THOUGHT U WANTED TO *ENJOY THE* ELD! WE ARE ON A TRAIN IGHT NOW WITH THE *MAN* E ARE HUNTING! LET'S HUNT HIM!
BAD GUYS ARE OUT THERE TOO.
I HAVE A WATCH THAT SHOOTS MISSILES. WE'LL BE FINE.
...
SORRY.
OH IT'S--
I'M NOT WEARING HAND MASKS.
GLOVES?
L PUT ON GLOVES.
I TOLD YOU. YOU DON'T HAVE TO DO THAT WHEN IT'S JUST ME.
LET'S CHECK OUT THE CAFE CAR. YOU CAN BUY ME A DRINK.

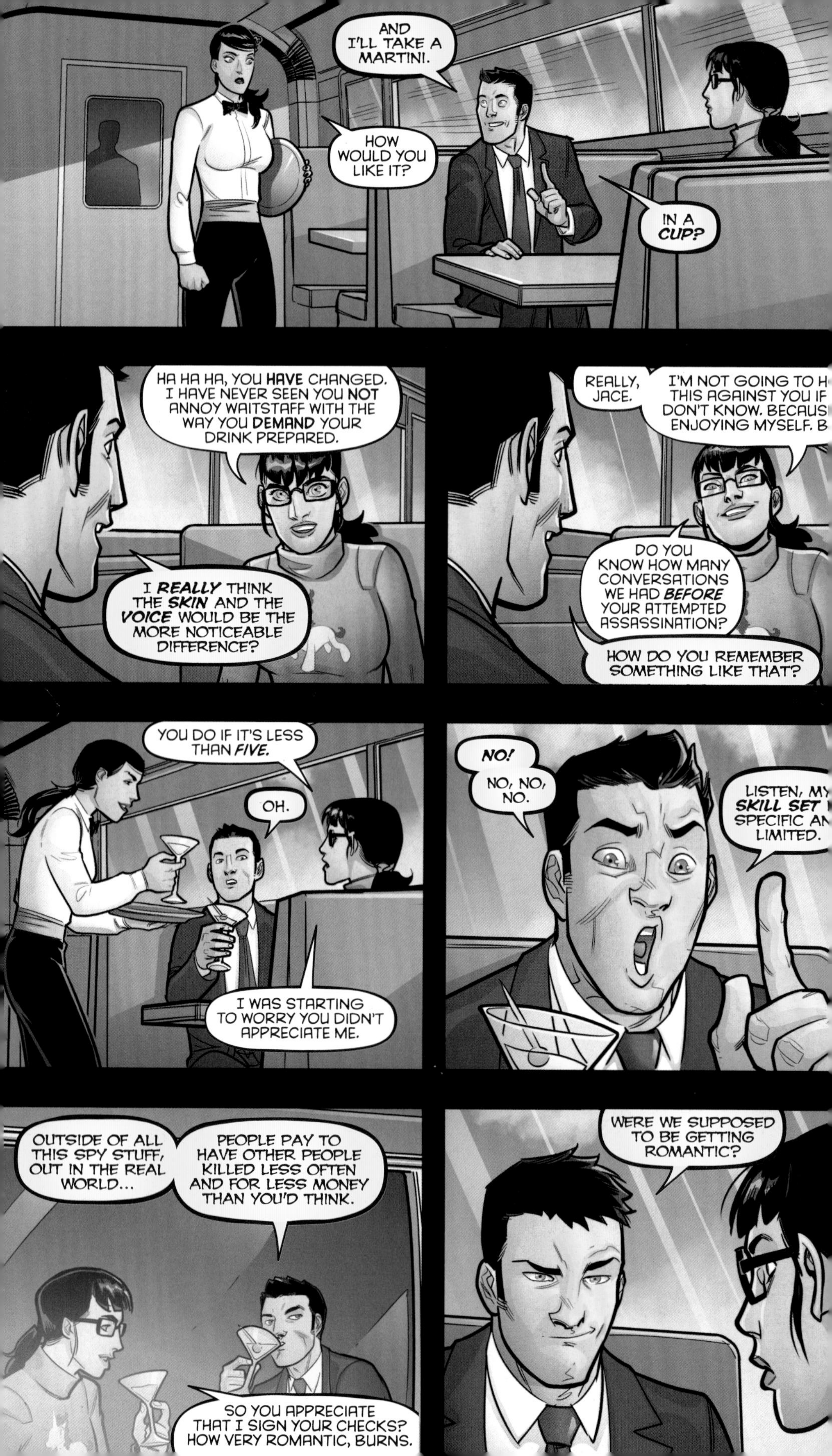
AND I'LL TAKE A MARTINI.
HOW WOULD YOU LIKE IT?
IN A CUP?
HA HA HA, YOU HAVE CHANGED. I HAVE NEVER SEEN YOU NOT ANNOY WAITSTAFF WITH THE WAY YOU DEMAND YOUR DRINK PREPARED.
I REALLY THINK THE SKIN AND THE VOICE WOULD BE THE MORE NOTICEABLE DIFFERENCE?
REALLY, JACE.
DO YOU KNOW HOW MANY CONVERSATIONS WE HAD BEFORE YOUR ATTEMPTED ASSASSINATION?
HOW DO YOU REMEMBER SOMETHING LIKE THAT?
YOU DO IF IT'S LESS THAN FIVE.
OH.
I WAS STARTING TO WORRY YOU DIDN'T APPRECIATE ME.
NO!
NO, NO, NO.
OUTSIDE OF ALL THIS SPY STUFF, OUT IN THE REAL WORLD...
PEOPLE PAY TO HAVE OTHER PEOPLE KILLED LESS OFTEN AND FOR LESS MONEY THAN YOU'D THINK.
SO YOU APPRECIATE THAT I SIGN YOUR CHECKS? HOW VERY ROMANTIC, BURNS.
WERE WE SUPPOSED TO BE GETTING ROMANTIC?

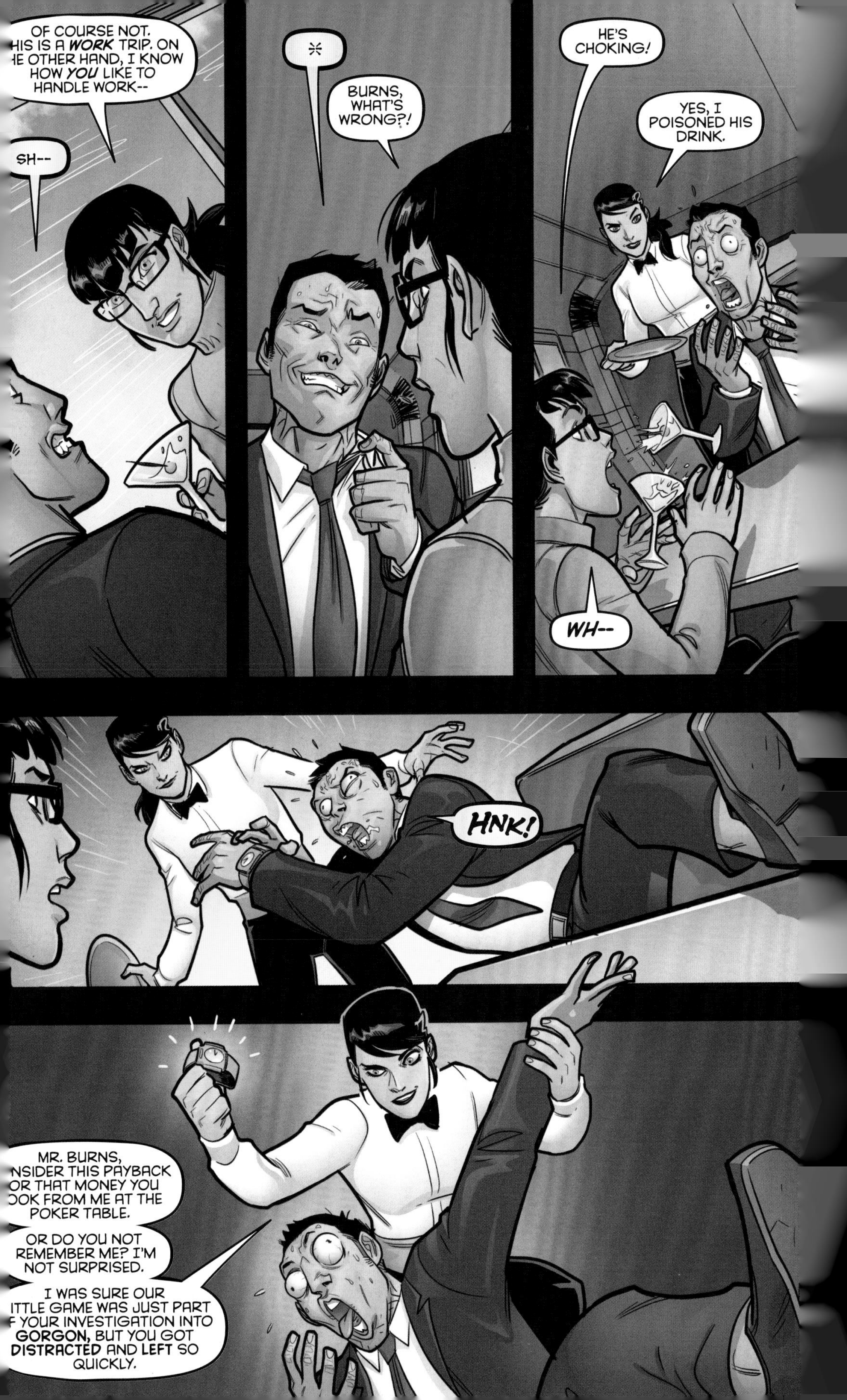
OF COURSE NOT. HIS IS A WORK TRIP. ON IE OTHER HAND, I KNOW HOW YOU LIKE TO HANDLE WORK--
SH--
BURNS, WHAT'S WRONG?!
HE'S CHOKING!
YES, I POISONED HIS DRINK.
WH--
HNK!
MR. BURNS, NSIDER THIS PAYBACK OR THAT MONEY YOU OOK FROM ME AT THE POKER TABLE.
OR DO YOU NOT REMEMBER ME? I'M NOT SURPRISED.
I WAS SURE OUR ITTLE GAME WAS JUST PART F YOUR INVESTIGATION INTO GORGON, BUT YOU GOT DISTRACTED AND LEFT SO QUICKLY.

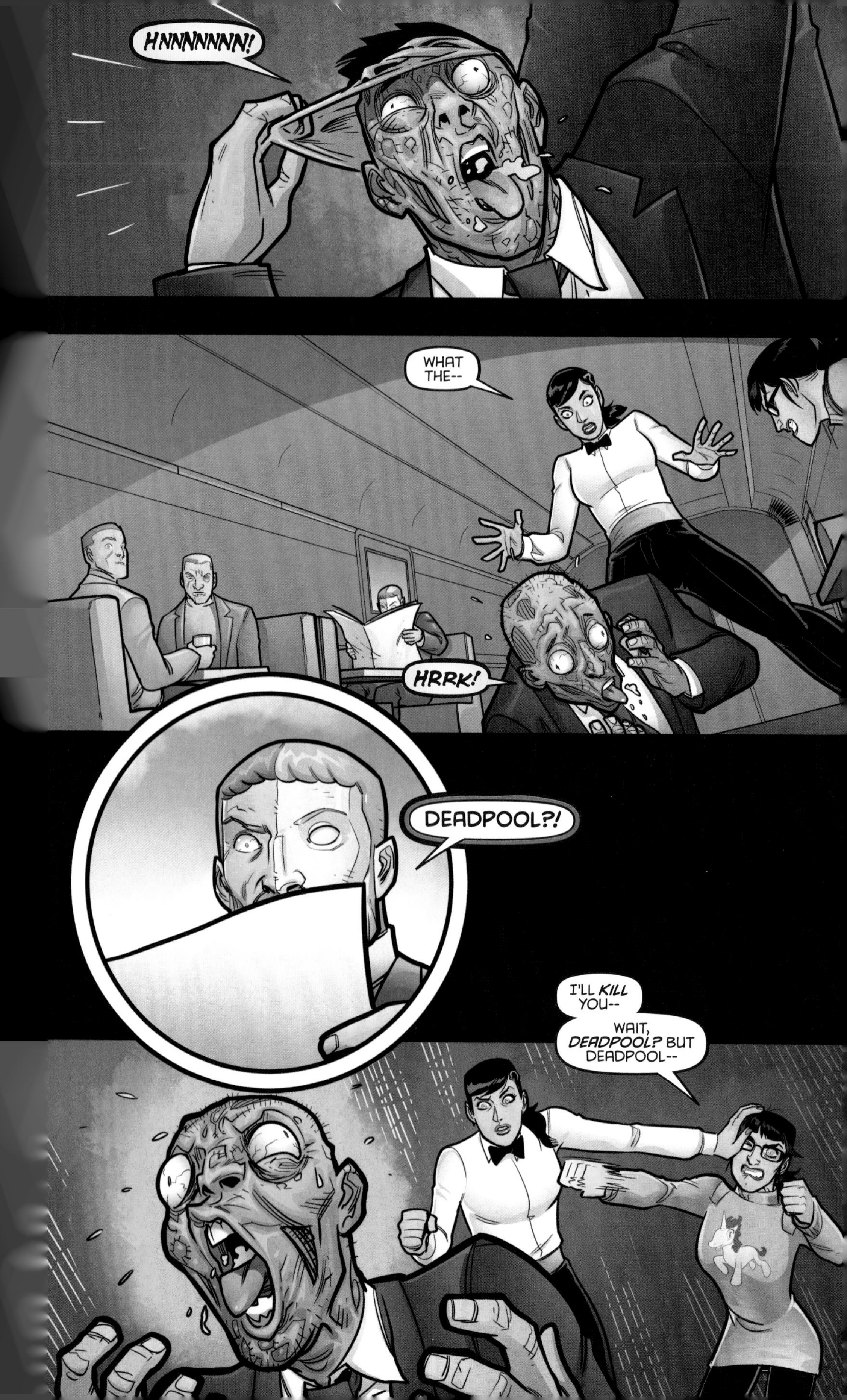
HNNNNNNN!
WHAT THE--
HRRK!
DEADPOOL?!
I'LL KILL YOU--
WAIT, DEADPOOL? BUT DEADPOOL--

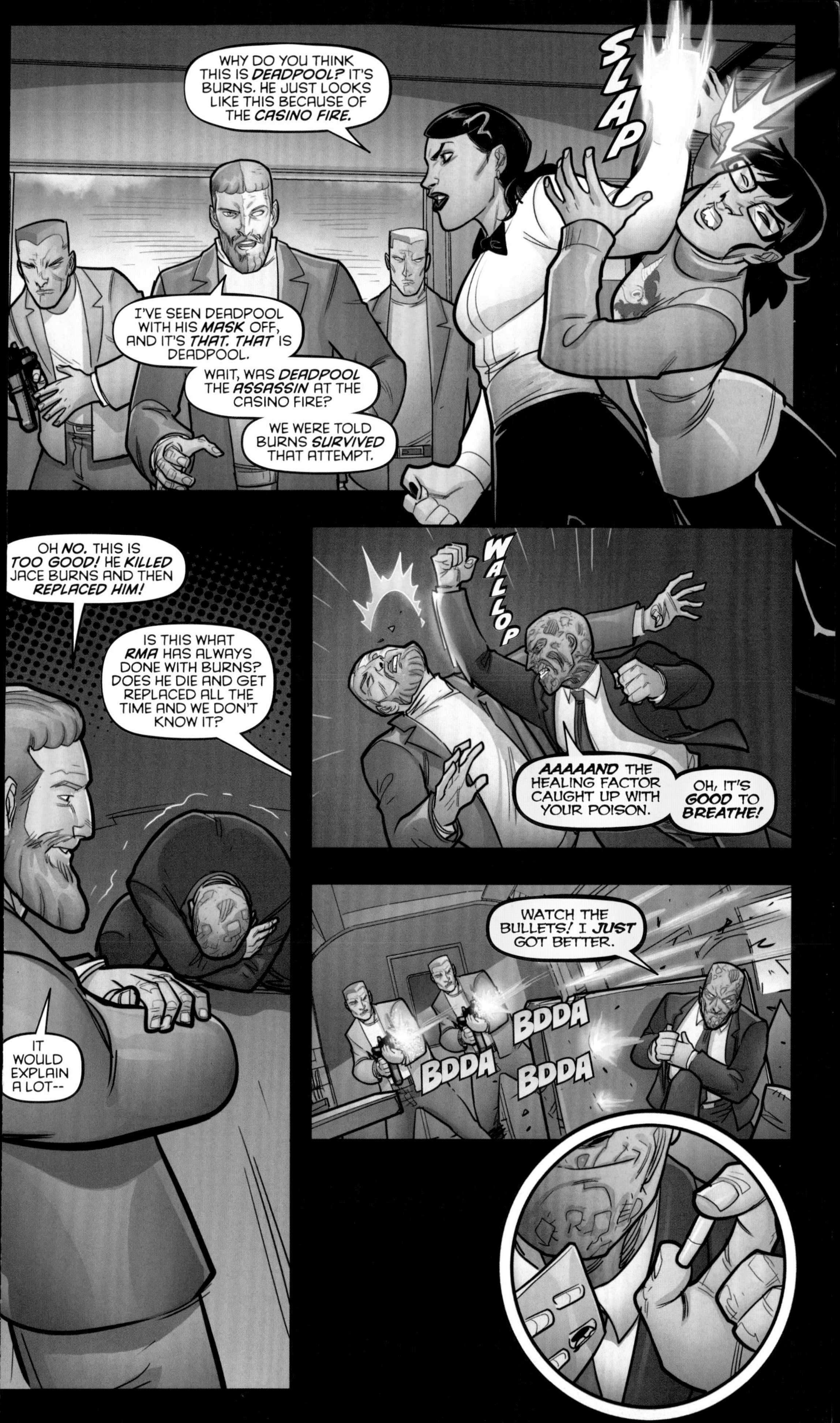
SLAP
WHY DO YOU THINK THIS IS DEADPOOL? IT'S BURNS. HE JUST LOOKS LIKE THIS BECAUSE OF THE CASINO FIRE.
I'VE SEEN DEADPOOL WITH HIS MASK OFF, AND IT'S THAT. THAT IS DEADPOOL.
WAIT, WAS DEADPOOL THE ASSASSIN AT THE CASINO FIRE?
WE WERE TOLD BURNS SURVIVED THAT ATTEMPT.
OH NO. THIS IS TOO GOOD! HE KILLED JACE BURNS AND THEN REPLACED HIM!
IS THIS WHAT RMA HAS ALWAYS DONE WITH BURNS? DOES HE DIE AND GET REPLACED ALL THE TIME AND WE DON'T KNOW IT?
IT WOULD EXPLAIN A LOT--
WALLOP
AAAAAND THE HEALING FACTOR CAUGHT UP WITH YOUR POISON.
OH, IT'S GOOD TO BREATHE!
WATCH THE BULLETS! I JUST GOT BETTER.
BDDA
BDDA
BDDA

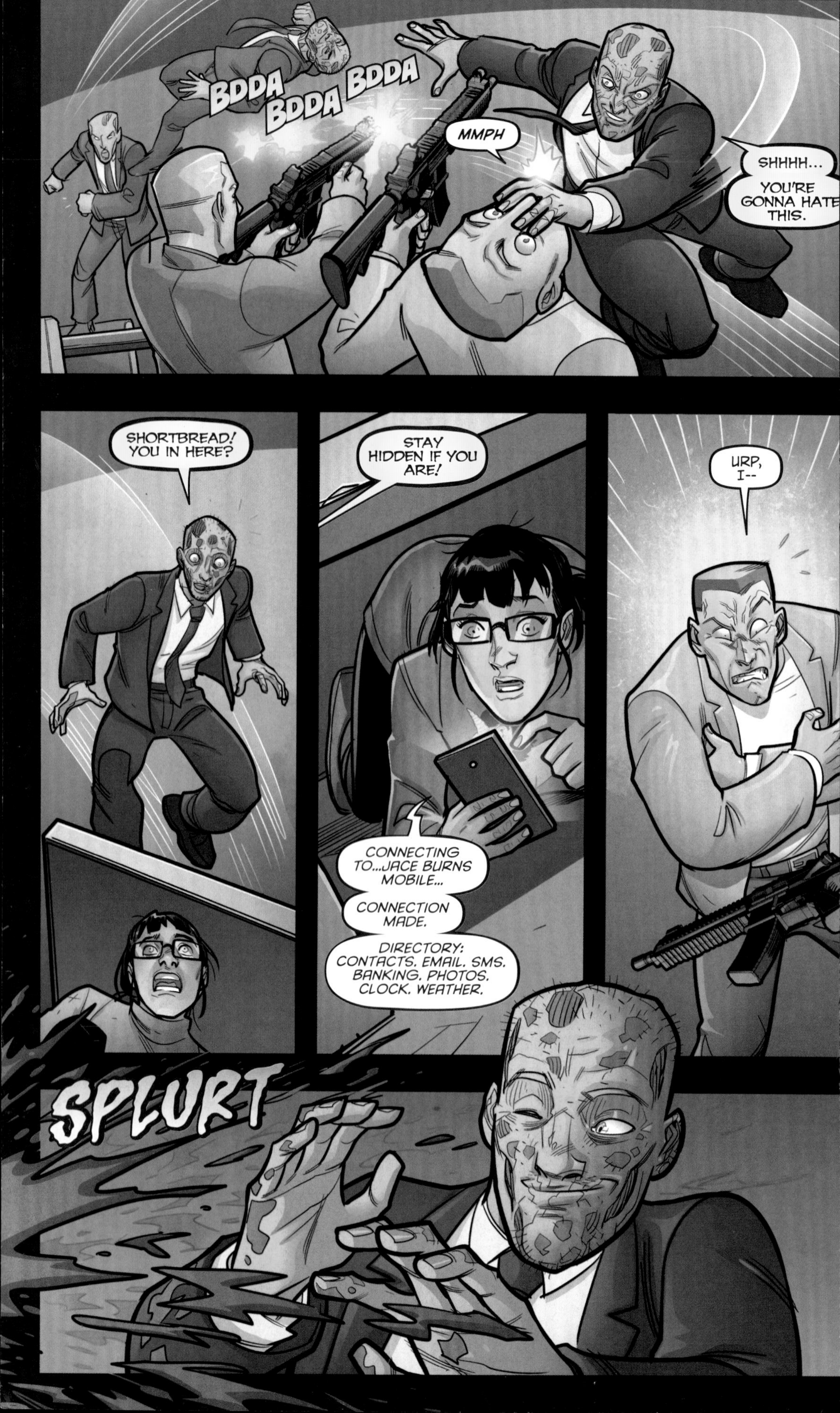
BDDA
BDDA
BDDA
MMPH
SHHHH...
YOU'RE GONNA HATE THIS.
SHORTBREAD! YOU IN HERE?
STAY HIDDEN IF YOU ARE!
CONNECTING TO...JACE BURNS MOBILE...
CONNECTION MADE.
DIRECTORY: CONTACTS. EMAIL. SMS. BANKING. PHOTOS. CLOCK. WEATHER.
URP, I--
SPLURT

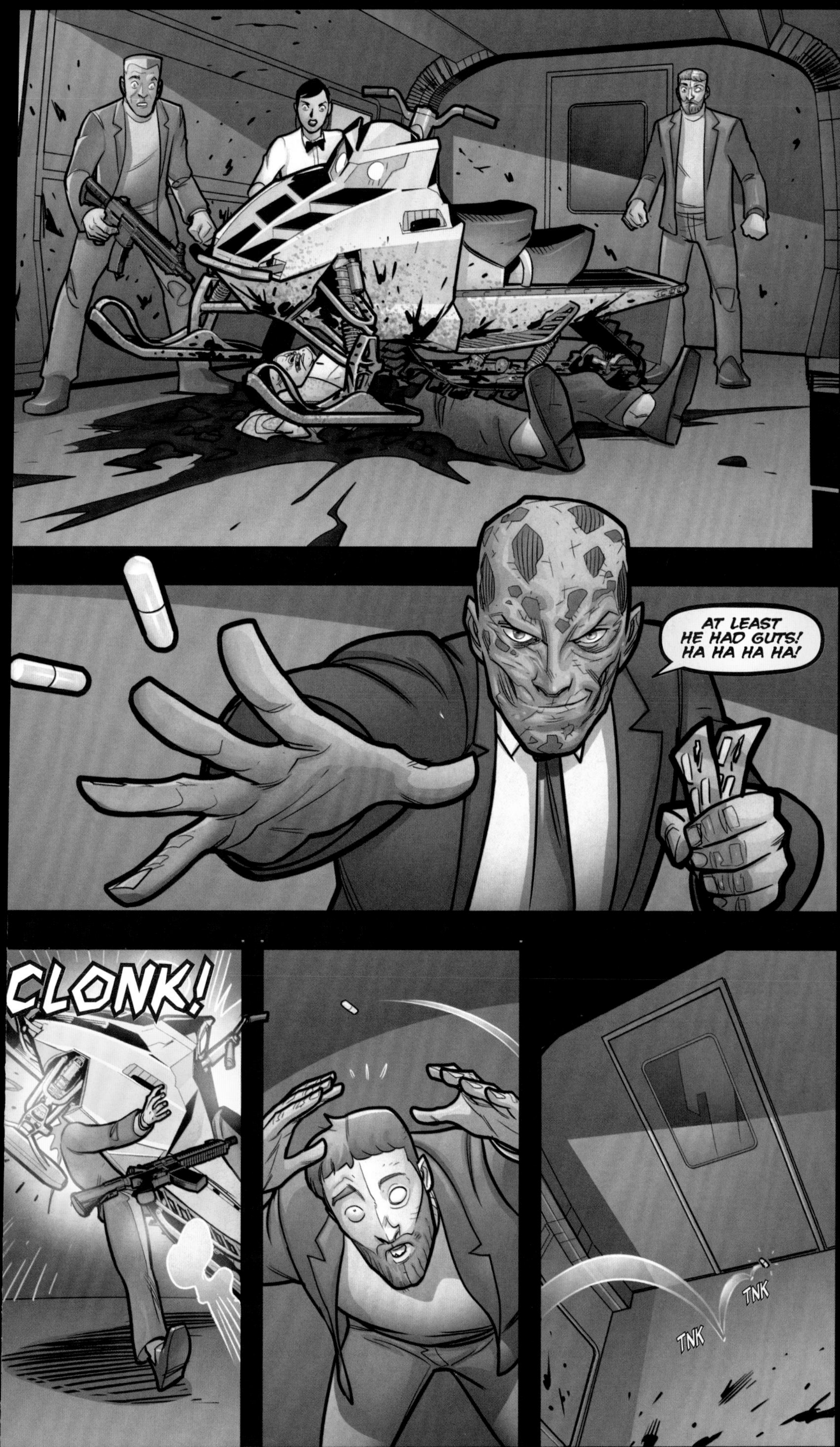
AT LEAST HE HAD GUTS! HA HA HA HA!
CLONK!
TNK
TNK

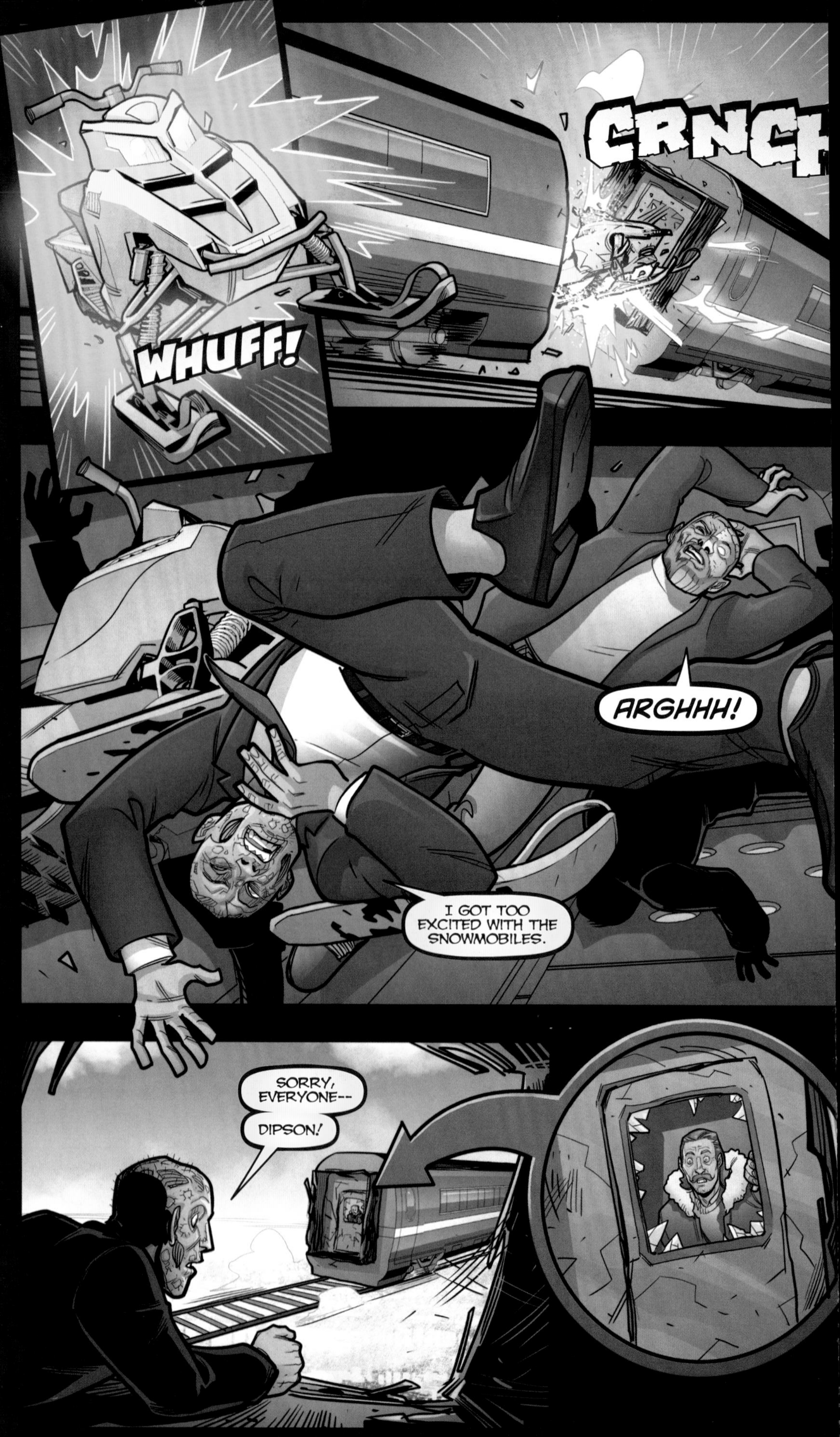
WHUFF!
CRNCH
ARGHHH!
I GOT TOO EXCITED WITH THE SNOWMOBILES.
SORRY, EVERYONE--
DIPSON!

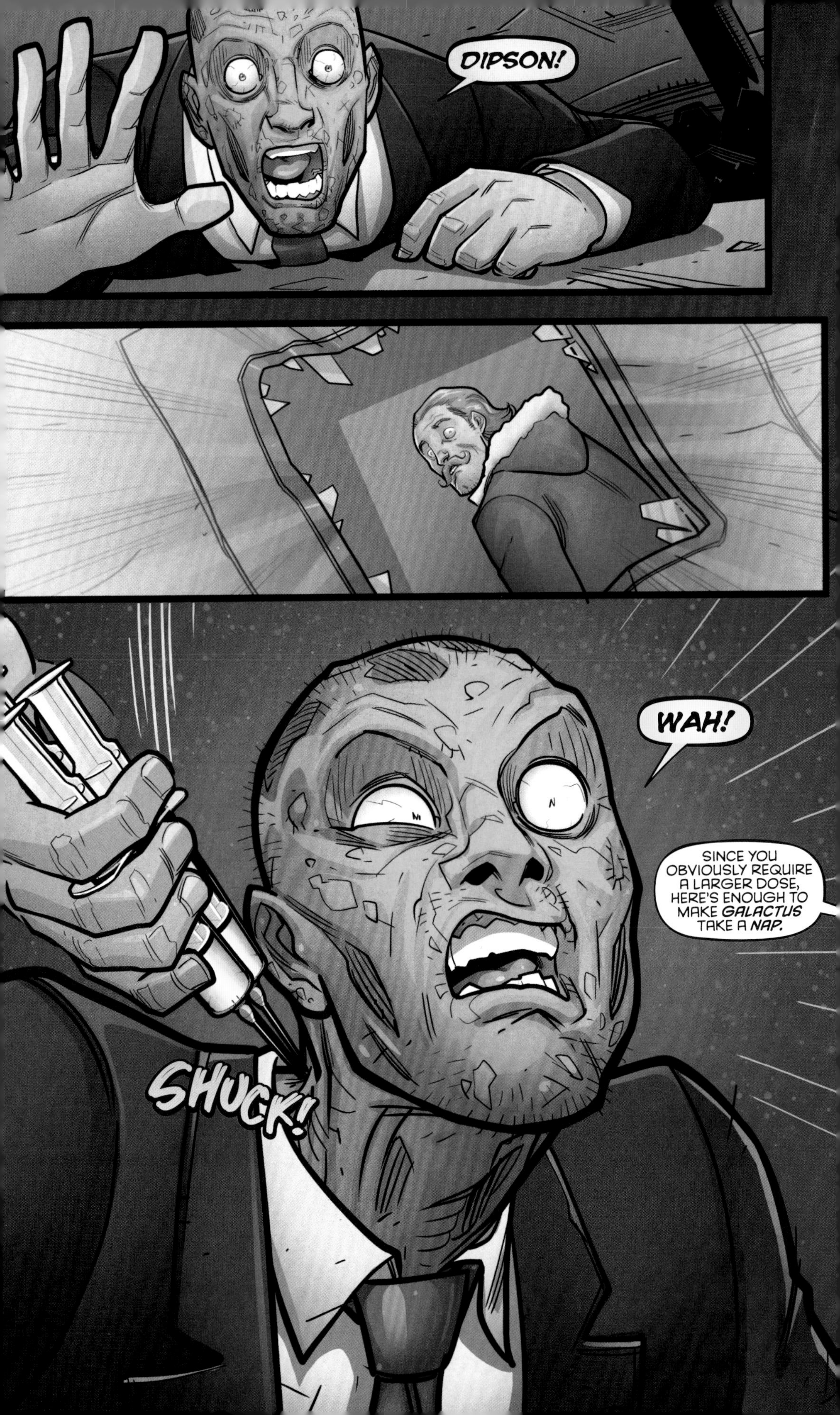

DIPSON!
WAH!
SINCE YOU OBVIOUSLY REQUIRE A LARGER DOSE, HERE'S ENOUGH TO MAKE *GALACTUS* TAKE A *NAP.*
SHUCK!

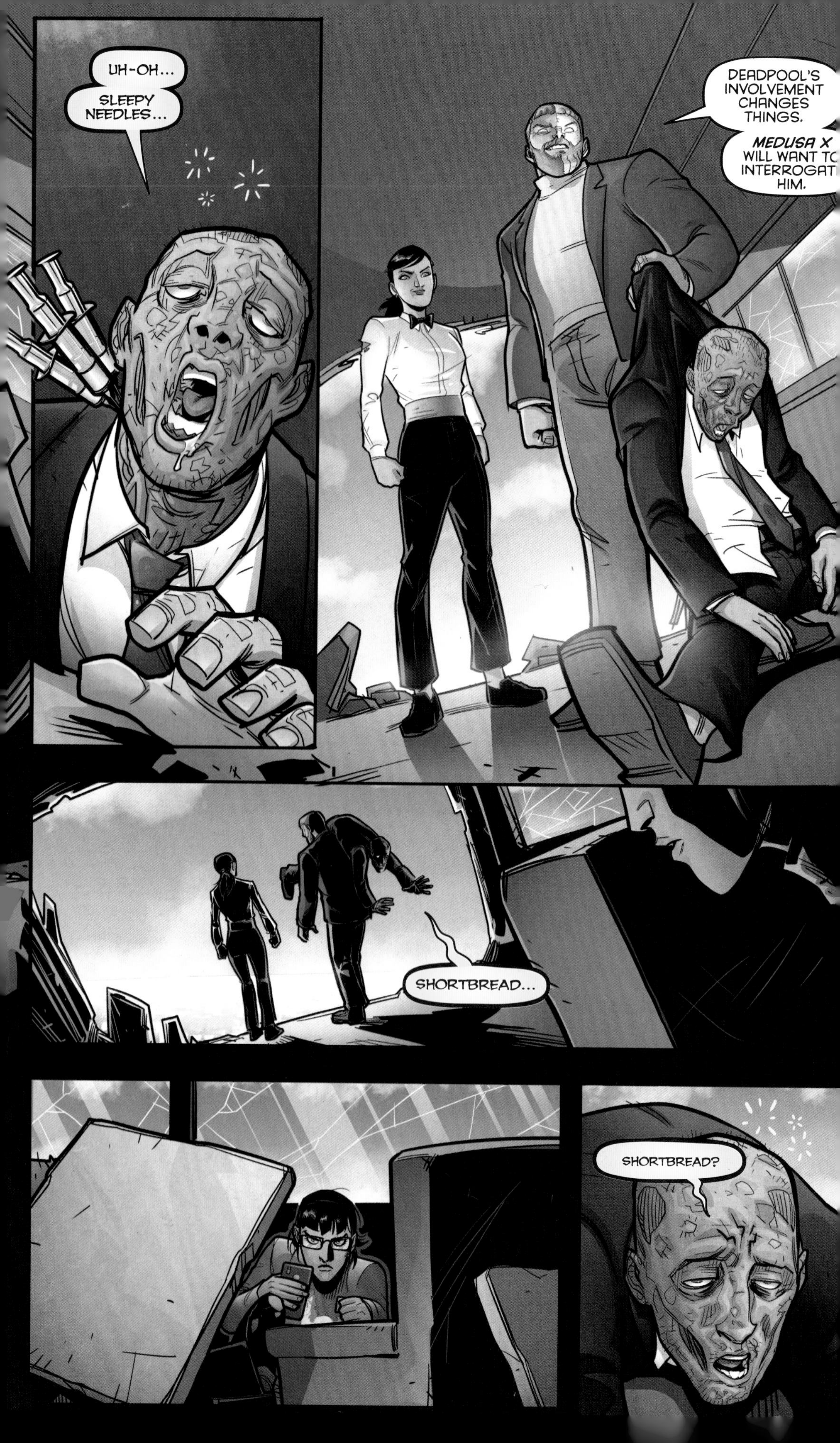

UH-OH...
SLEEPY NEEDLES...
DEADPOOL'S INVOLVEMENT CHANGES THINGS.
MEDUSA X WILL WANT TO INTERROGATE HIM.
SHORTBREAD...
SHORTBREAD?

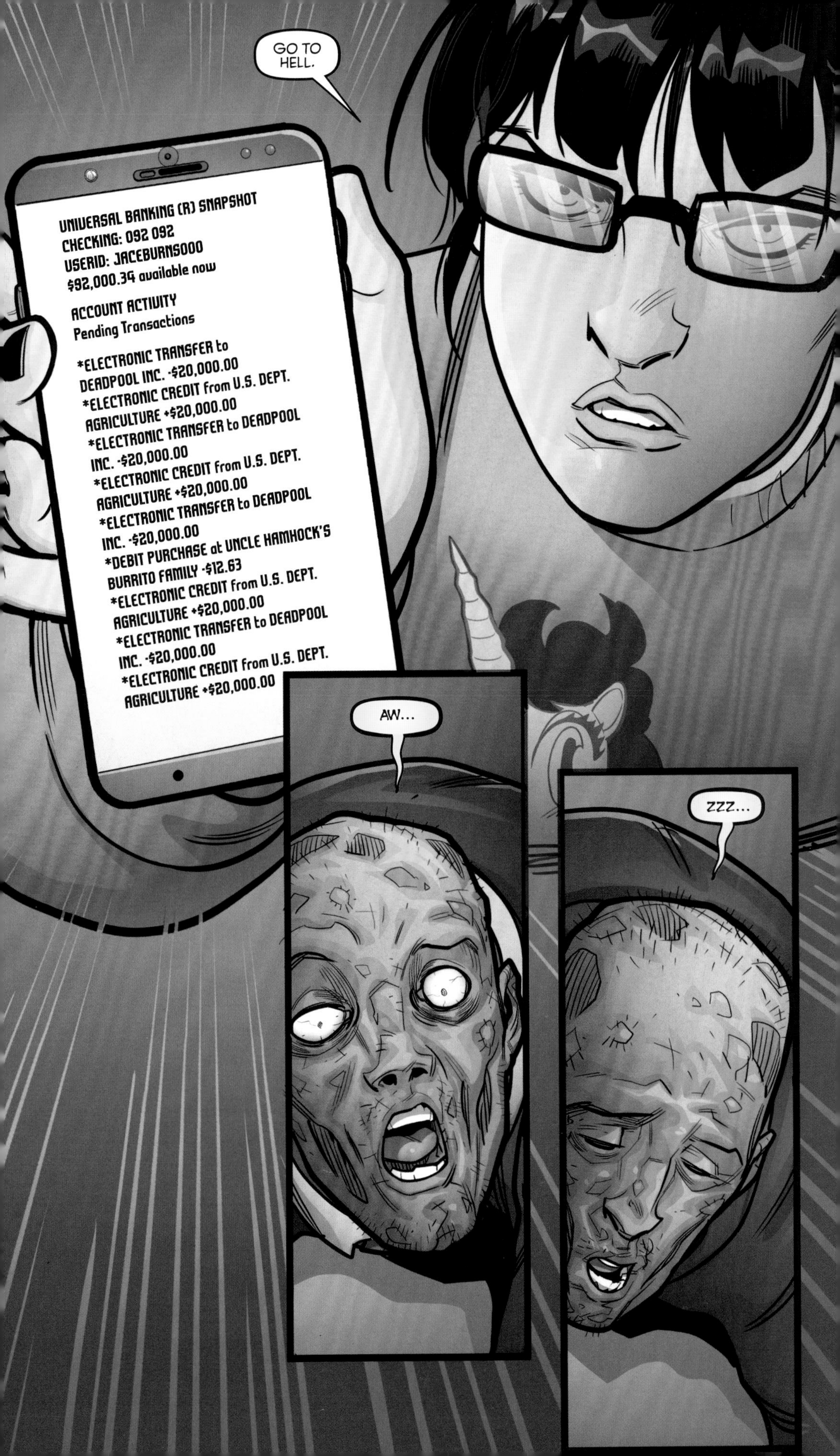
GO TO HELL.
UNIVERSAL BANKING (R) SNAPSHOT
CHECKING: 092 092
USERID: JACEBURNS000
$92,000.34 available now
ACCOUNT ACTIVITY
Pending Transactions
*ELECTRONIC TRANSFER to DEADPOOL INC. -$20,000.00
*ELECTRONIC CREDIT from U.S. DEPT. AGRICULTURE +$20,000.00
*ELECTRONIC TRANSFER to DEADPOOL INC. -$20,000.00
*ELECTRONIC CREDIT from U.S. DEPT. AGRICULTURE +$20,000.00
*ELECTRONIC TRANSFER to DEADPOOL INC. -$20,000.00
*DEBIT PURCHASE at UNCLE HAMHOCK'S BURRITO FAMILY -$12.63
*ELECTRONIC CREDIT from U.S. DEPT. AGRICULTURE +$20,000.00
*ELECTRONIC TRANSFER to DEADPOOL INC. -$20,000.00
*ELECTRONIC CREDIT from U.S. DEPT. AGRICULTURE +$20,000.00
AW...
ZZZ...

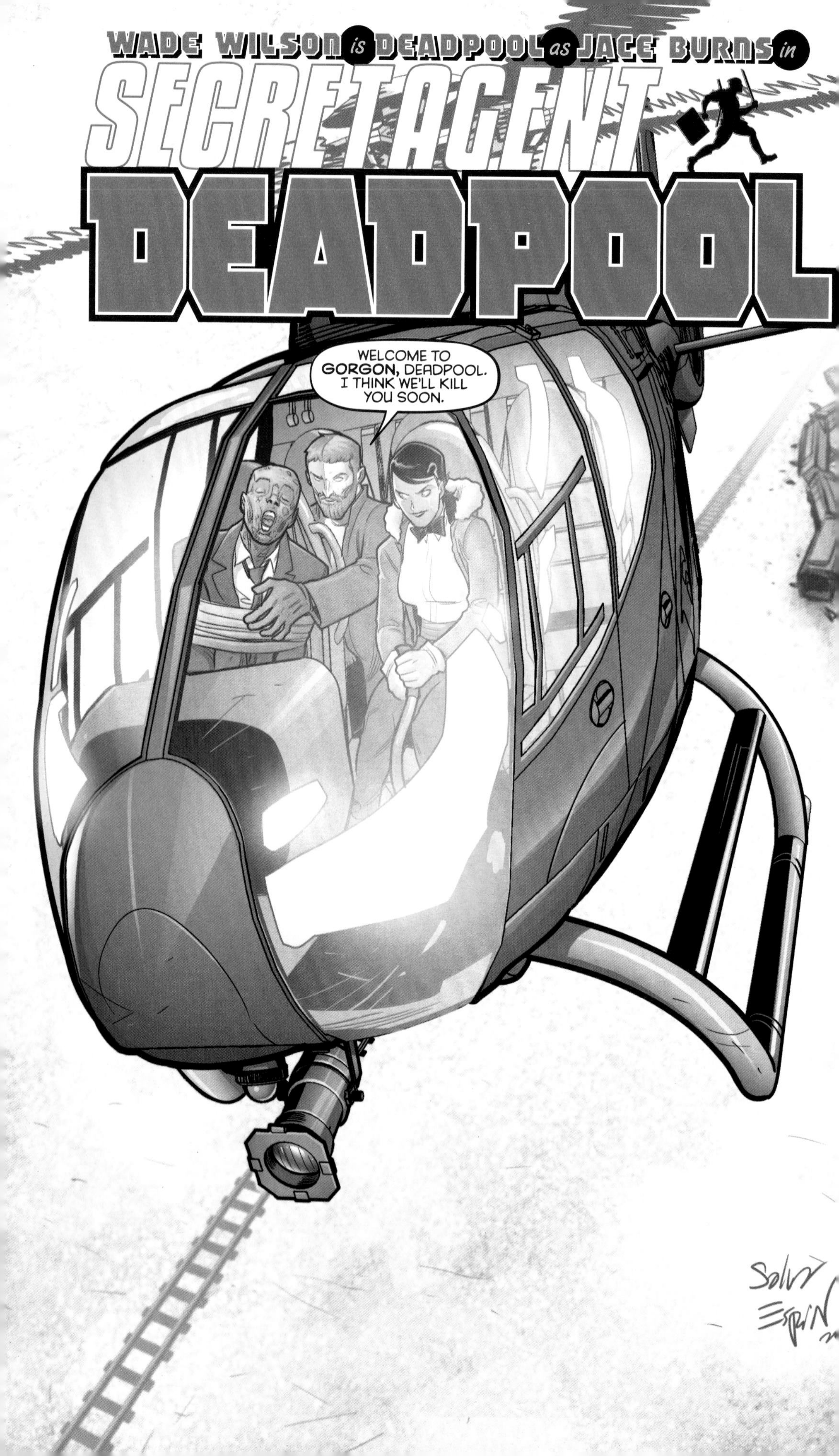
WADE WILSON is DEADPOOL as JACE BURNS in
SECRET AGENT DEADPOOL
WELCOME TO GORGON, DEADPOOL. I THINK WE'LL KILL YOU SOON.
Salva Espin

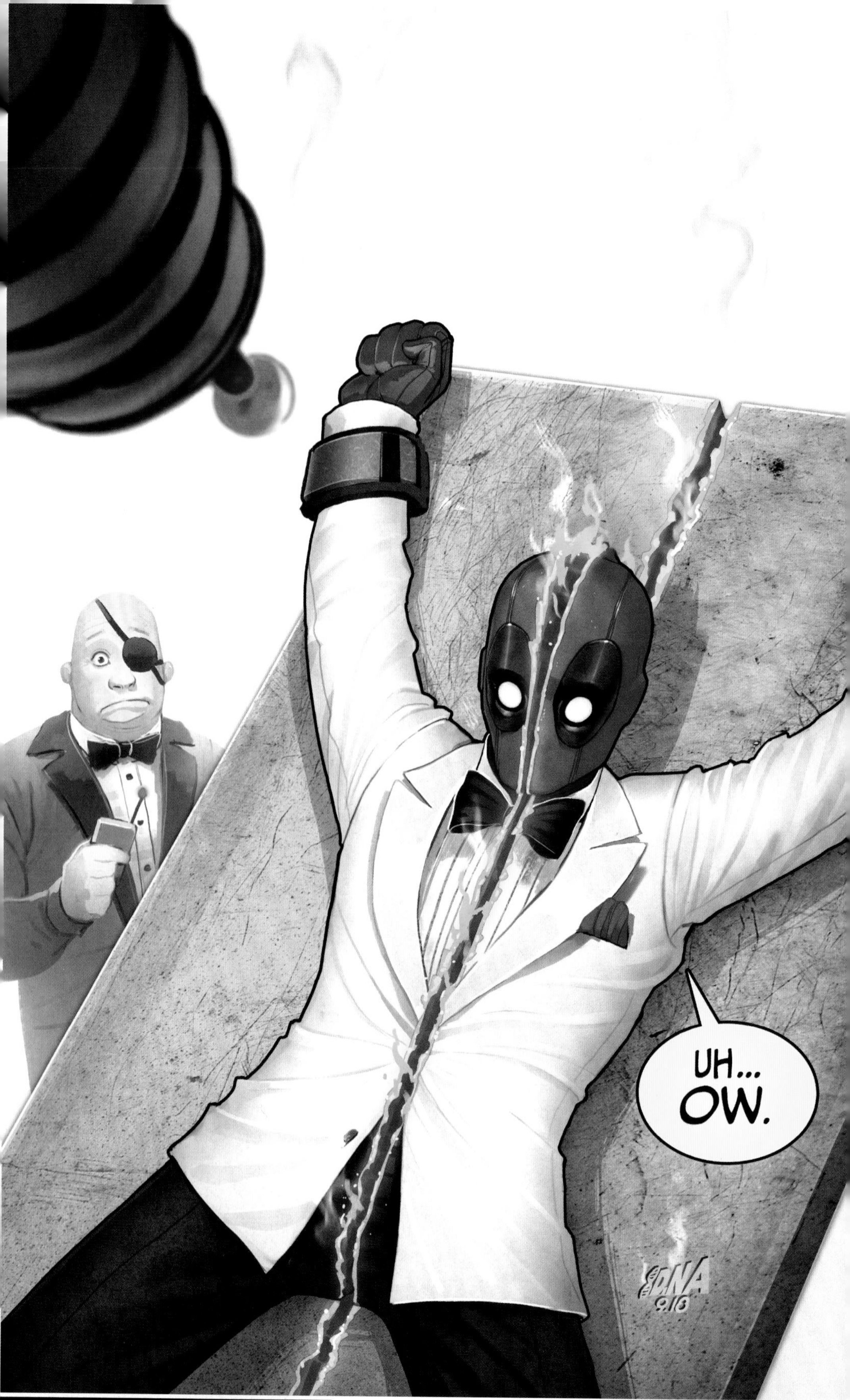
UH... OW.

4

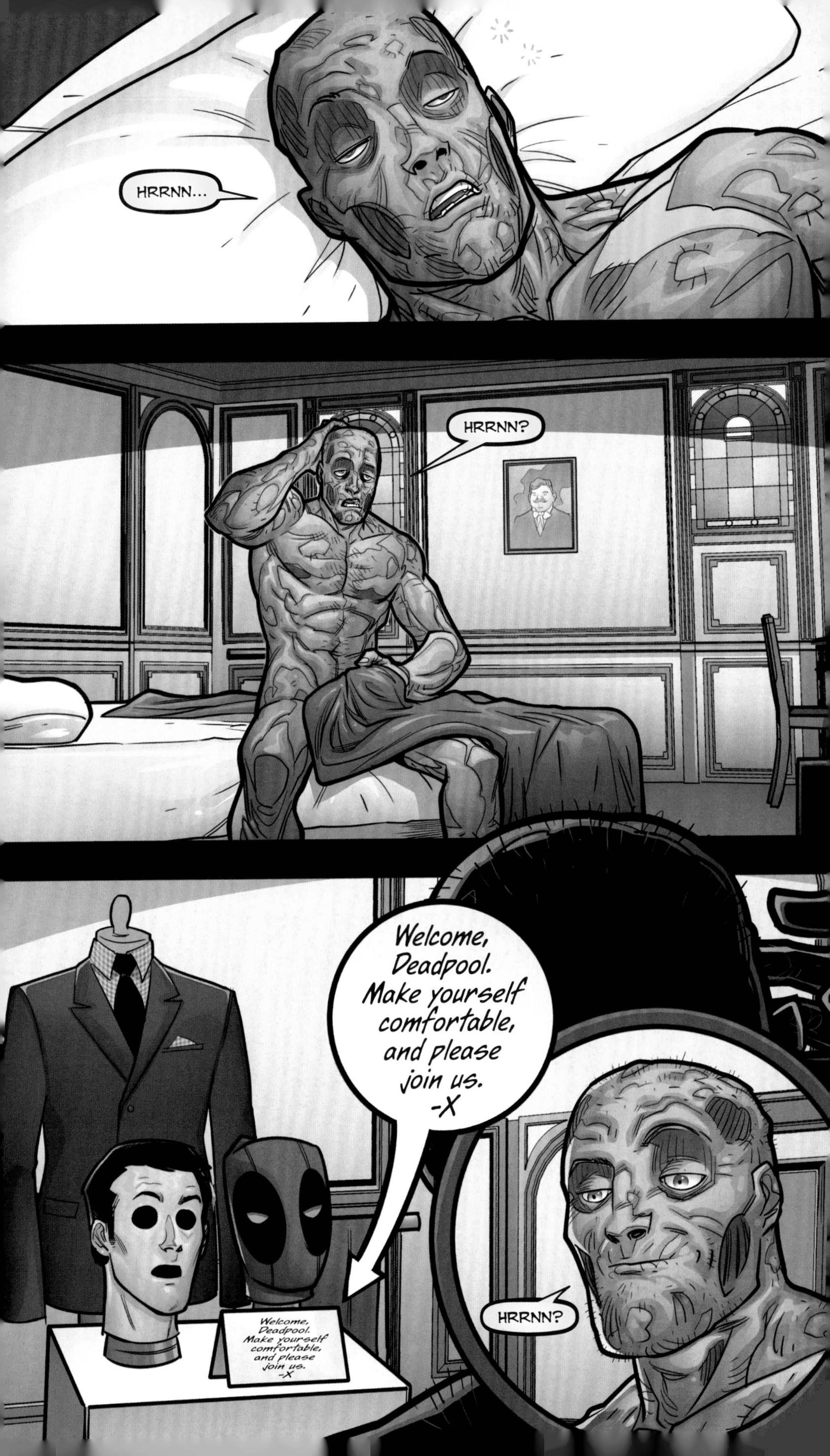
HRRNN...
HRRNN?
Welcome, Deadpool. Make yourself comfortable, and please join us. -X
Welcome, Deadpool. Make yourself comfortable, and please join us. -X
HRRNN?

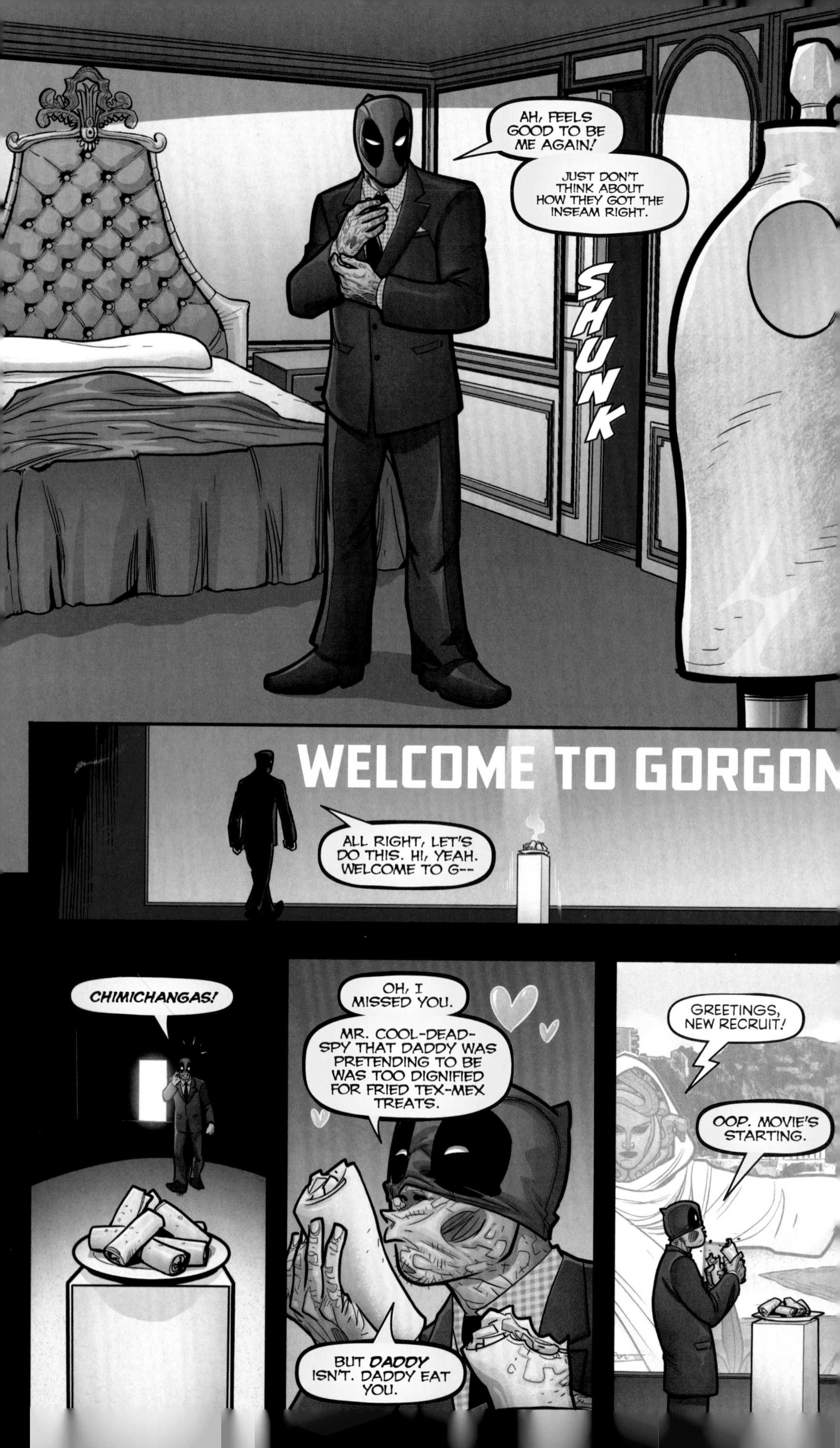
AH, FEELS GOOD TO BE ME AGAIN!
JUST DON'T THINK ABOUT HOW THEY GOT THE INSEAM RIGHT.
SHUNK
WELCOME TO GORGON
ALL RIGHT, LET'S DO THIS. HI, YEAH. WELCOME TO G--
CHIMICHANGAS!
OH, I MISSED YOU.
MR. COOL-DEAD-SPY THAT DADDY WAS PRETENDING TO BE WAS TOO DIGNIFIED FOR FRIED TEX-MEX TREATS.
BUT DADDY ISN'T. DADDY EAT YOU.
GREETINGS, NEW RECRUIT!
OOP. MOVIE'S STARTING.

WELCOME TO BEAUTIFUL GREECE! LAND OF LEGEND AND MYSTERY.

YOU ARE CURRENTLY DEEP UNDERGROUND IN **GORGON'S** PRIVATE COMPOUND.

I AM **MEDUSA X,** CURRENT HEAD OF **GORGON** OPERATIONS.

IF YOU'VE MADE IT THIS FAR, *CONGRATULATIONS!* **GORGON** RECOGNIZES YOU AS A SKILLED AND VALUABLE ASSET, WITH PRINCIPLES THAT MIRROR THOSE OF OUR ORIGINAL FOUNDER, *MEDUSA.*

THOUSANDS OF YEARS AGO, MEDUSA WAS A BEAUTIFUL WOMAN, WRONGED BY THE GODS. SHE WAS CURSED WITH A CROWN OF SNAKES AND A GAZE THAT WOULD TURN MEN TO STONE.

HEARD OF HER...

THERE ARE MANY STORIES OF MEDUSA, BUT ONE LESS TOLD IS HER FORMATION OF A SECRET SOCIETY...

OHHHH...

...AN ORGANIZATION DICATED TO STRIKING BACK GAINST THE UNJUST GODS WHO CURSED MEDUSA.

OPERATING IN CRET, **GORGON** WORKED CONSOLIDATE POWER AND RIKE WHERE IT COULD TO RIGHT THE WRONGS OF A CRUEL AND PETTY PANTHEON.

AS YEARS WENT BY, THE GODS WERE FORGOTTEN. BUT POWER...

...*UNJUST* POWER...

...ALWAYS REMAINS.

AND GORGON HAS ALWAYS BEEN THERE TO FIGHT IT.

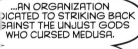

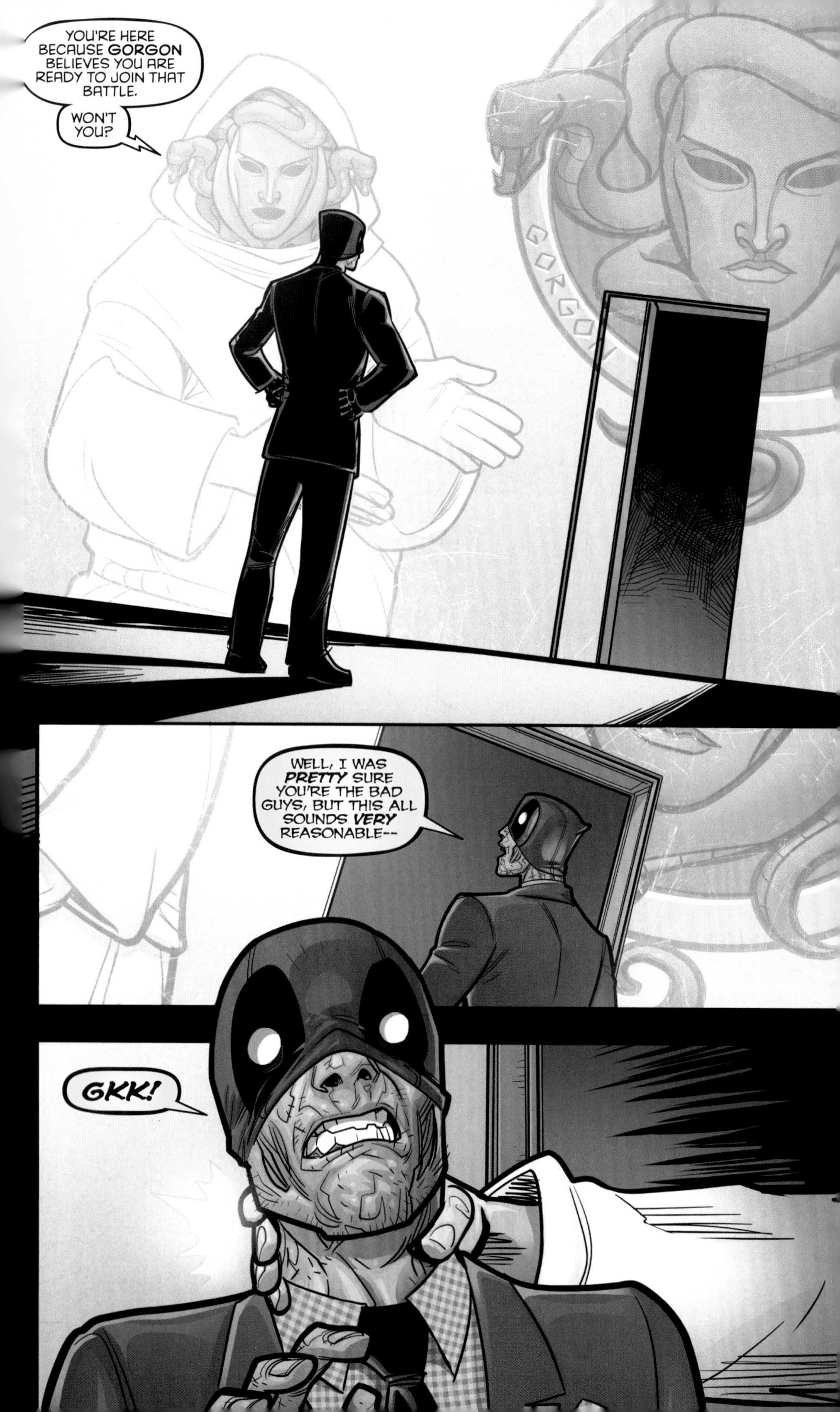
YOU'RE HERE BECAUSE **GORGON** BELIEVES YOU ARE READY TO JOIN THAT BATTLE.
WON'T YOU?
GORGON
WELL, I WAS ***PRETTY*** SURE YOU'RE THE BAD GUYS, BUT THIS ALL SOUNDS ***VERY*** REASONABLE--
GKK!

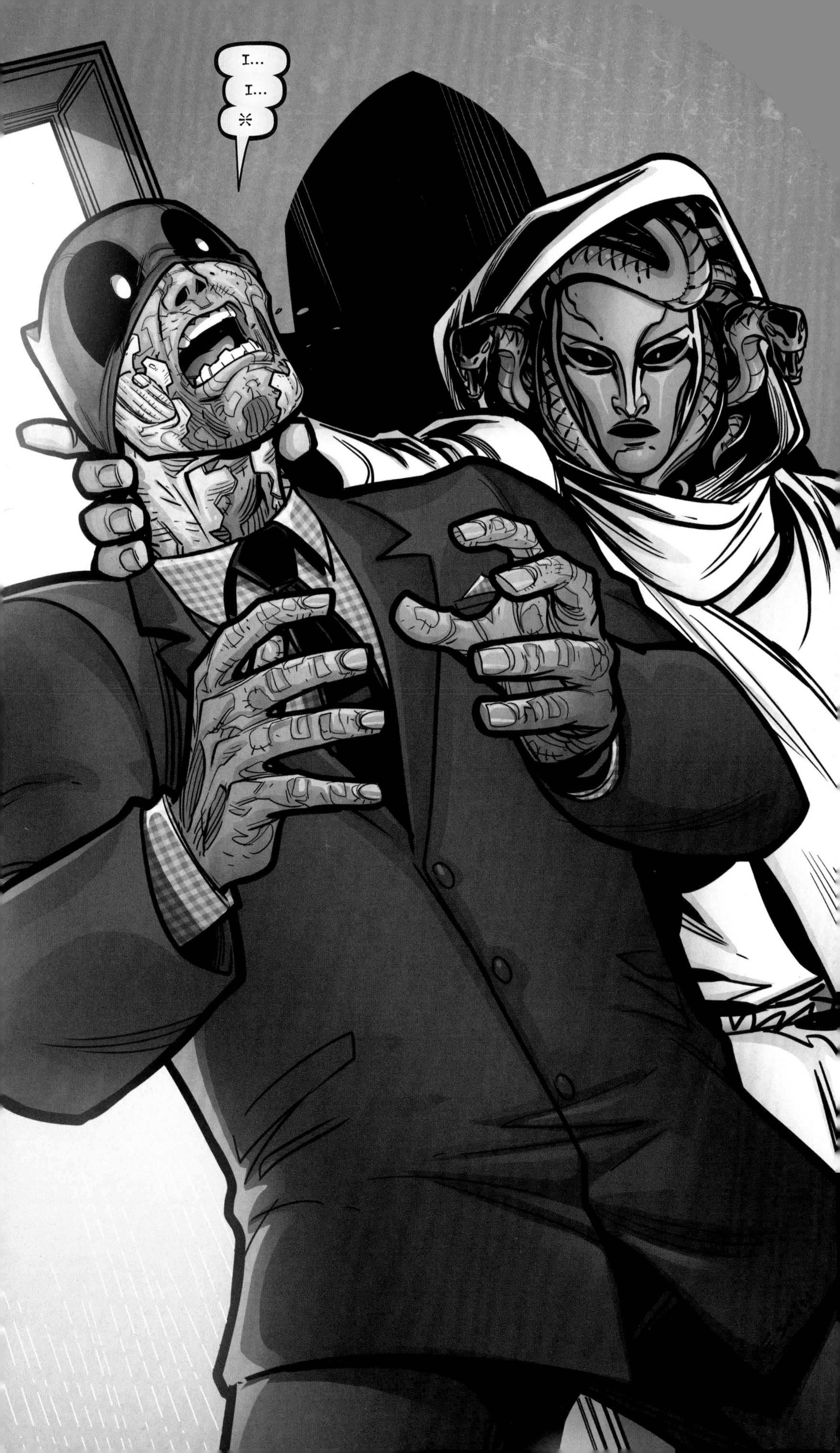
I...
I...
*

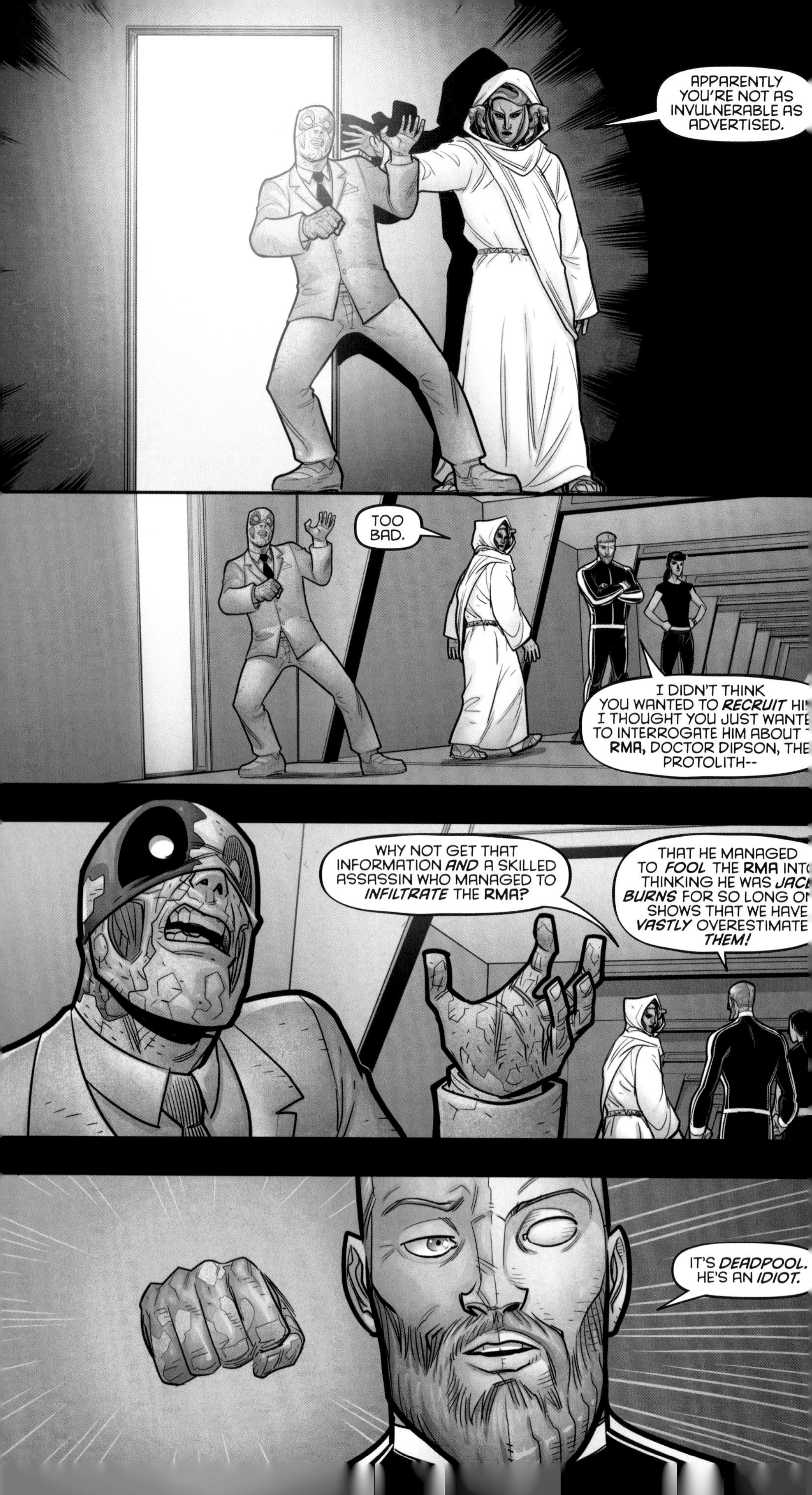
APPARENTLY YOU'RE NOT AS INVULNERABLE AS ADVERTISED.
TOO BAD.
I DIDN'T THINK YOU WANTED TO *RECRUIT* HI I THOUGHT YOU JUST WANTE TO INTERROGATE HIM ABOUT **RMA,** DOCTOR DIPSON, THE PROTOLITH--
WHY NOT GET THAT INFORMATION ***AND*** A SKILLED ASSASSIN WHO MANAGED TO *INFILTRATE* THE **RMA?**
THAT HE MANAGED TO *FOOL* THE **RMA** INT THINKING HE WAS *JAC BURNS* FOR SO LONG O SHOWS THAT WE HAVE *VASTLY* OVERESTIMATE *THEM!*
IT'S *DEADPOOL.* HE'S AN *IDIOT.*

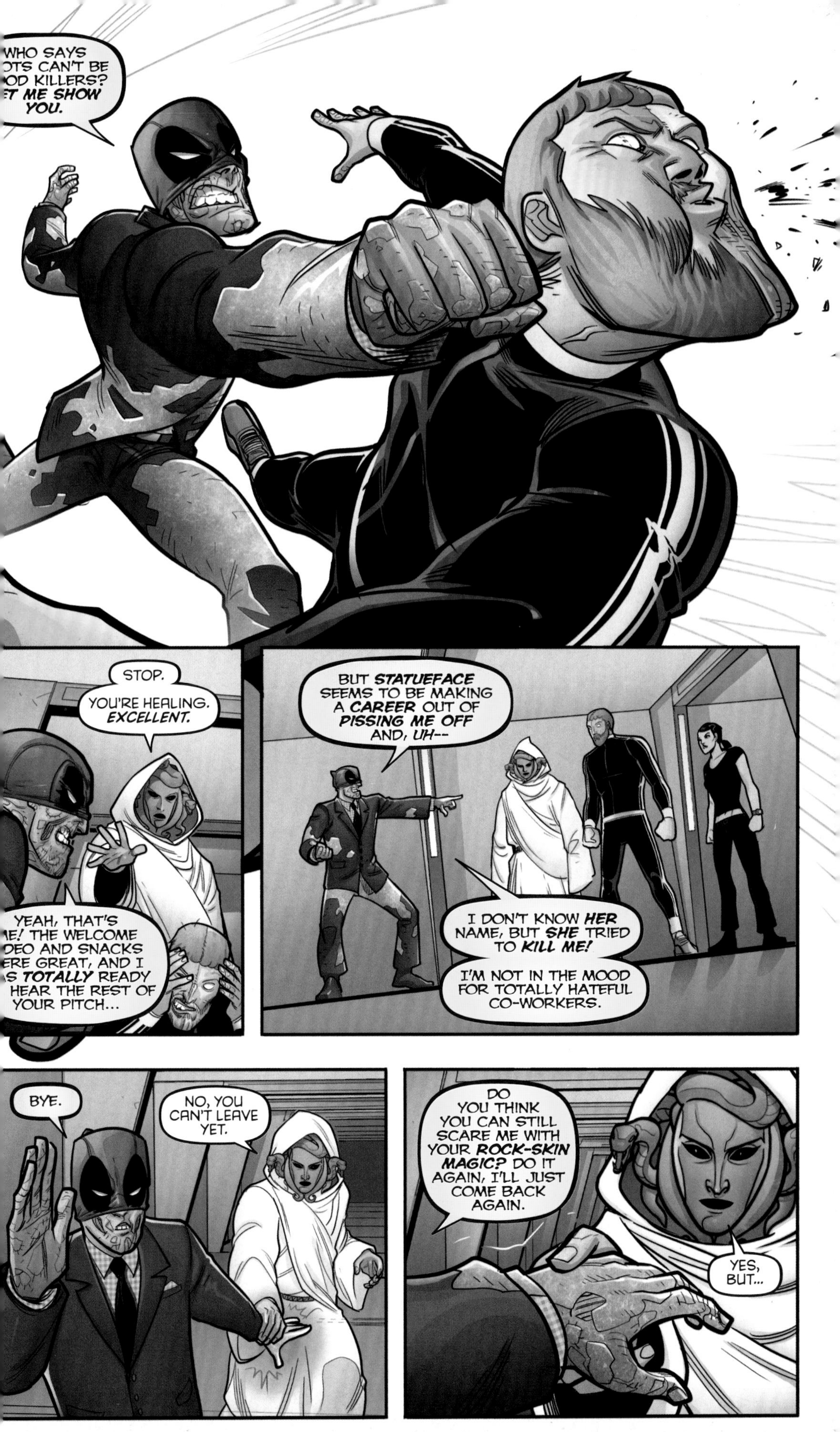
WHO SAYS
OTS CAN'T BE
OD KILLERS?
T ME SHOW
YOU.
STOP.
YOU'RE HEALING. EXCELLENT.
YEAH, THAT'S
E! THE WELCOME
DEO AND SNACKS
ERE GREAT, AND I
S TOTALLY READY
HEAR THE REST OF
YOUR PITCH...
BUT STATUEFACE SEEMS TO BE MAKING A CAREER OUT OF PISSING ME OFF AND, UH--
I DON'T KNOW HER NAME, BUT SHE TRIED TO KILL ME!
I'M NOT IN THE MOOD FOR TOTALLY HATEFUL CO-WORKERS.
BYE.
NO, YOU CAN'T LEAVE YET.
DO YOU THINK YOU CAN STILL SCARE ME WITH YOUR ROCK-SKIN MAGIC? DO IT AGAIN, I'LL JUST COME BACK AGAIN.
YES, BUT...

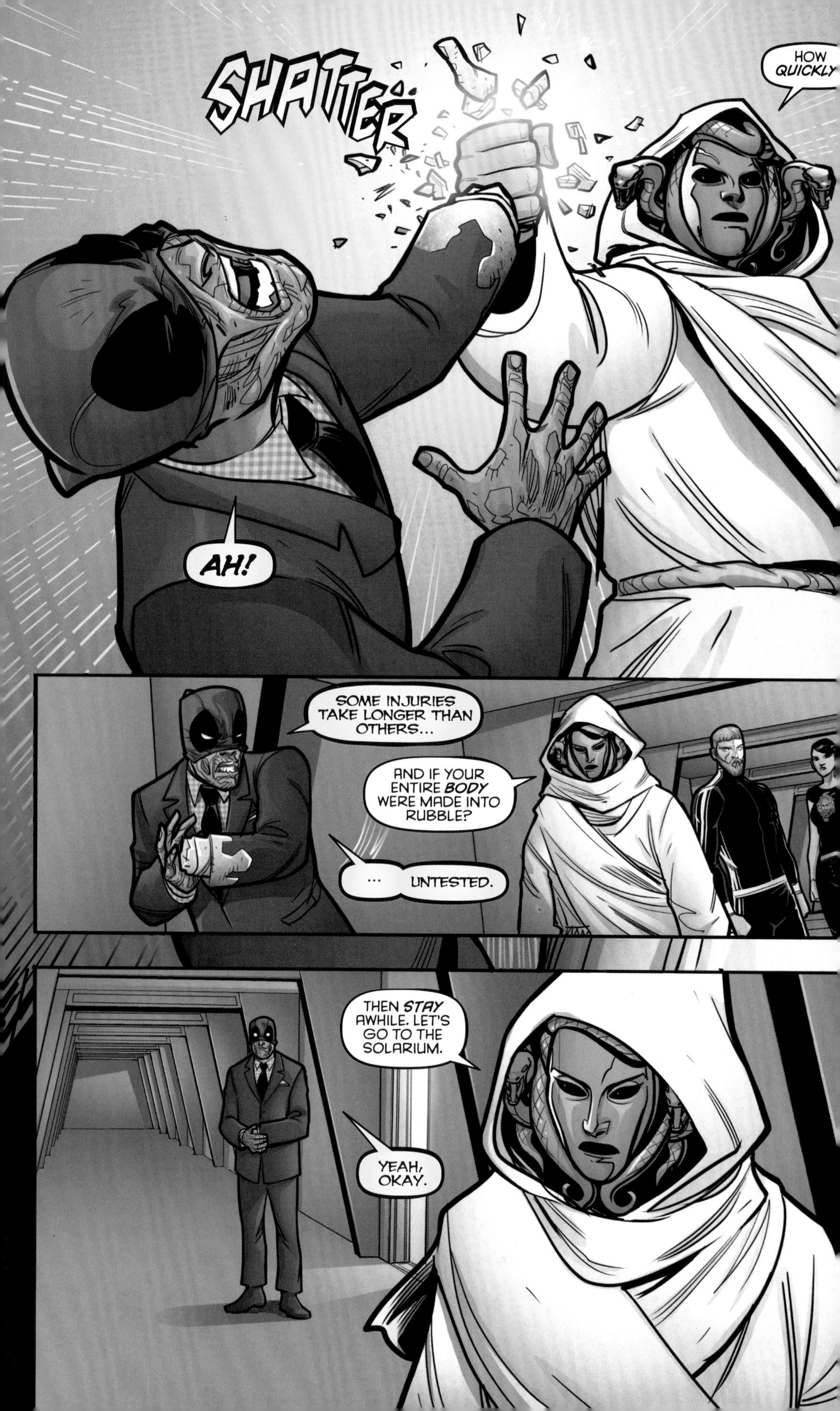
SHATTER
HOW QUICKLY
AH!
SOME INJURIES TAKE LONGER THAN OTHERS...
AND IF YOUR ENTIRE *BODY* WERE MADE INTO RUBBLE?
... UNTESTED.
THEN *STAY* AWHILE. LET'S GO TO THE SOLARIUM.
YEAH, OKAY.

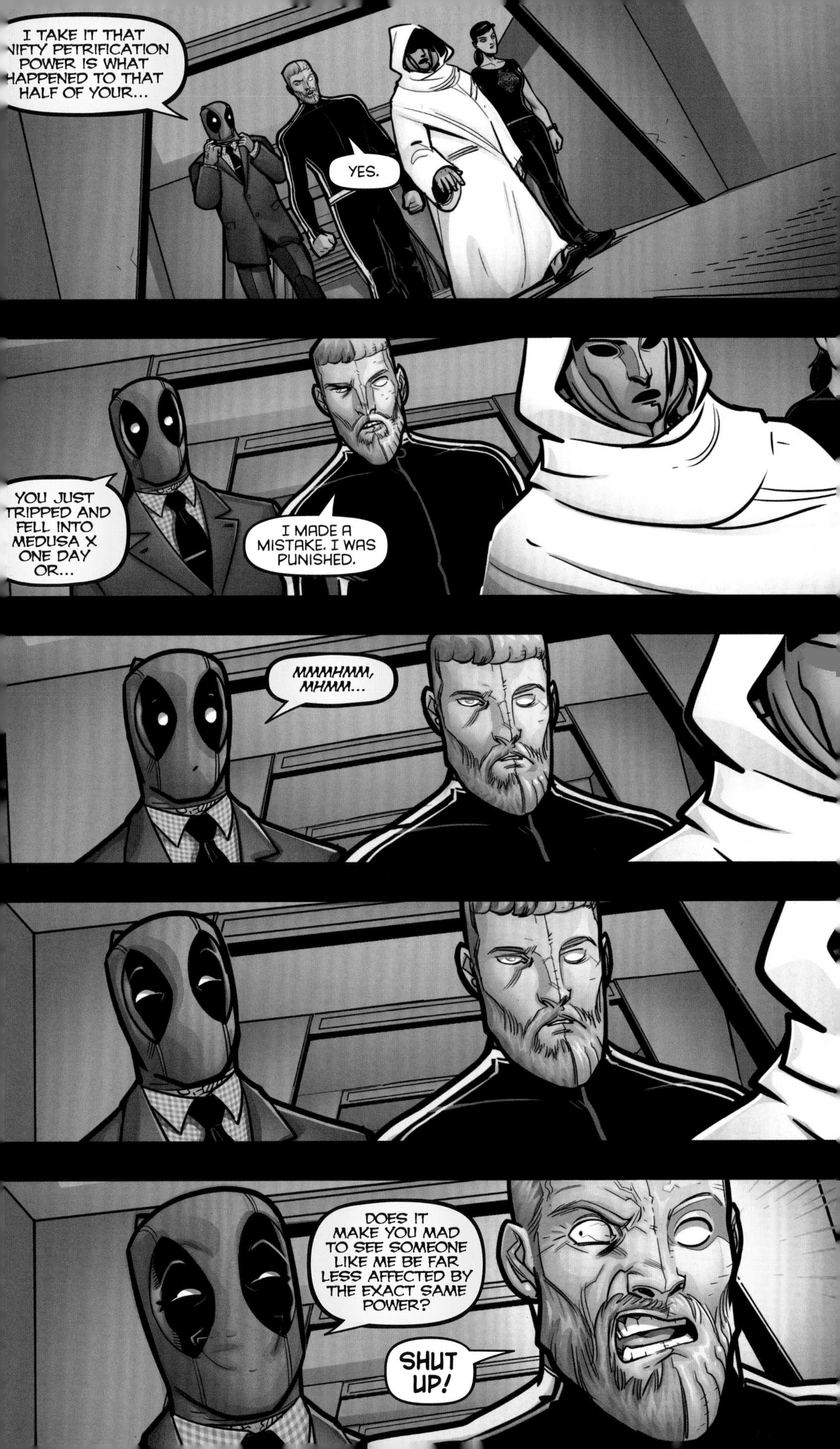
I TAKE IT THAT NIFTY PETRIFICATION POWER IS WHAT HAPPENED TO THAT HALF OF YOUR...
YES.
YOU JUST TRIPPED AND FELL INTO MEDUSA X ONE DAY OR...
I MADE A MISTAKE. I WAS PUNISHED.
MMMHMM, MHMM...
DOES IT MAKE YOU MAD TO SEE SOMEONE LIKE ME BE FAR LESS AFFECTED BY THE EXACT SAME POWER?
SHUT UP!

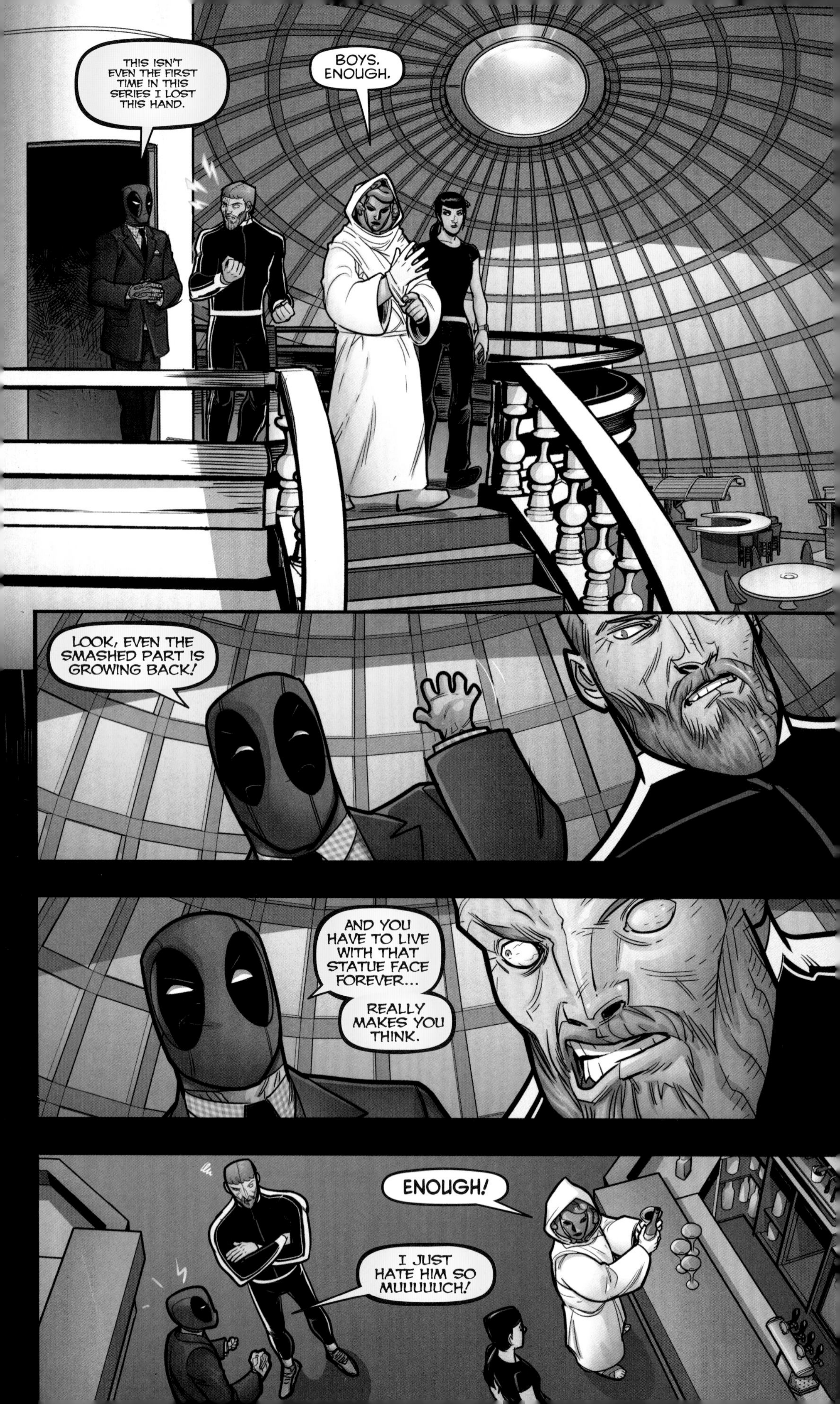
THIS ISN'T EVEN THE FIRST TIME IN THIS SERIES I LOST THIS HAND.
BOYS. ENOUGH.
LOOK, EVEN THE SMASHED PART IS GROWING BACK!
AND YOU HAVE TO LIVE WITH THAT STATUE FACE FOREVER...
REALLY MAKES YOU THINK.
ENOUGH!
I JUST HATE HIM SO MUUUUUCH!

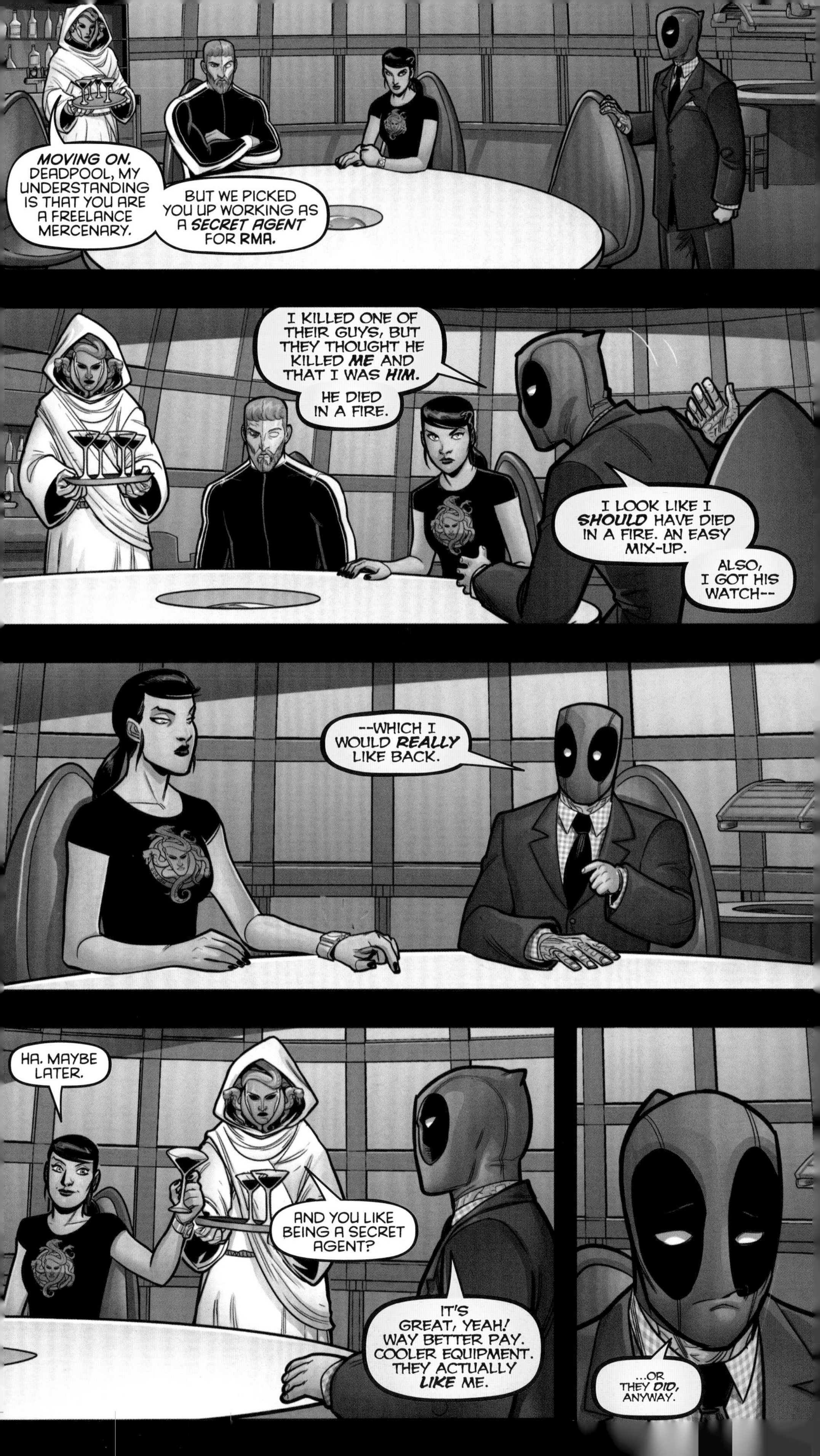
MOVING ON. DEADPOOL, MY UNDERSTANDING IS THAT YOU ARE A FREELANCE MERCENARY.
BUT WE PICKED YOU UP WORKING AS A SECRET AGENT FOR RMA.
I KILLED ONE OF THEIR GUYS, BUT THEY THOUGHT HE KILLED ME AND THAT I WAS HIM.
HE DIED IN A FIRE.
I LOOK LIKE I SHOULD HAVE DIED IN A FIRE. AN EASY MIX-UP.
ALSO, I GOT HIS WATCH--
--WHICH I WOULD REALLY LIKE BACK.
HA. MAYBE LATER.
AND YOU LIKE BEING A SECRET AGENT?
IT'S GREAT, YEAH! WAY BETTER PAY. COOLER EQUIPMENT. THEY ACTUALLY LIKE ME.
...OR THEY DID, ANYWAY.

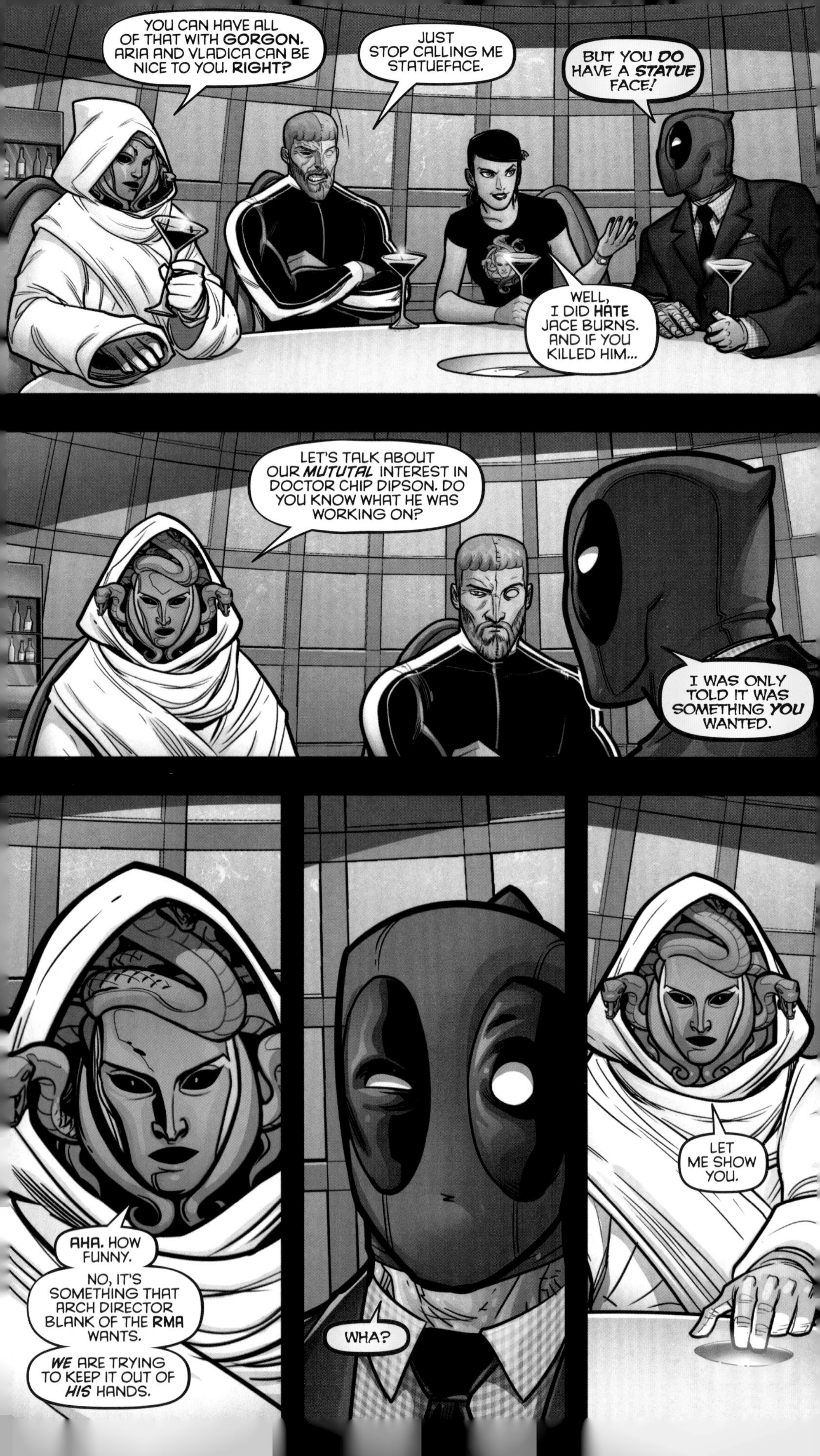
YOU CAN HAVE ALL OF THAT WITH GORGON. ARIA AND VLADICA CAN BE NICE TO YOU. RIGHT?
JUST STOP CALLING ME STATUEFACE.
BUT YOU DO HAVE A STATUE FACE!
WELL, I DID HATE JACE BURNS. AND IF YOU KILLED HIM...
LET'S TALK ABOUT OUR MUTUTAL INTEREST IN DOCTOR CHIP DIPSON. DO YOU KNOW WHAT HE WAS WORKING ON?
I WAS ONLY TOLD IT WAS SOMETHING YOU WANTED.
AHA. HOW FUNNY.
NO, IT'S SOMETHING THAT ARCH DIRECTOR BLANK OF THE RMA WANTS.
WE ARE TRYING TO KEEP IT OUT OF HIS HANDS.
WHA?
LET ME SHOW YOU.

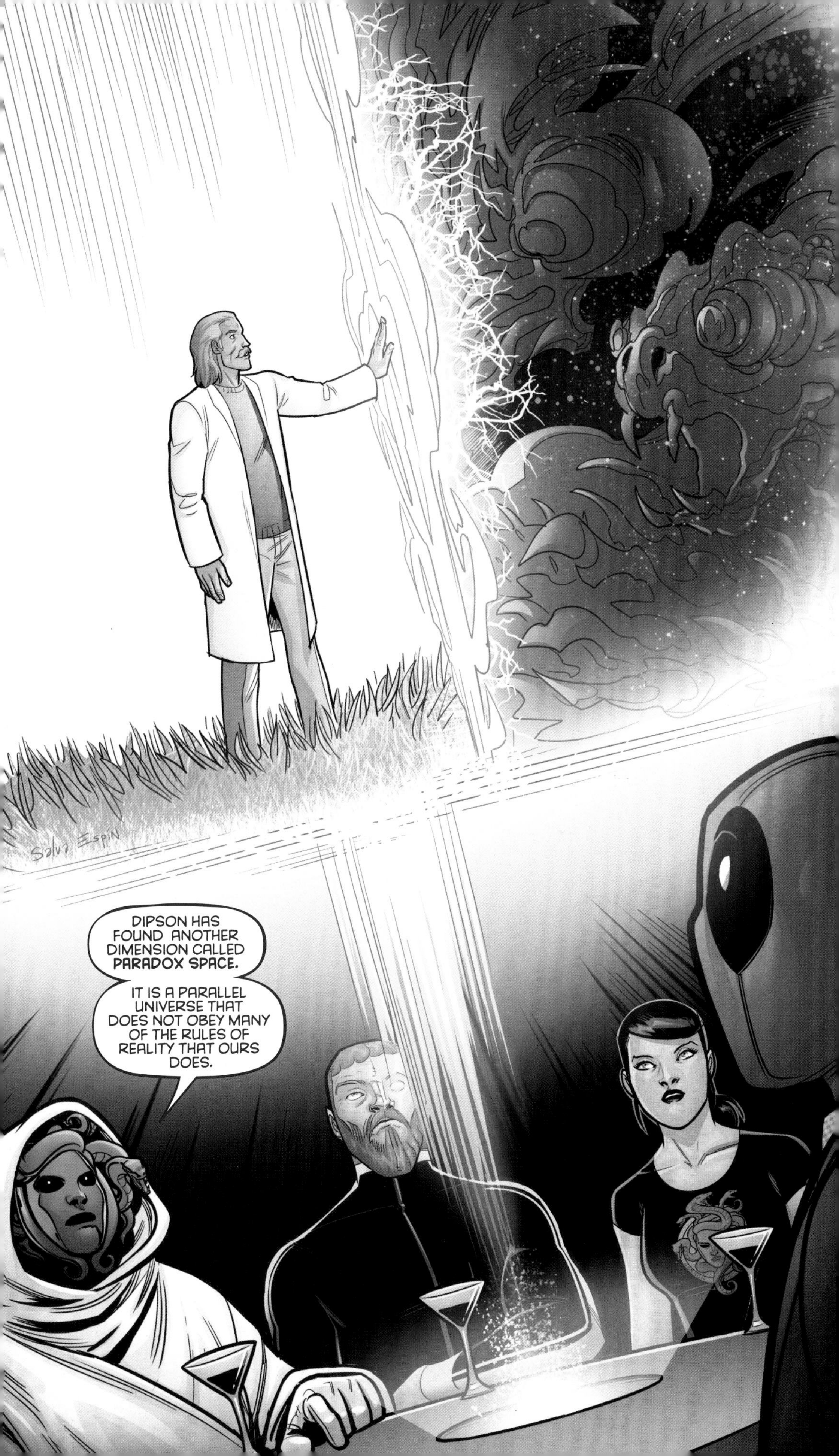
DIPSON HAS FOUND ANOTHER DIMENSION CALLED PARADOX SPACE.
IT IS A PARALLEL UNIVERSE THAT DOES NOT OBEY MANY OF THE RULES OF REALITY THAT OURS DOES.

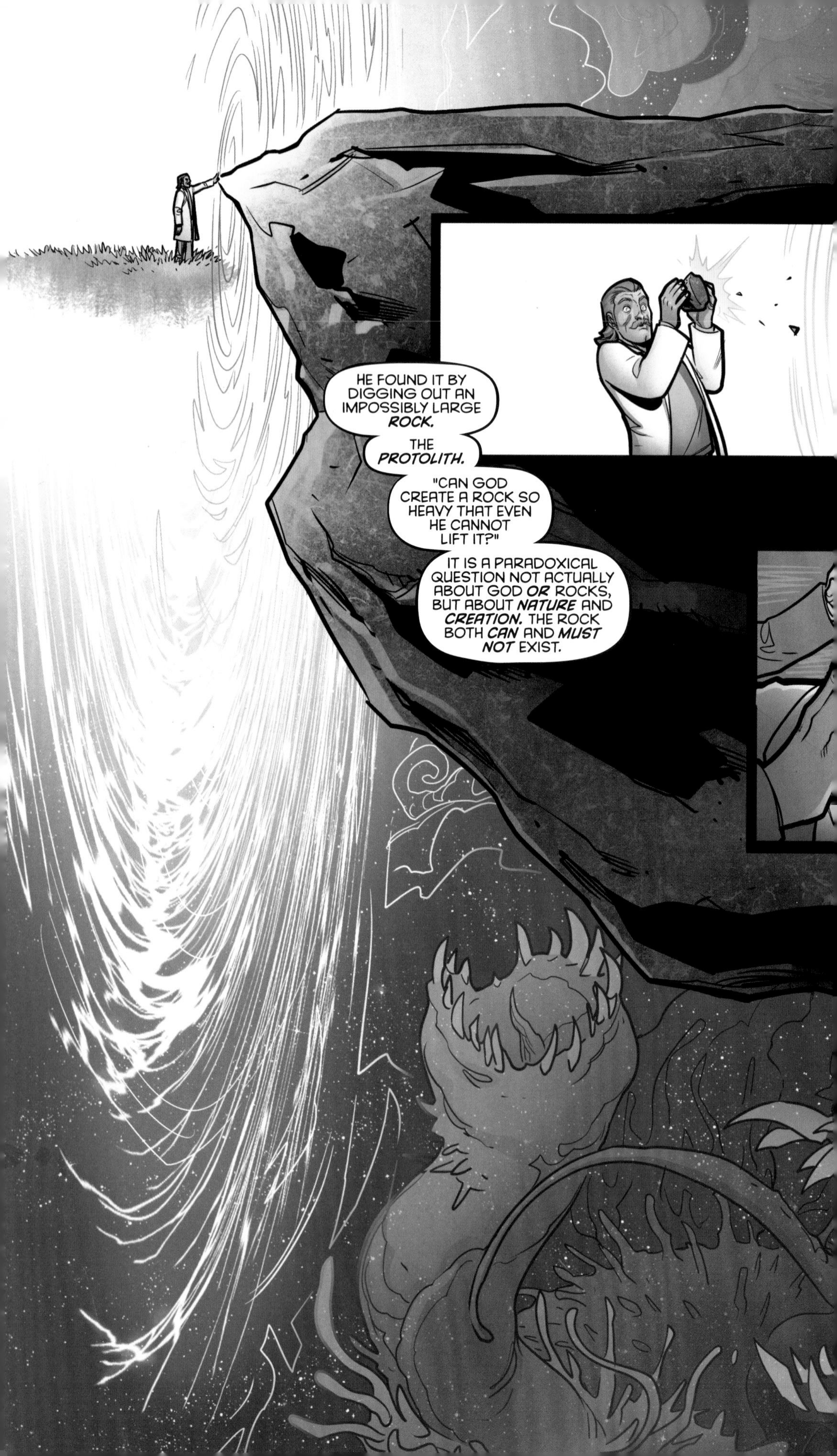
HE FOUND IT BY DIGGING OUT AN IMPOSSIBLY LARGE *ROCK.*
THE *PROTOLITH.*
"CAN GOD CREATE A ROCK SO HEAVY THAT EVEN HE CANNOT LIFT IT?"
IT IS A PARADOXICAL QUESTION NOT ACTUALLY ABOUT GOD *OR* ROCKS, BUT ABOUT *NATURE* AND *CREATION.* THE ROCK BOTH *CAN* AND *MUST NOT* EXIST.

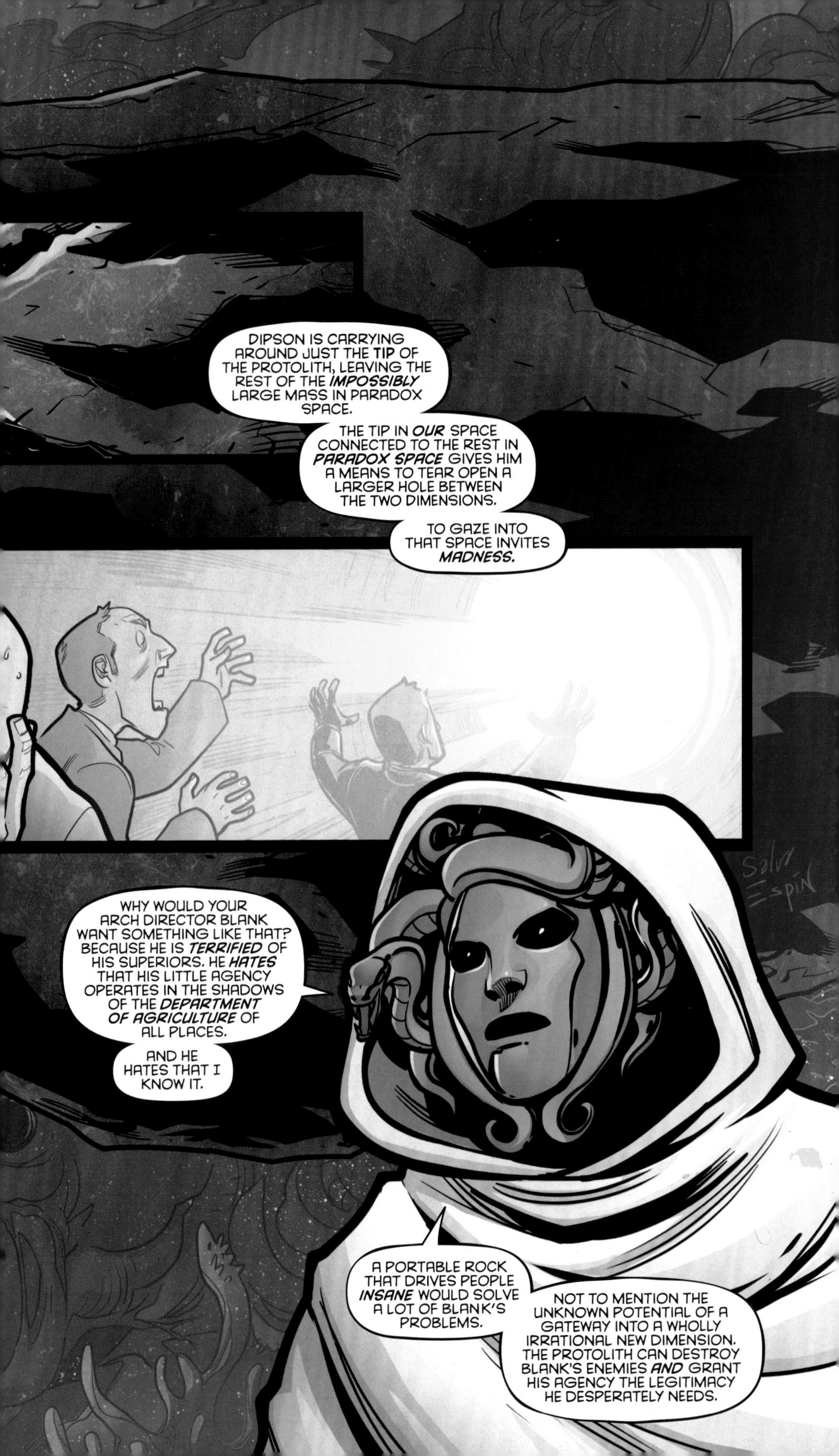
DIPSON IS CARRYING AROUND JUST THE TIP OF THE PROTOLITH, LEAVING THE REST OF THE IMPOSSIBLY LARGE MASS IN PARADOX SPACE.
THE TIP IN OUR SPACE CONNECTED TO THE REST IN PARADOX SPACE GIVES HIM A MEANS TO TEAR OPEN A LARGER HOLE BETWEEN THE TWO DIMENSIONS.
TO GAZE INTO THAT SPACE INVITES MADNESS.
WHY WOULD YOUR ARCH DIRECTOR BLANK WANT SOMETHING LIKE THAT? BECAUSE HE IS TERRIFIED OF HIS SUPERIORS. HE HATES THAT HIS LITTLE AGENCY OPERATES IN THE SHADOWS OF THE DEPARTMENT OF AGRICULTURE OF ALL PLACES.
AND HE HATES THAT I KNOW IT.
A PORTABLE ROCK THAT DRIVES PEOPLE INSANE WOULD SOLVE A LOT OF BLANK'S PROBLEMS.
NOT TO MENTION THE UNKNOWN POTENTIAL OF A GATEWAY INTO A WHOLLY IRRATIONAL NEW DIMENSION. THE PROTOLITH CAN DESTROY BLANK'S ENEMIES AND GRANT HIS AGENCY THE LEGITIMACY HE DESPERATELY NEEDS.
Salva Espin

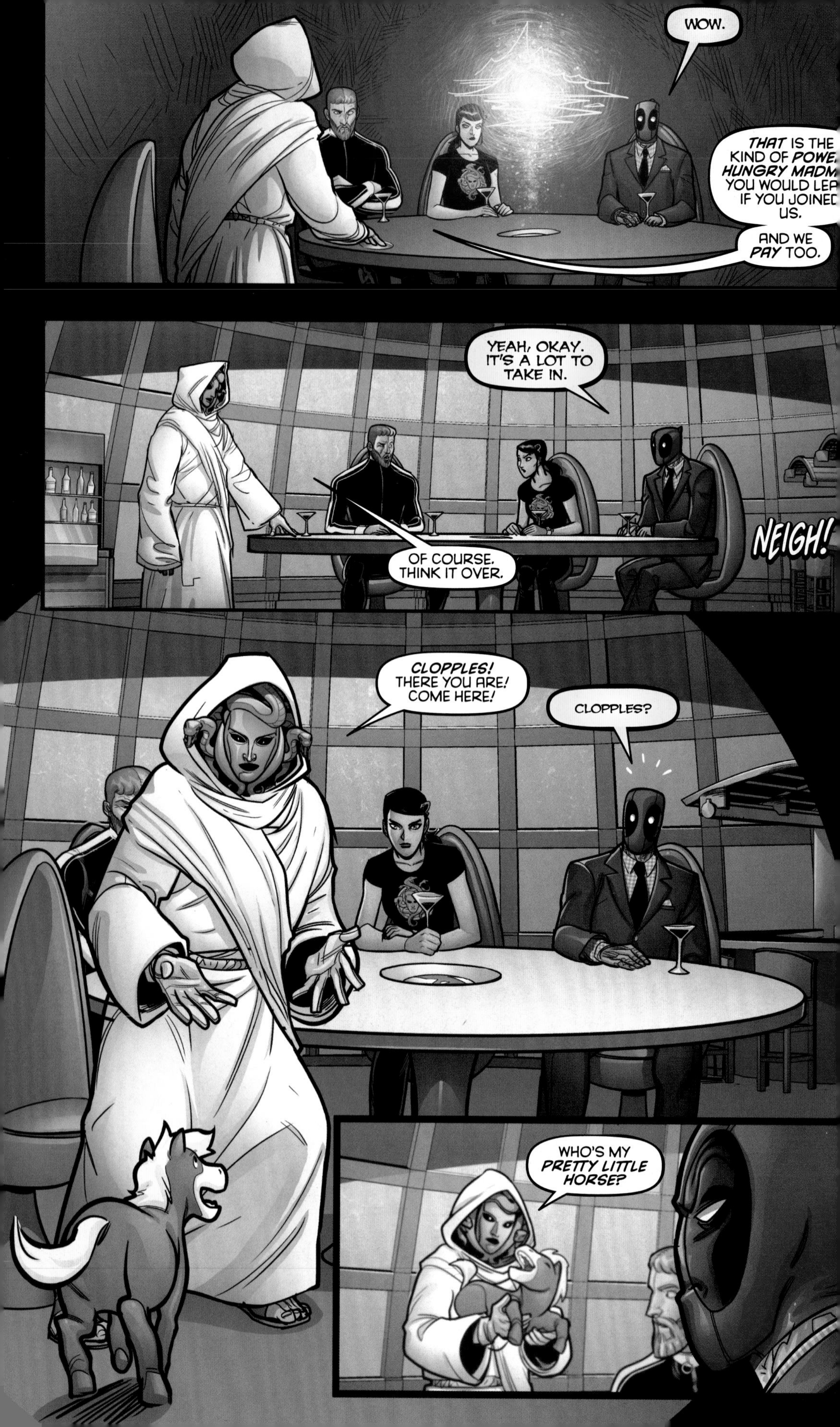
WOW.
THAT IS THE KIND OF POWE HUNGRY MADM YOU WOULD LEA IF YOU JOINED US.
AND WE PAY TOO.
YEAH, OKAY. IT'S A LOT TO TAKE IN.
OF COURSE. THINK IT OVER.
NEIGH!
CLOPPLES! THERE YOU ARE! COME HERE!
CLOPPLES?
WHO'S MY PRETTY LITTLE HORSE?

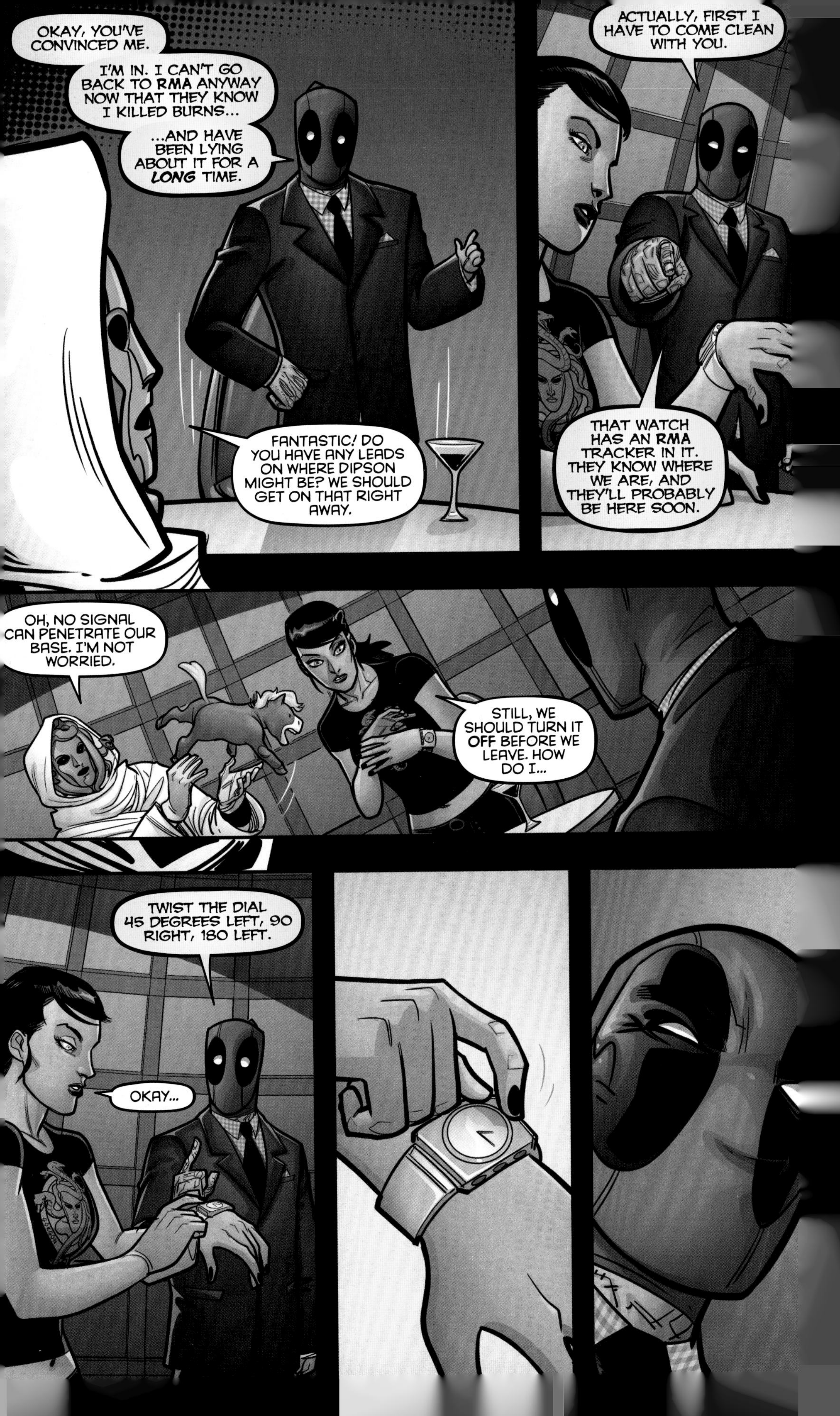
OKAY, YOU'VE CONVINCED ME.
I'M IN. I CAN'T GO BACK TO RMA ANYWAY NOW THAT THEY KNOW I KILLED BURNS...
...AND HAVE BEEN LYING ABOUT IT FOR A LONG TIME.
FANTASTIC! DO YOU HAVE ANY LEADS ON WHERE DIPSON MIGHT BE? WE SHOULD GET ON THAT RIGHT AWAY.
ACTUALLY, FIRST I HAVE TO COME CLEAN WITH YOU.
THAT WATCH HAS AN RMA TRACKER IN IT. THEY KNOW WHERE WE ARE, AND THEY'LL PROBABLY BE HERE SOON.
OH, NO SIGNAL CAN PENETRATE OUR BASE. I'M NOT WORRIED.
STILL, WE SHOULD TURN IT OFF BEFORE WE LEAVE. HOW DO I...
TWIST THE DIAL 45 DEGREES LEFT, 90 RIGHT, 180 LEFT.
OKAY...

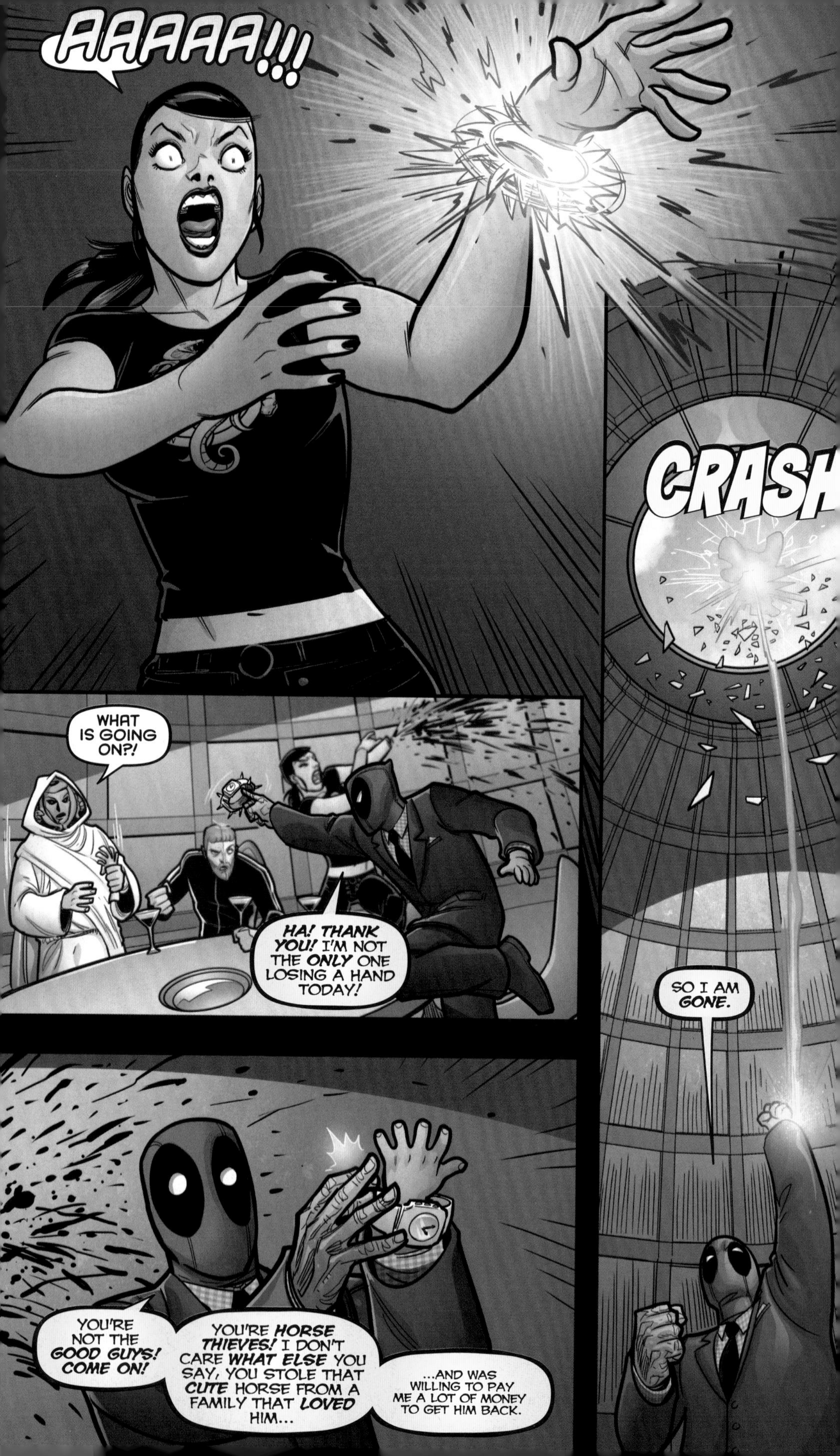
AAAAAA!!!
CRASH
WHAT IS GOING ON?!
HA! THANK YOU! I'M NOT THE ONLY ONE LOSING A HAND TODAY!
YOU'RE NOT THE GOOD GUYS! COME ON!
YOU'RE HORSE THIEVES! I DON'T CARE WHAT ELSE YOU SAY, YOU STOLE THAT CUTE HORSE FROM A FAMILY THAT LOVED HIM...
...AND WAS WILLING TO PAY ME A LOT OF MONEY TO GET HIM BACK.
SO I AM GONE.

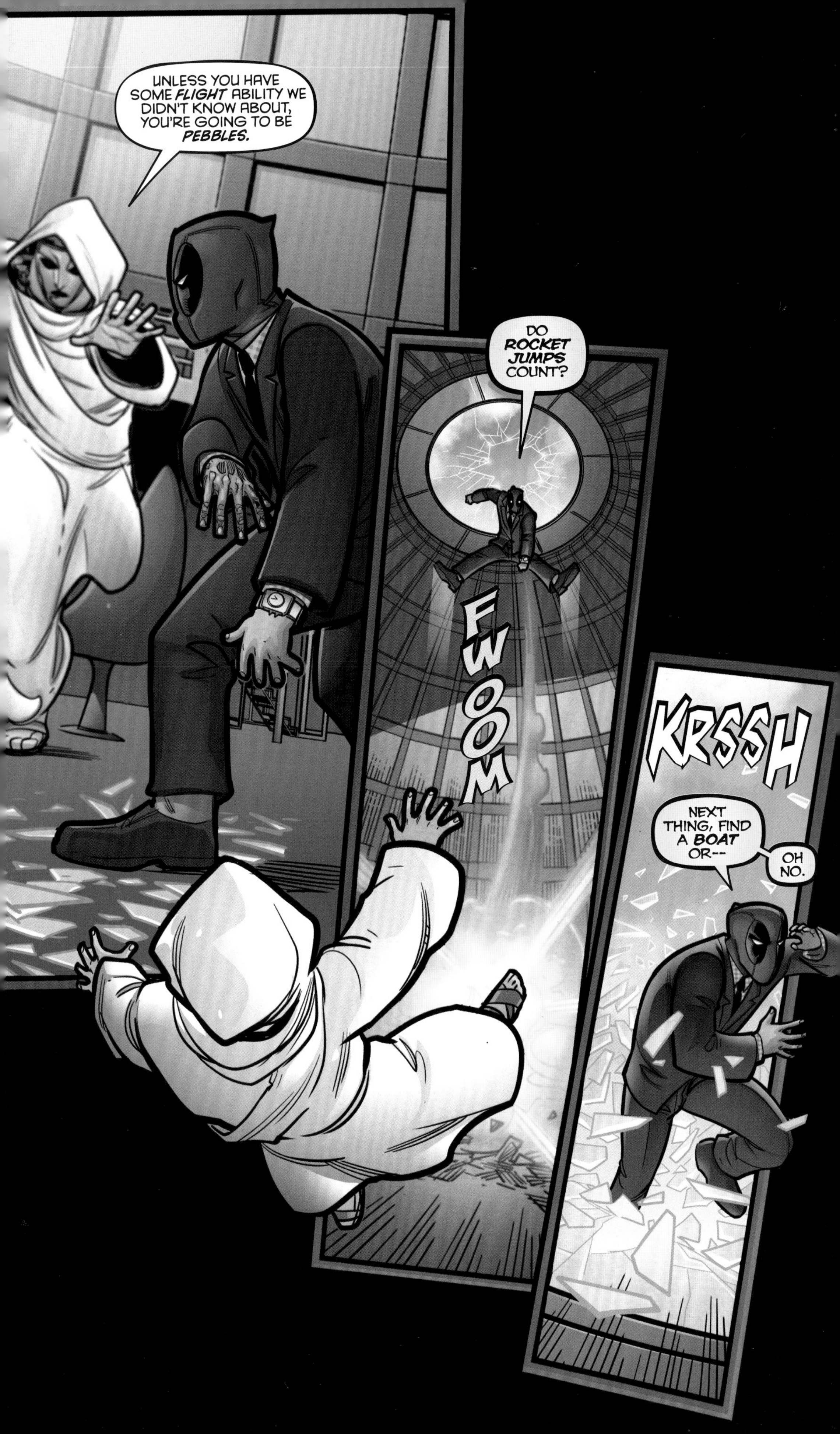
UNLESS YOU HAVE SOME FLIGHT ABILITY WE DIDN'T KNOW ABOUT, YOU'RE GOING TO BE PEBBLES.
DO ROCKET JUMPS COUNT?
FWOOM
KRSSH
NEXT THING, FIND A BOAT OR--
OH NO.

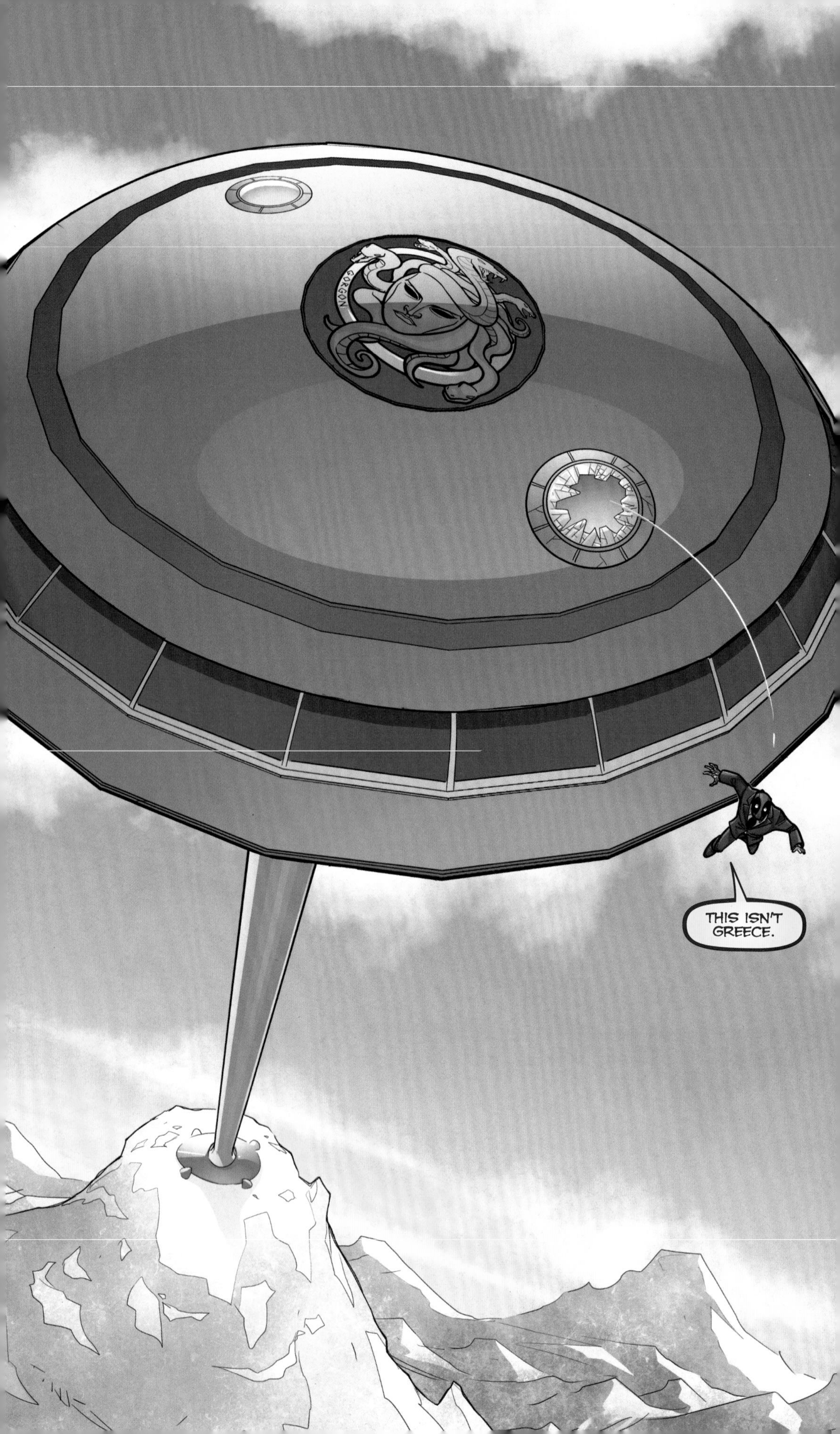
THIS ISN'T GREECE.

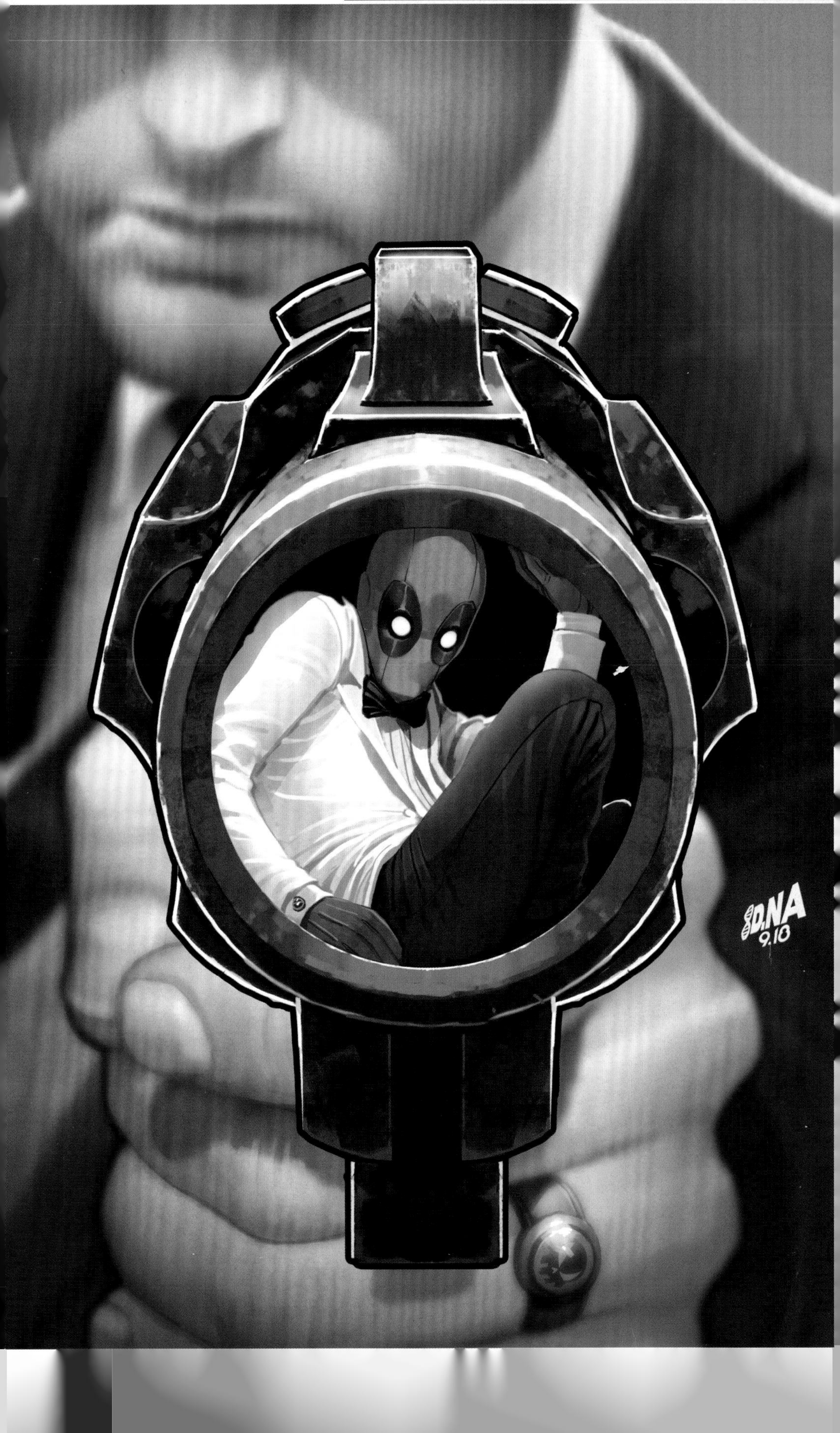
D.NA
9.18

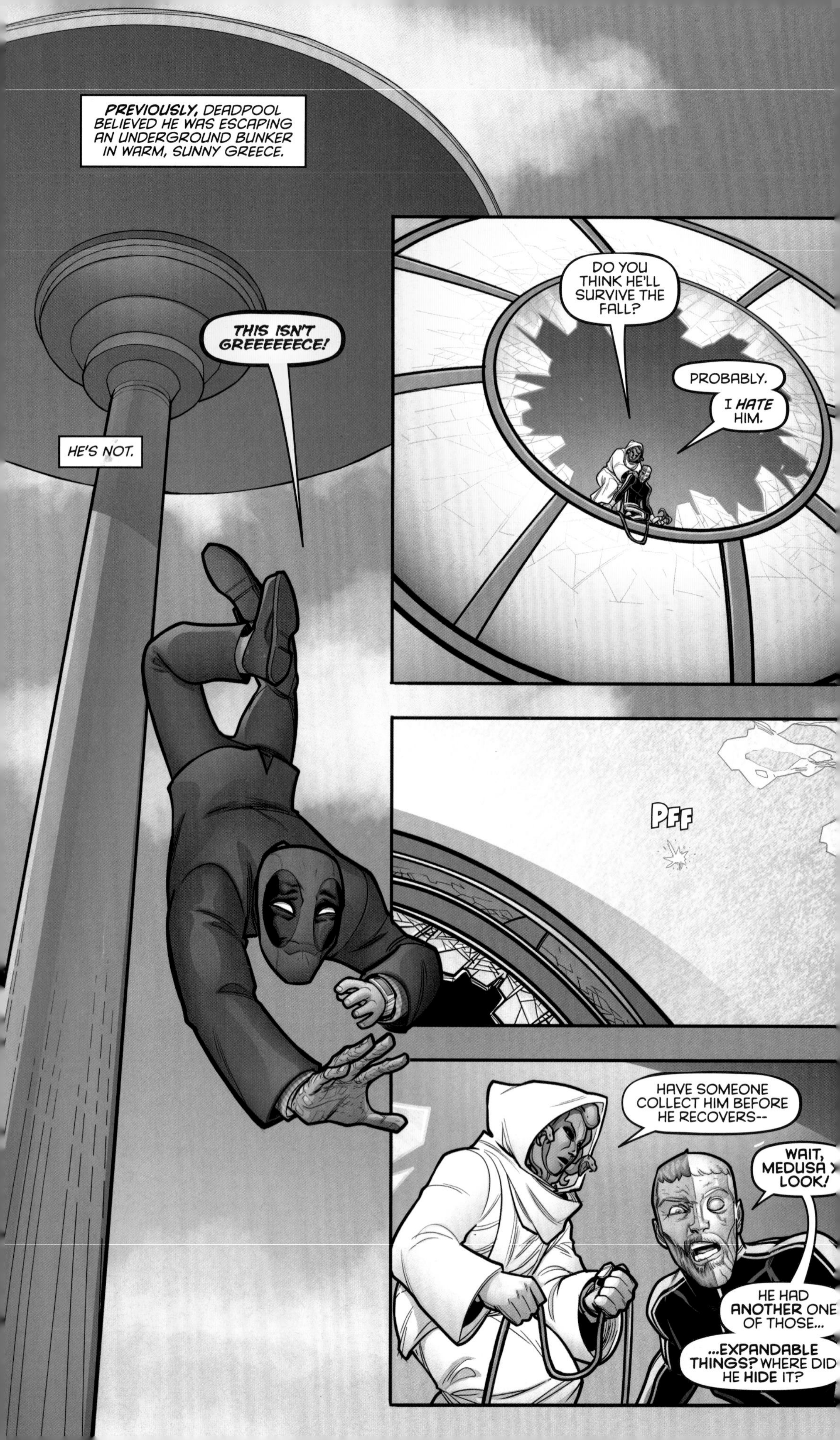

PREVIOUSLY, DEADPOOL BELIEVED HE WAS ESCAPING AN UNDERGROUND BUNKER IN WARM, SUNNY GREECE.
THIS ISN'T GREEEEEECE!
HE'S NOT.
DO YOU THINK HE'LL SURVIVE THE FALL?
PROBABLY.
I HATE HIM.
PFF
HAVE SOMEONE COLLECT HIM BEFORE HE RECOVERS--
WAIT, MEDUSA LOOK!
HE HAD ANOTHER ONE OF THOSE...
...EXPANDABLE THINGS? WHERE DID HE HIDE IT?

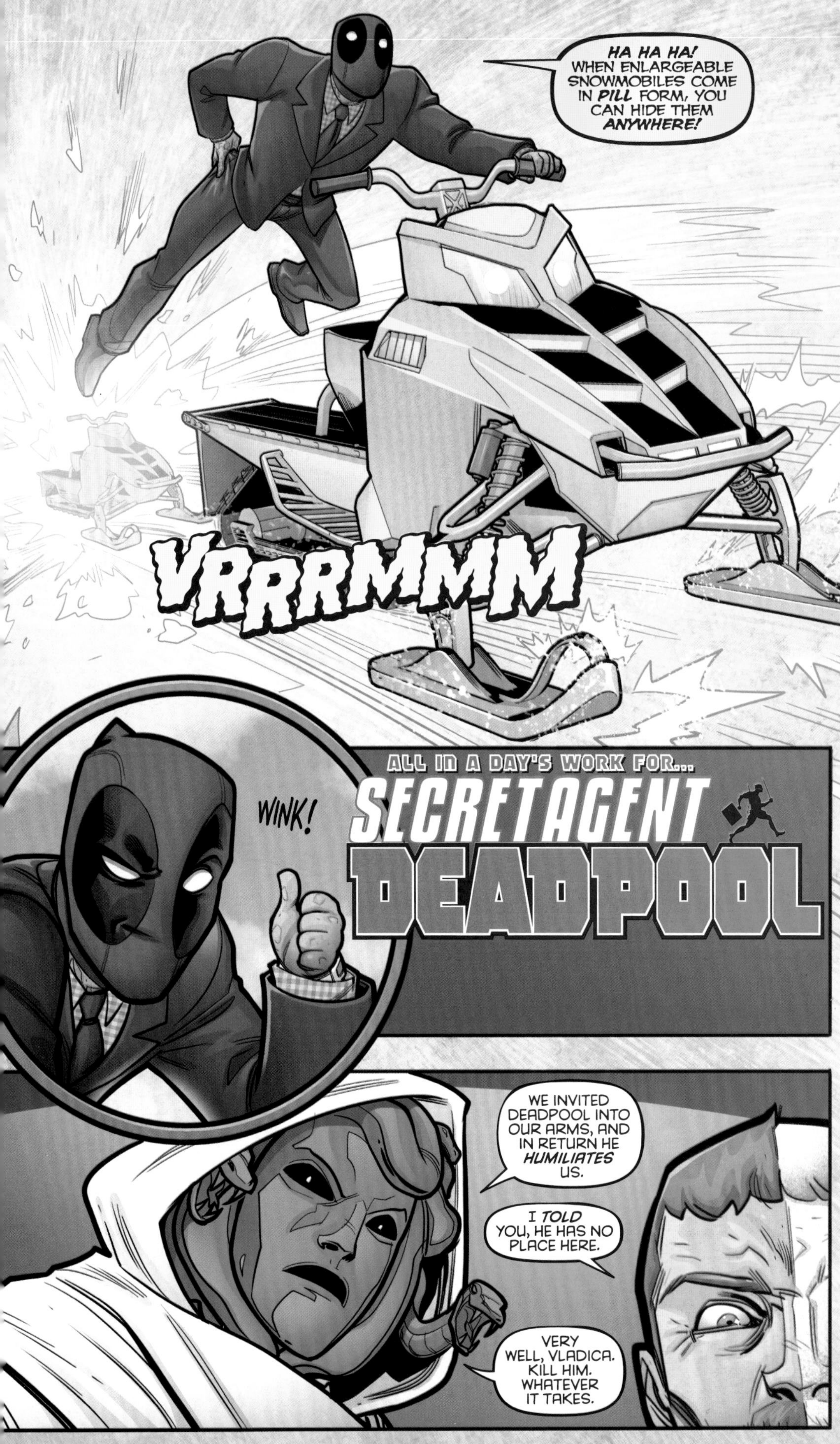
HA HA HA! WHEN ENLARGEABLE SNOWMOBILES COME IN PILL FORM, YOU CAN HIDE THEM ANYWHERE!
VRRRMMMM
WINK!
ALL IN A DAY'S WORK FOR...
SECRET AGENT DEADPOOL
WE INVITED DEADPOOL INTO OUR ARMS, AND IN RETURN HE HUMILIATES US.
I TOLD YOU, HE HAS NO PLACE HERE.
VERY WELL, VLADICA. KILL HIM. WHATEVER IT TAKES.

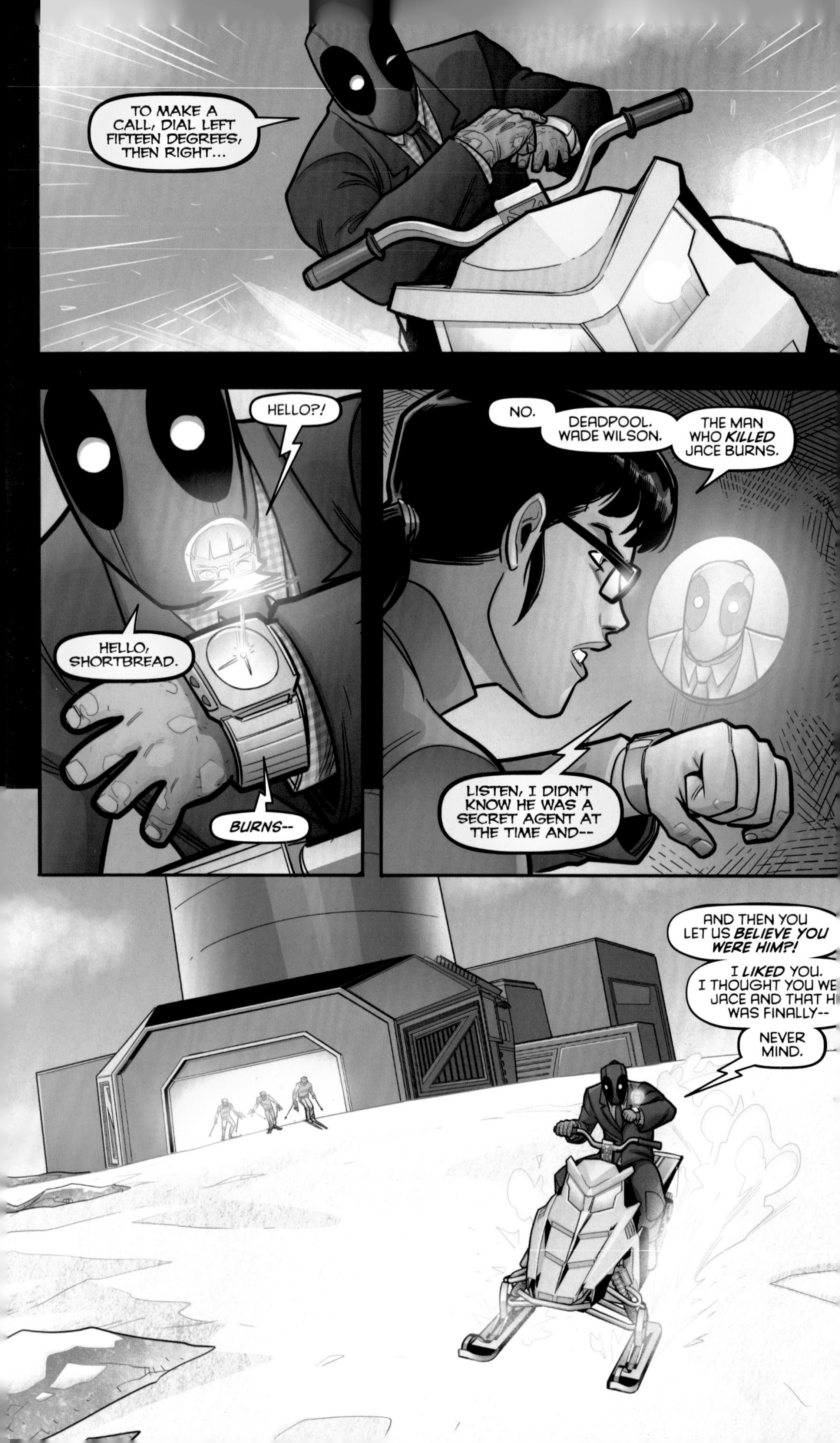
TO MAKE A CALL, DIAL LEFT FIFTEEN DEGREES, THEN RIGHT...
HELLO?!
HELLO, SHORTBREAD.
BURNS--
NO.
DEADPOOL. WADE WILSON.
THE MAN WHO KILLED JACE BURNS.
LISTEN, I DIDN'T KNOW HE WAS A SECRET AGENT AT THE TIME AND--
AND THEN YOU LET US BELIEVE YOU WERE HIM?!
I LIKED YOU. I THOUGHT YOU WE JACE AND THAT H WAS FINALLY--
NEVER MIND.

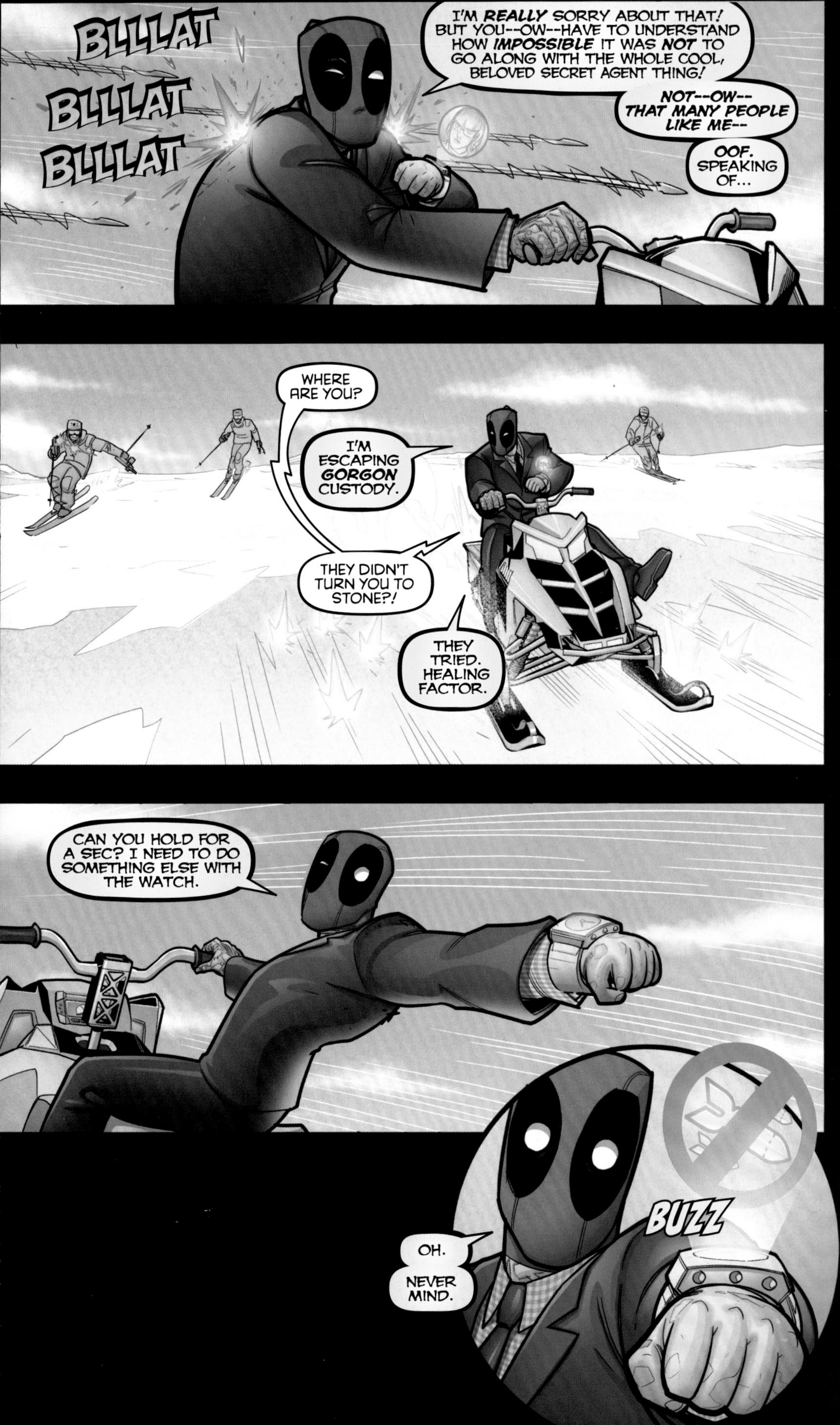
BLLLAT
BLLLAT
BLLLAT
I'M REALLY SORRY ABOUT THAT! BUT YOU--OW--HAVE TO UNDERSTAND HOW IMPOSSIBLE IT WAS NOT TO GO ALONG WITH THE WHOLE COOL, BELOVED SECRET AGENT THING!
NOT--OW-- THAT MANY PEOPLE LIKE ME--
OOF. SPEAKING OF...
WHERE ARE YOU?
I'M ESCAPING GORGON CUSTODY.
THEY DIDN'T TURN YOU TO STONE?!
THEY TRIED. HEALING FACTOR.
CAN YOU HOLD FOR A SEC? I NEED TO DO SOMETHING ELSE WITH THE WATCH.
BUZZ
OH.
NEVER MIND.

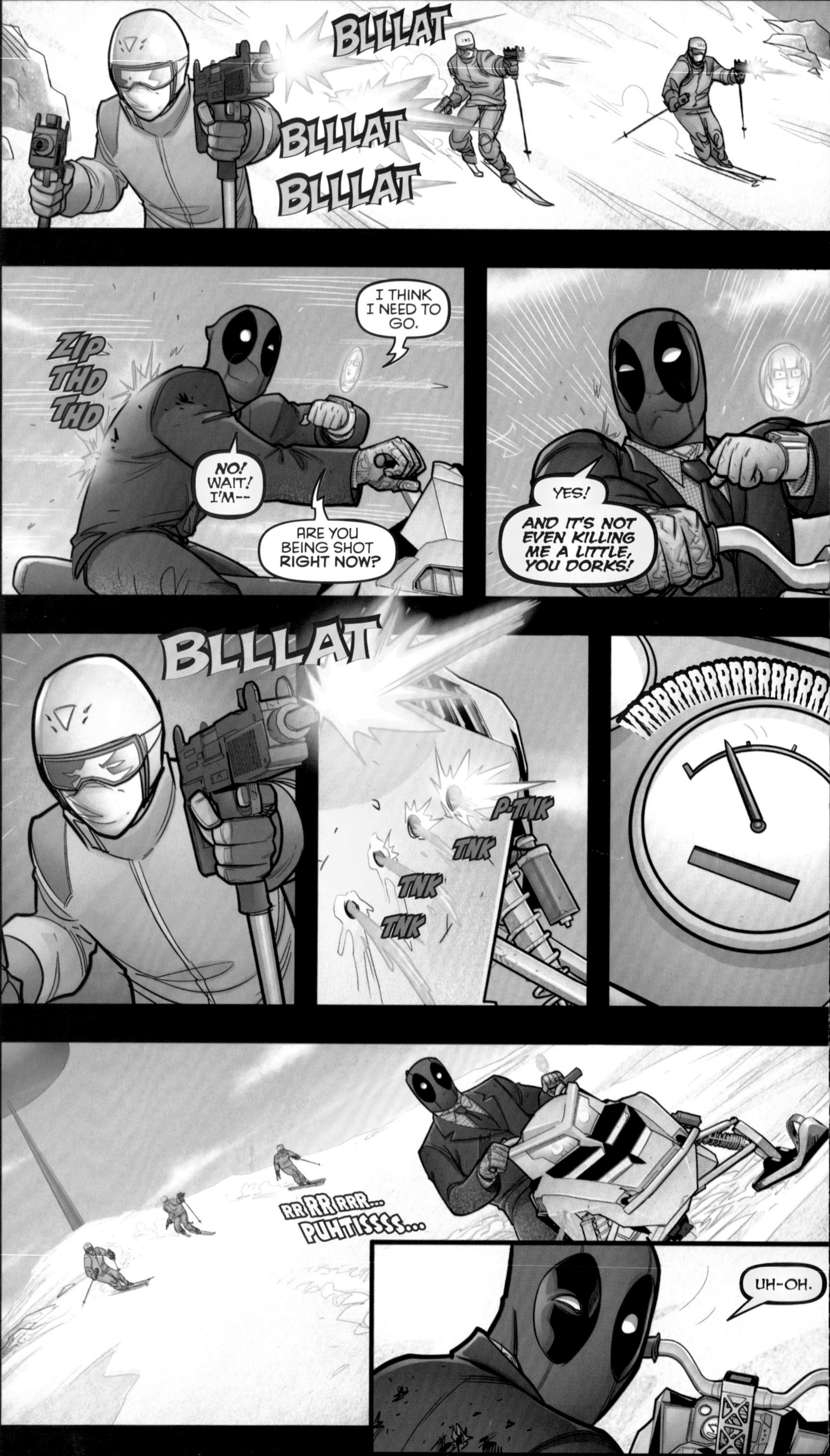
BLLLAT
BLLLAT
BLLLAT
ZIP
THD
THD
I THINK I NEED TO GO.
NO! WAIT! I'M--
ARE YOU BEING SHOT RIGHT NOW?
YES!
AND IT'S NOT EVEN KILLING ME A LITTLE, YOU DORKS!
BLLLAT
P-TNK
TNK
TNK
TNK
VRRRRRRRRRRRRRRRRR
RR RR RRR...
PUHTISSSS...
UH-OH.

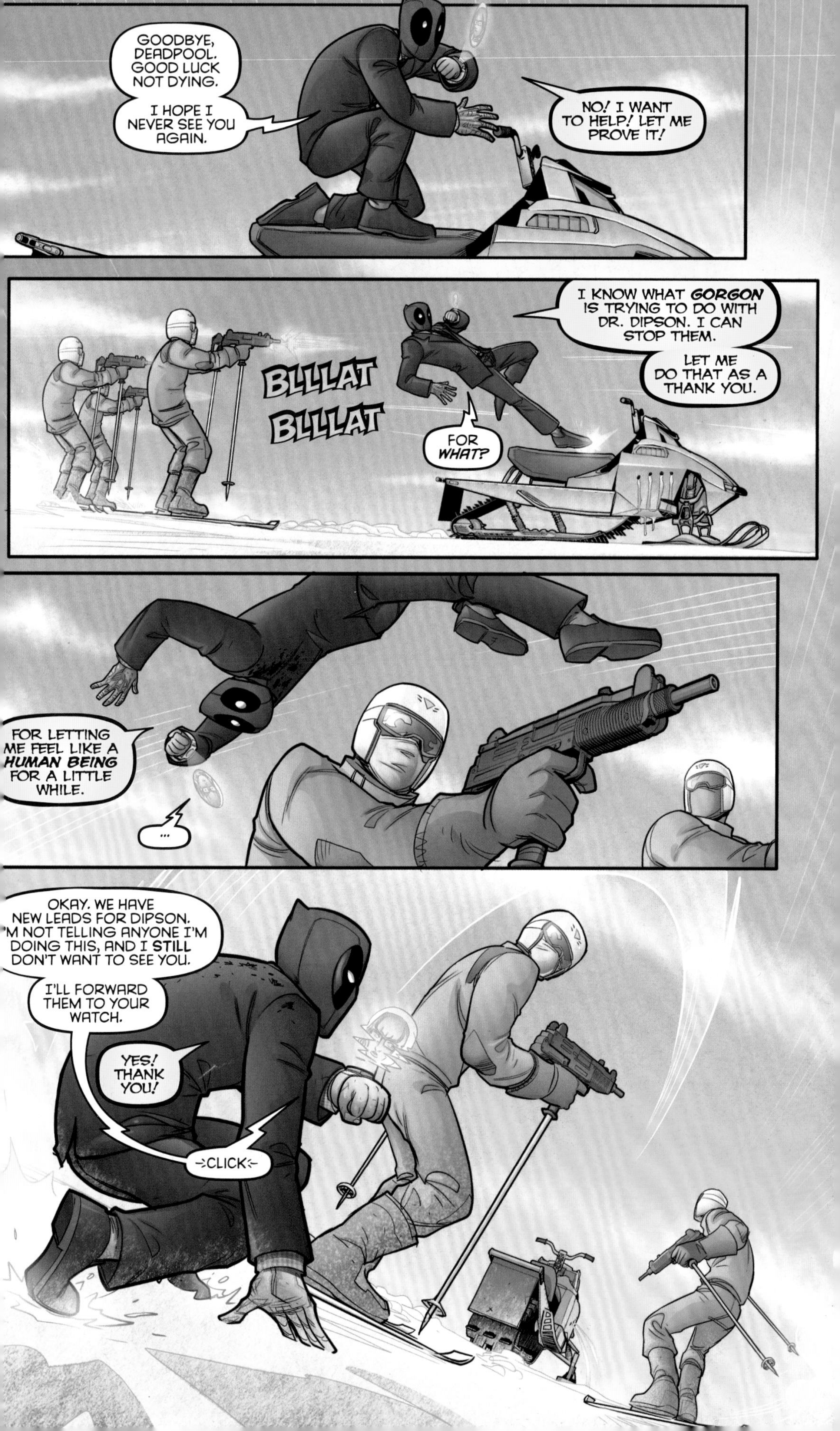
GOODBYE, DEADPOOL. GOOD LUCK NOT DYING.
I HOPE I NEVER SEE YOU AGAIN.
NO! I WANT TO HELP! LET ME PROVE IT!
I KNOW WHAT GORGON IS TRYING TO DO WITH DR. DIPSON. I CAN STOP THEM.
LET ME DO THAT AS A THANK YOU.
BLLLAT BLLLAT
FOR WHAT?
FOR LETTING ME FEEL LIKE A HUMAN BEING FOR A LITTLE WHILE.
...
OKAY. WE HAVE NEW LEADS FOR DIPSON. I'M NOT TELLING ANYONE I'M DOING THIS, AND I STILL DON'T WANT TO SEE YOU.
I'LL FORWARD THEM TO YOUR WATCH.
YES! THANK YOU!
CLICK

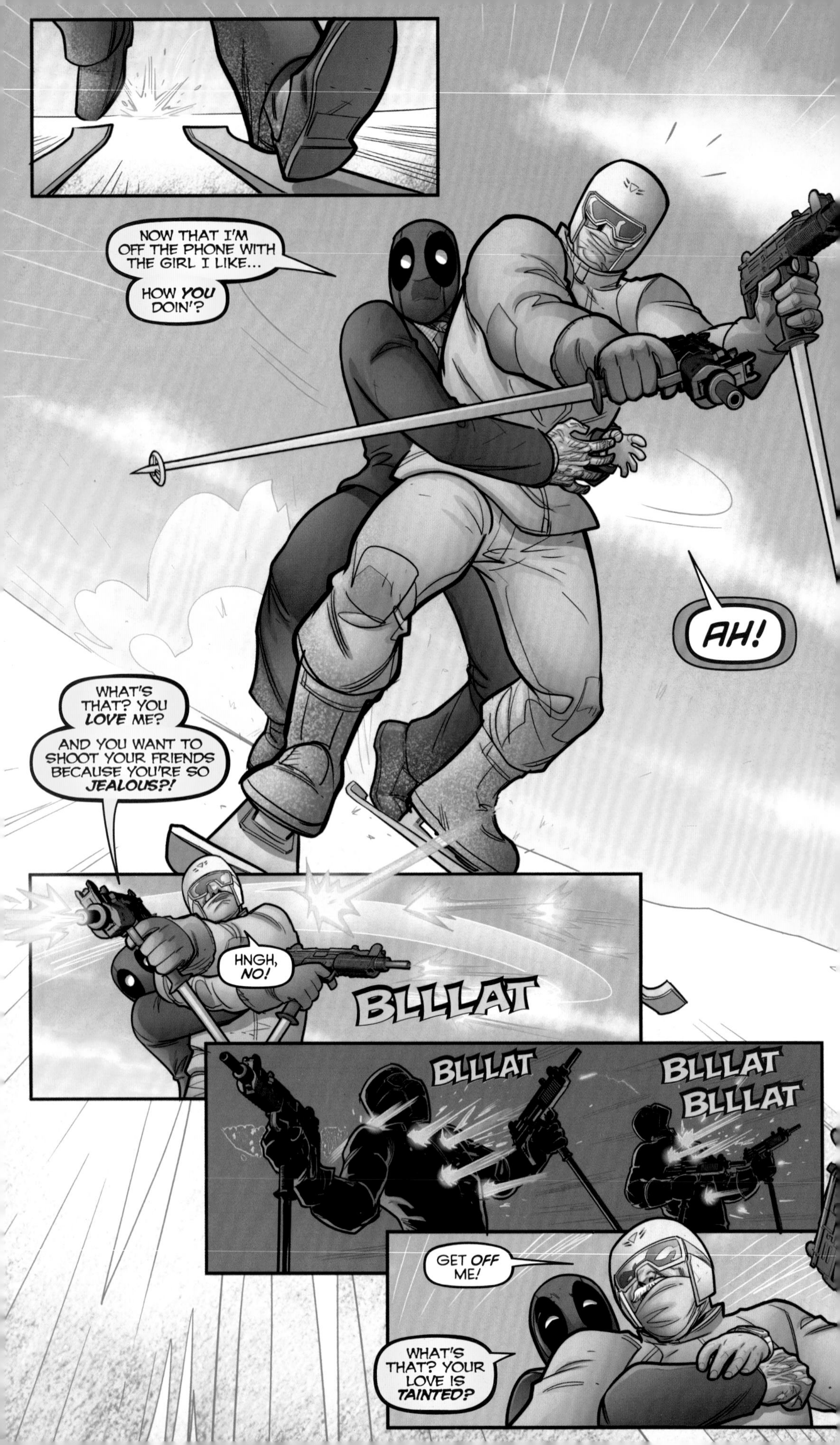
NOW THAT I'M OFF THE PHONE WITH THE GIRL I LIKE...
HOW YOU DOIN'?
AH!
WHAT'S THAT? YOU LOVE ME?
AND YOU WANT TO SHOOT YOUR FRIENDS BECAUSE YOU'RE SO JEALOUS?!
HNGH, NO!
BLLLAT
BLLLAT
BLLLAT
BLLLAT
GET OFF ME!
WHAT'S THAT? YOUR LOVE IS TAINTED?

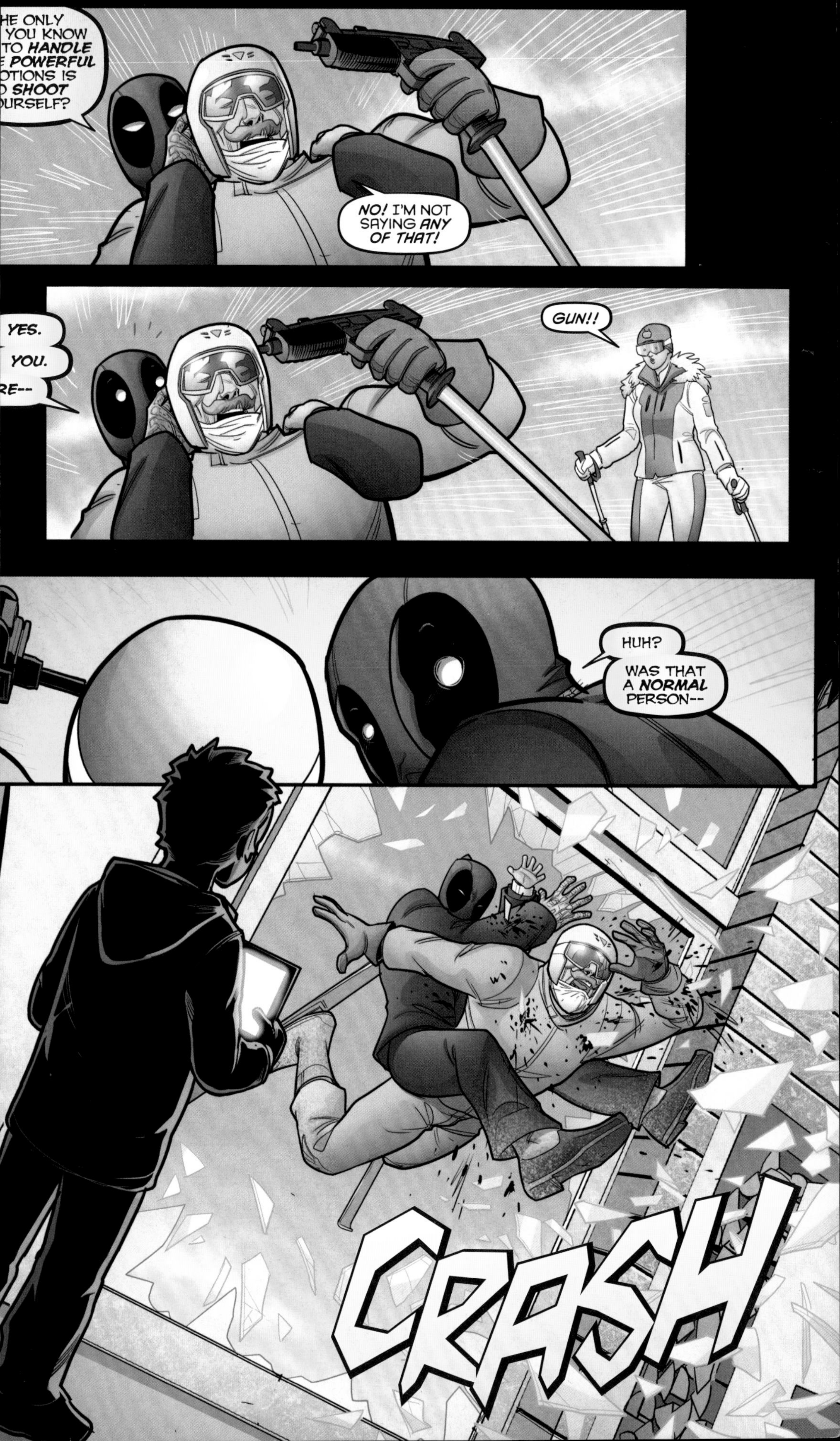
HE ONLY YOU KNOW TO HANDLE E POWERFUL OTIONS IS D SHOOT OURSELF?
NO! I'M NOT SAYING ANY OF THAT!
YES. YOU. RE--
GUN!!
HUH?
WAS THAT A NORMAL PERSON--
CRASH

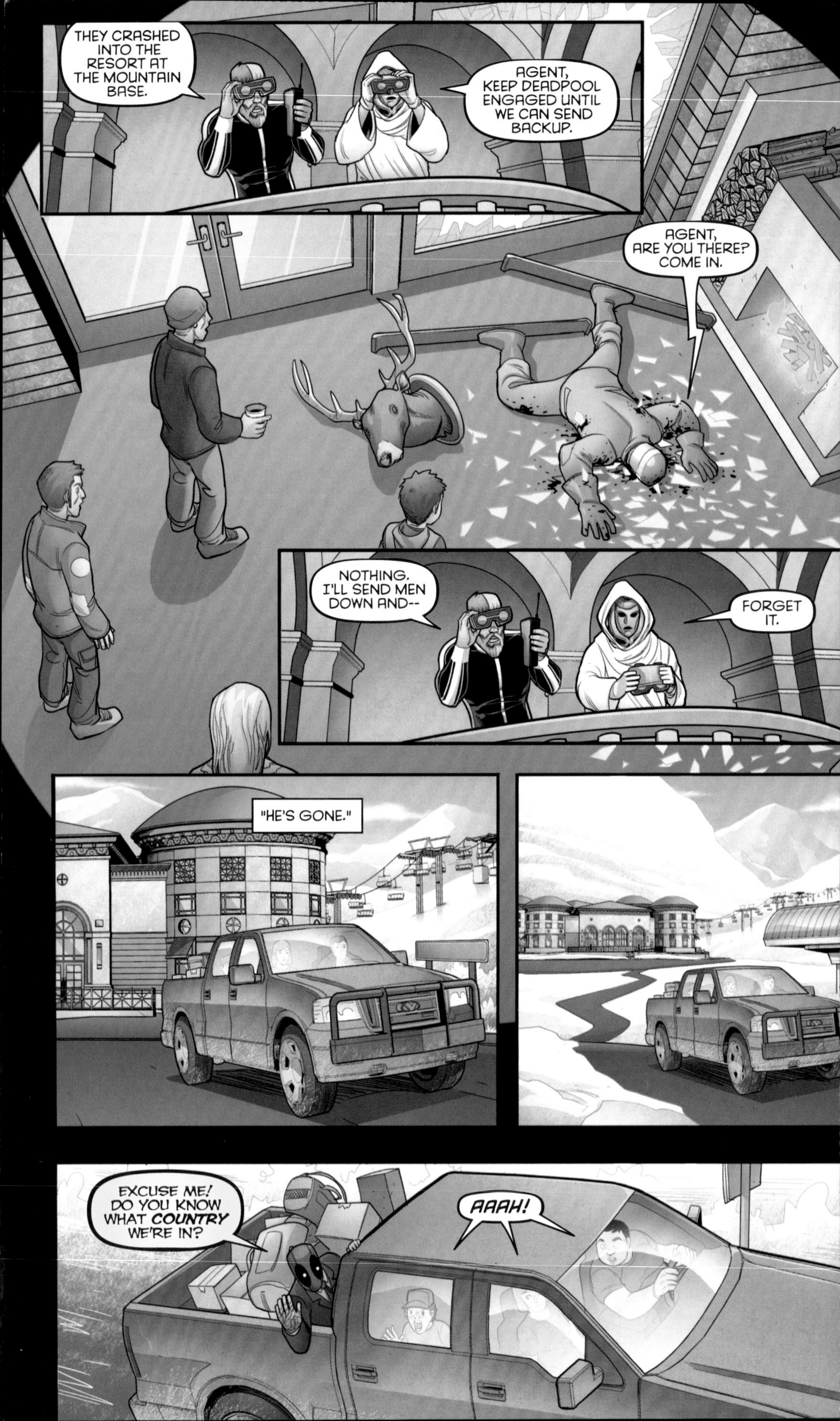
THEY CRASHED INTO THE RESORT AT THE MOUNTAIN BASE.
AGENT, KEEP DEADPOOL ENGAGED UNTIL WE CAN SEND BACKUP.
AGENT, ARE YOU THERE? COME IN.
NOTHING. I'LL SEND MEN DOWN AND--
FORGET IT.
"HE'S GONE."
EXCUSE ME! DO YOU KNOW WHAT COUNTRY WE'RE IN?
AAAH!

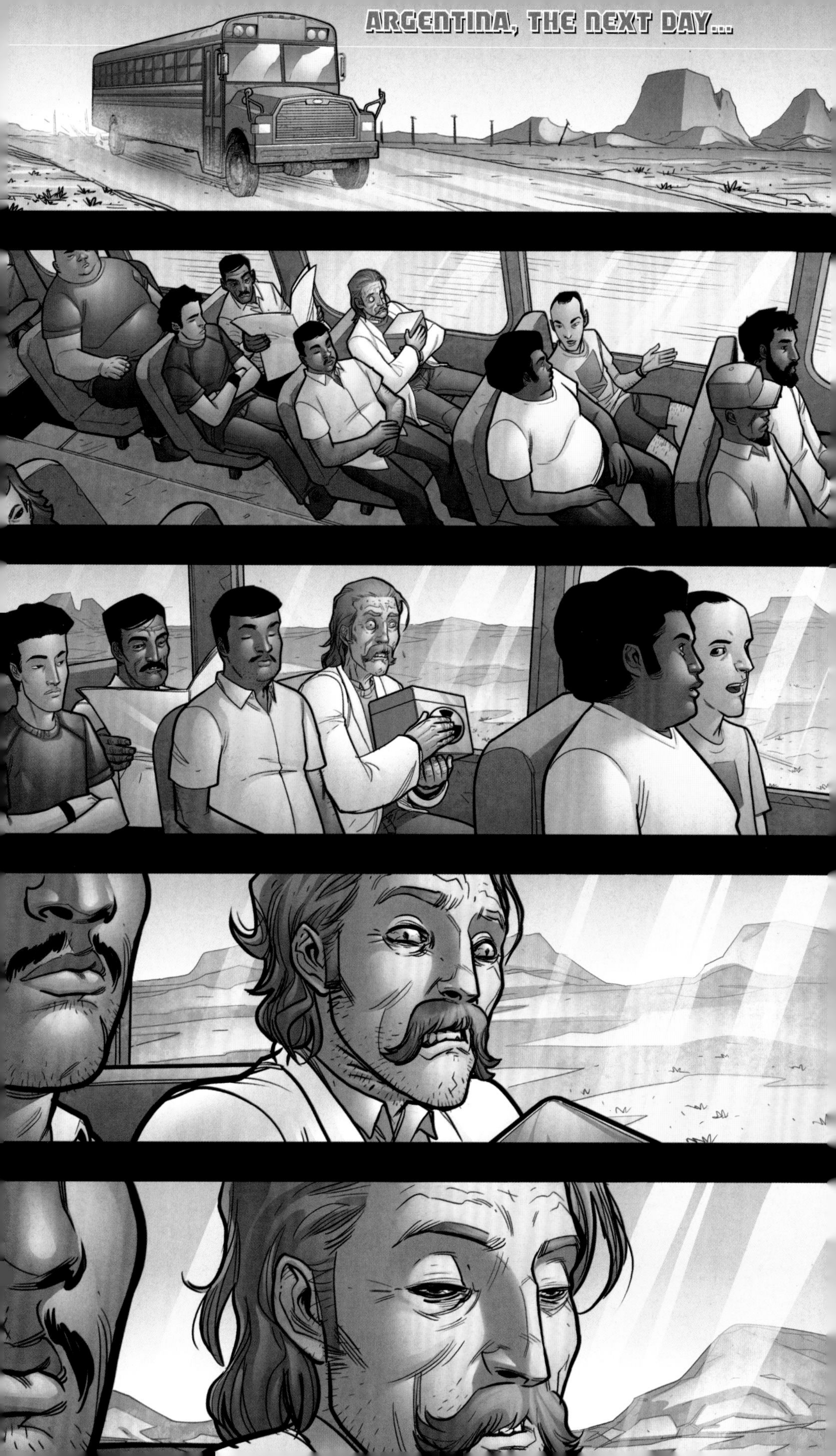
ARGENTINA, THE NEXT DAY...

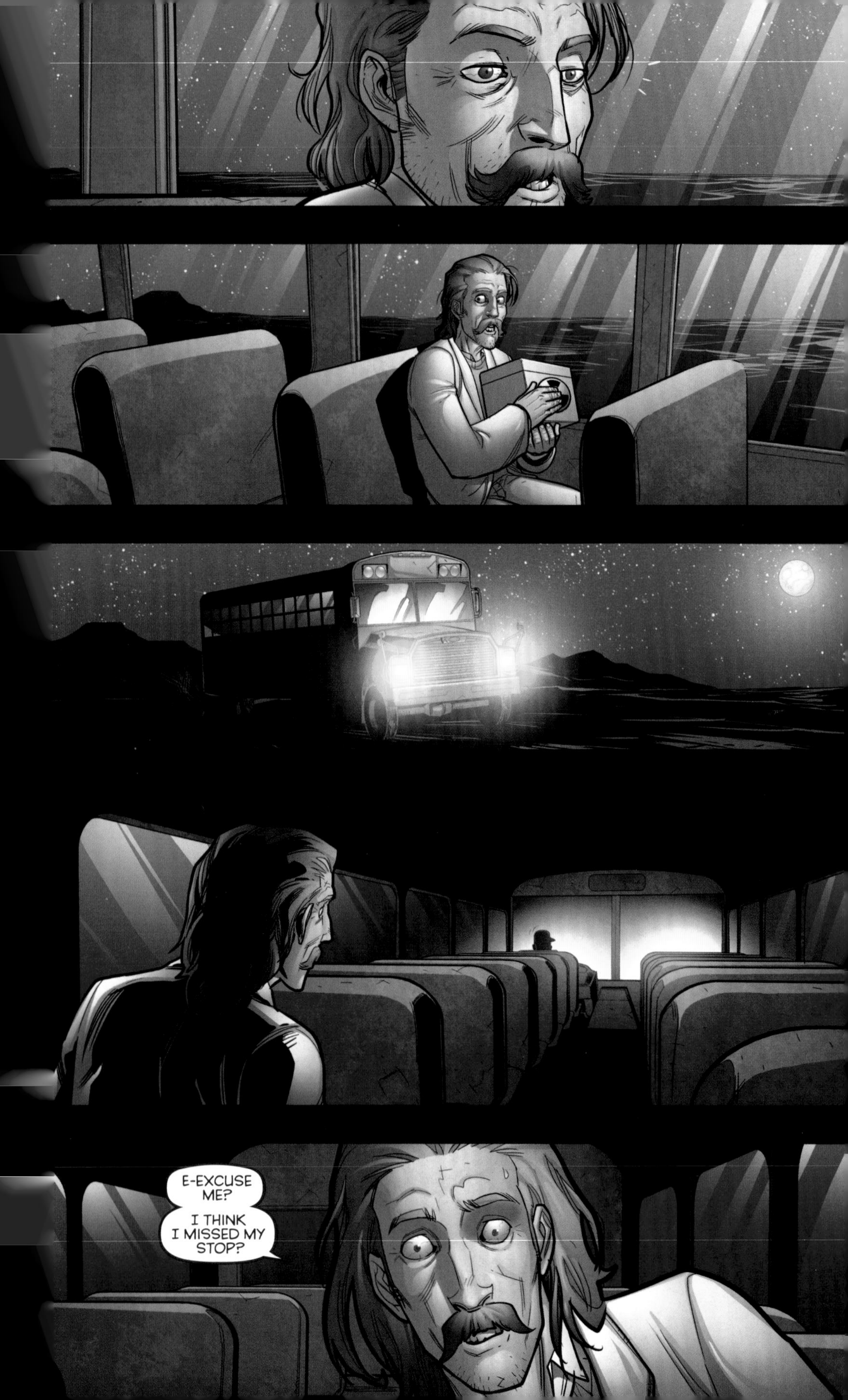
E-EXCUSE ME?
I THINK I MISSED MY STOP?

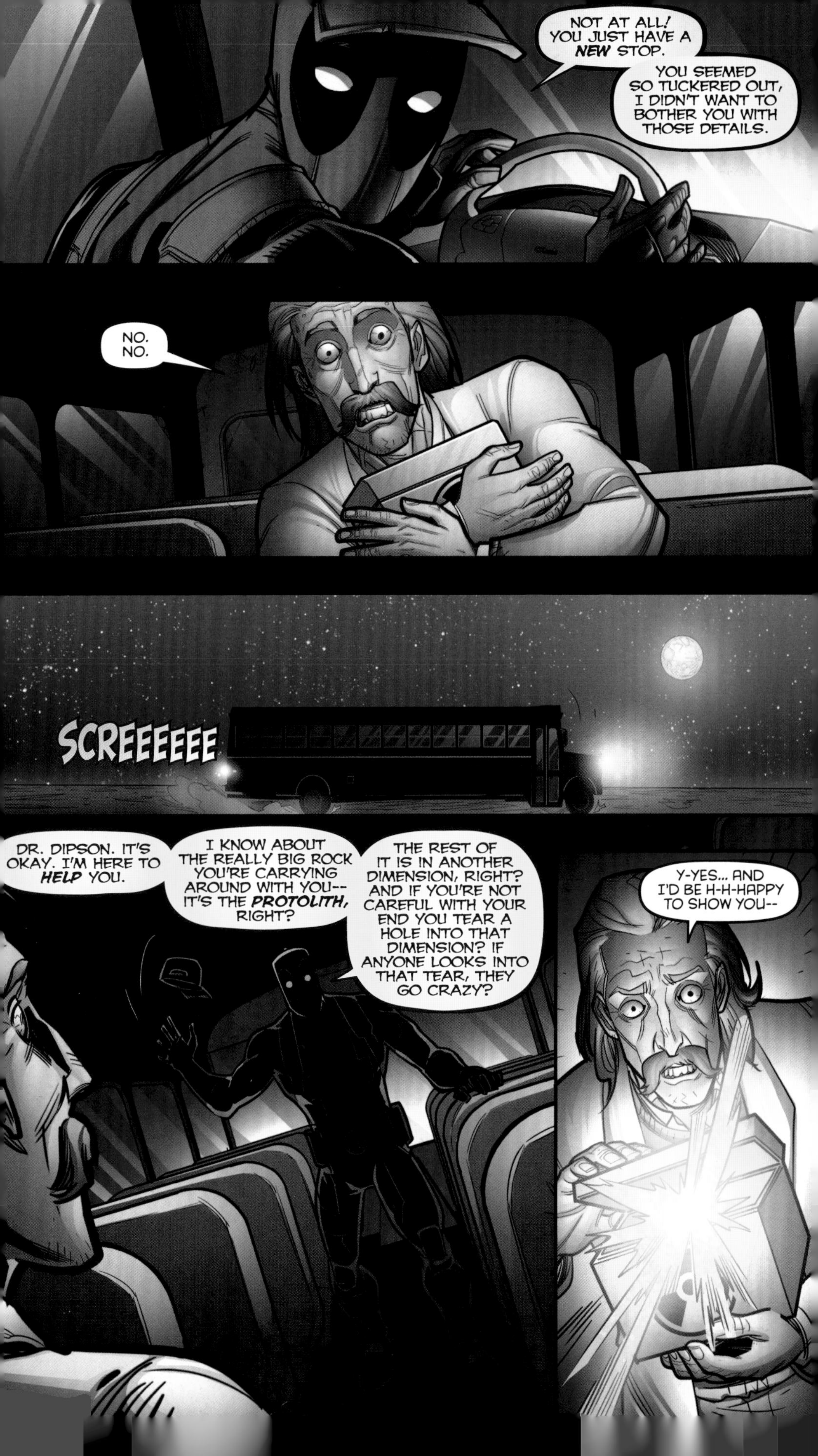
NOT AT ALL! YOU JUST HAVE A NEW STOP.
YOU SEEMED SO TUCKERED OUT, I DIDN'T WANT TO BOTHER YOU WITH THOSE DETAILS.
NO. NO.
SCREEEEEE
DR. DIPSON. IT'S OKAY. I'M HERE TO HELP YOU.
I KNOW ABOUT THE REALLY BIG ROCK YOU'RE CARRYING AROUND WITH YOU-- IT'S THE PROTOLITH, RIGHT?
THE REST OF IT IS IN ANOTHER DIMENSION, RIGHT? AND IF YOU'RE NOT CAREFUL WITH YOUR END YOU TEAR A HOLE INTO THAT DIMENSION? IF ANYONE LOOKS INTO THAT TEAR, THEY GO CRAZY?
Y-YES... AND I'D BE H-H-HAPPY TO SHOW YOU--

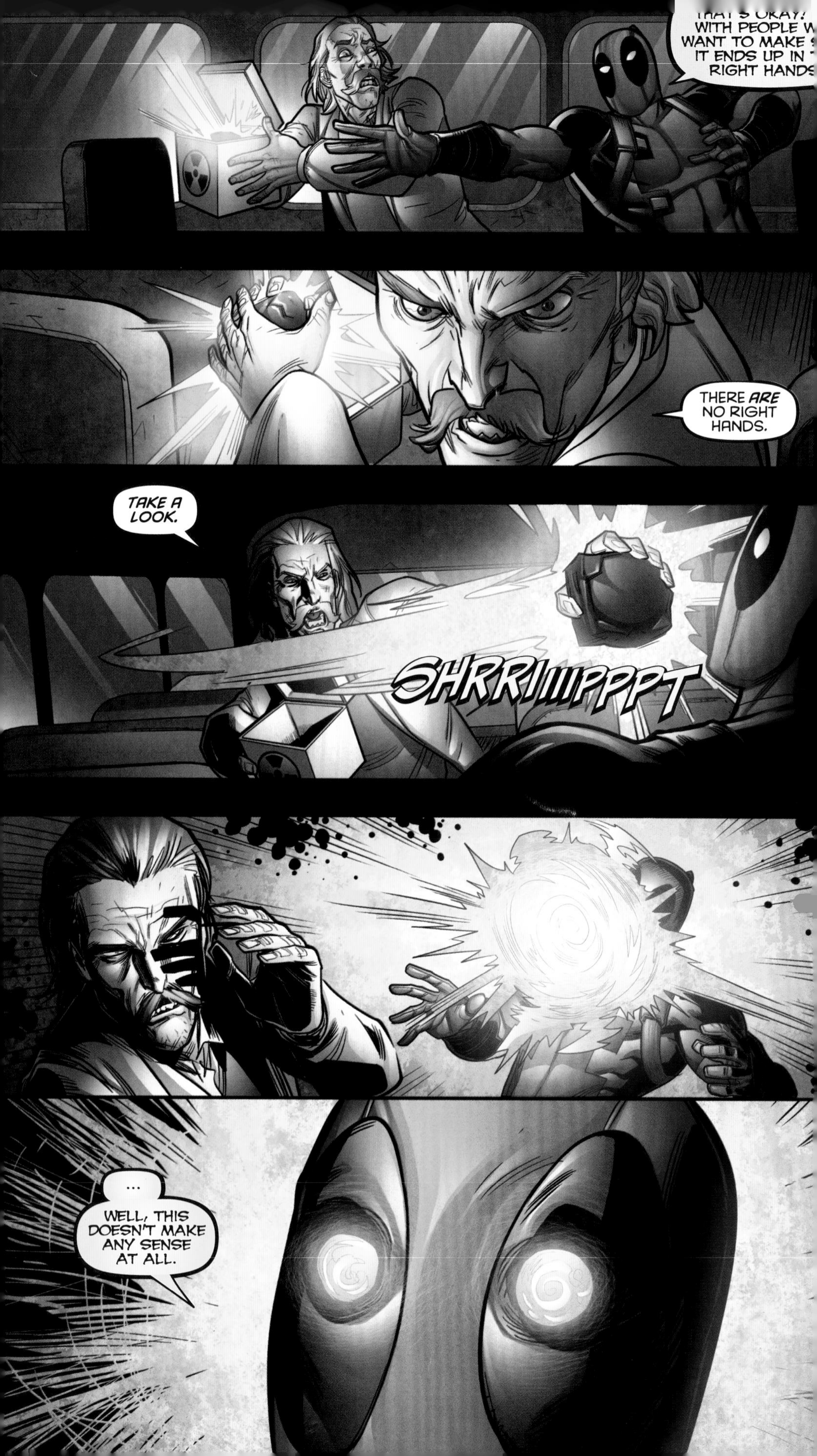
WITH PEOPLE W
WANT TO MAKE S
IT ENDS UP IN T
RIGHT HANDS
THERE *ARE* NO RIGHT HANDS.
TAKE A LOOK.
SHRRIIIIPPPPT
...
WELL, THIS DOESN'T MAKE ANY SENSE AT ALL.

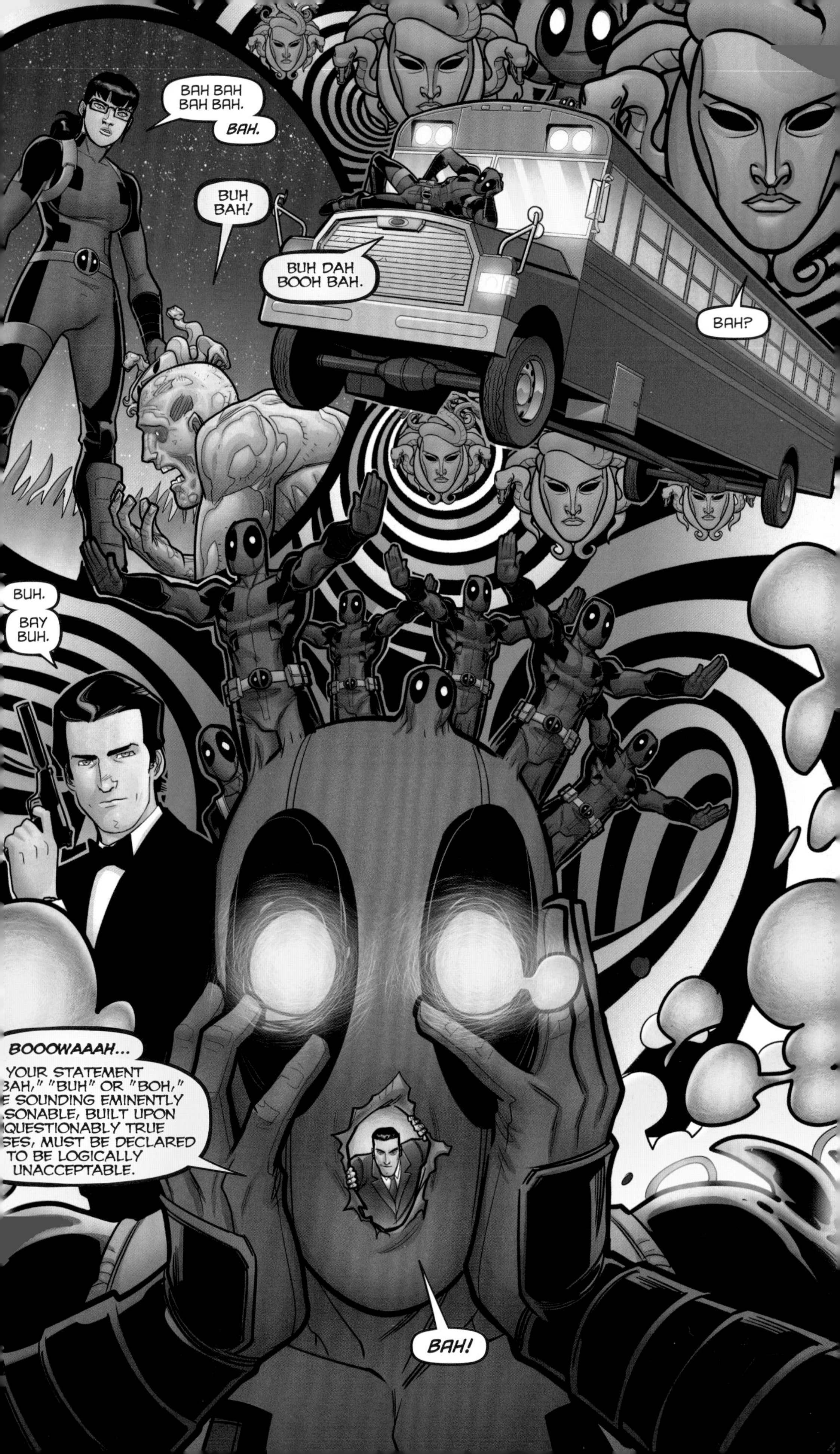

BAH BAH BAH BAH. BAH.
BUH BAH!
BUH DAH BOOH BAH.
BAH?
BUH.
BAY BUH.
BOOOWAAAH...
YOUR STATEMENT
BAH," "BUH" OR "BOH,"
E SOUNDING EMINENTLY
SONABLE, BUILT UPON
QUESTIONABLY TRUE
SES, MUST BE DECLARED
TO BE LOGICALLY
UNACCEPTABLE.
BAH!

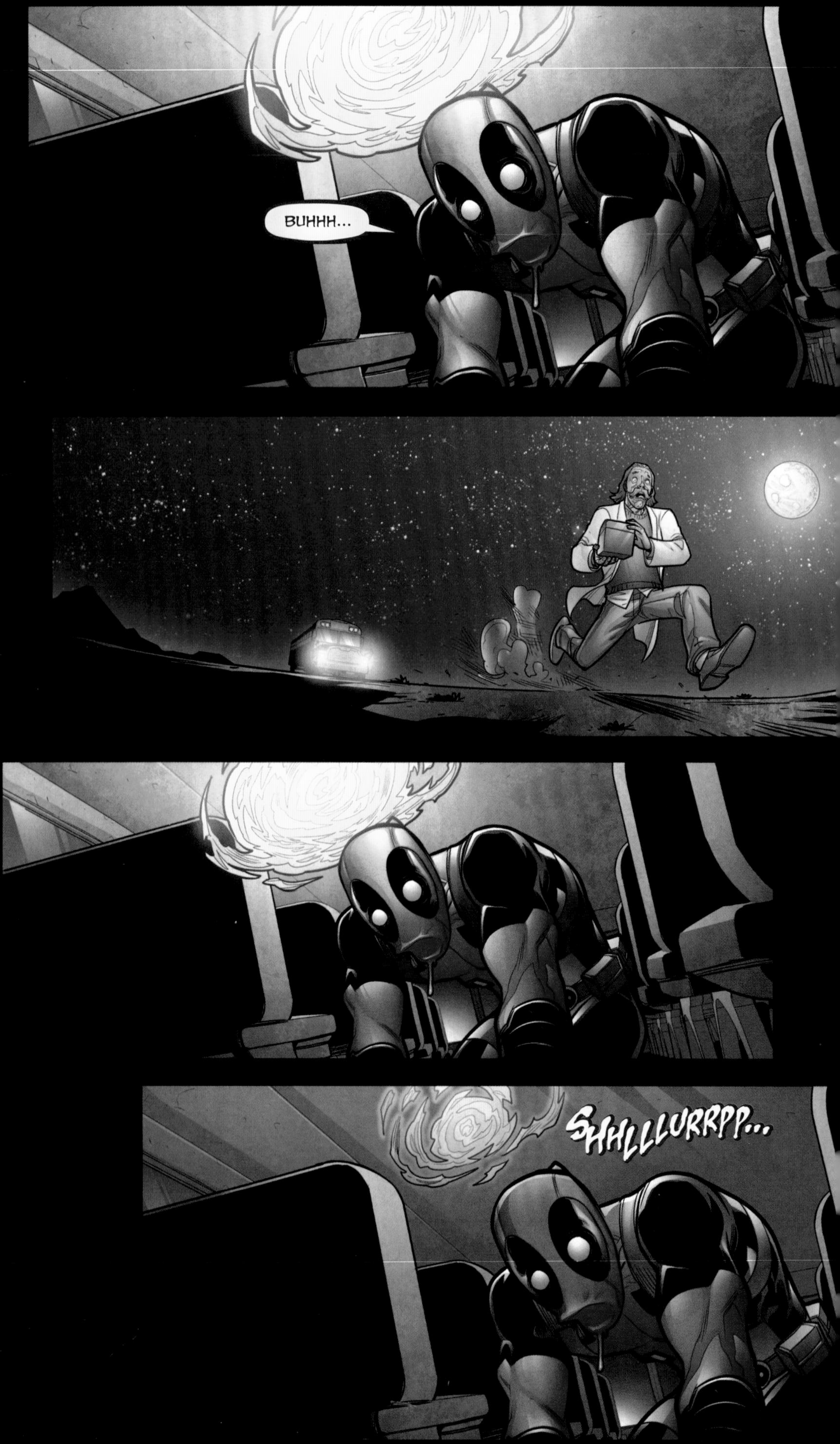
BUHHH...
SHHLLLURRPP...

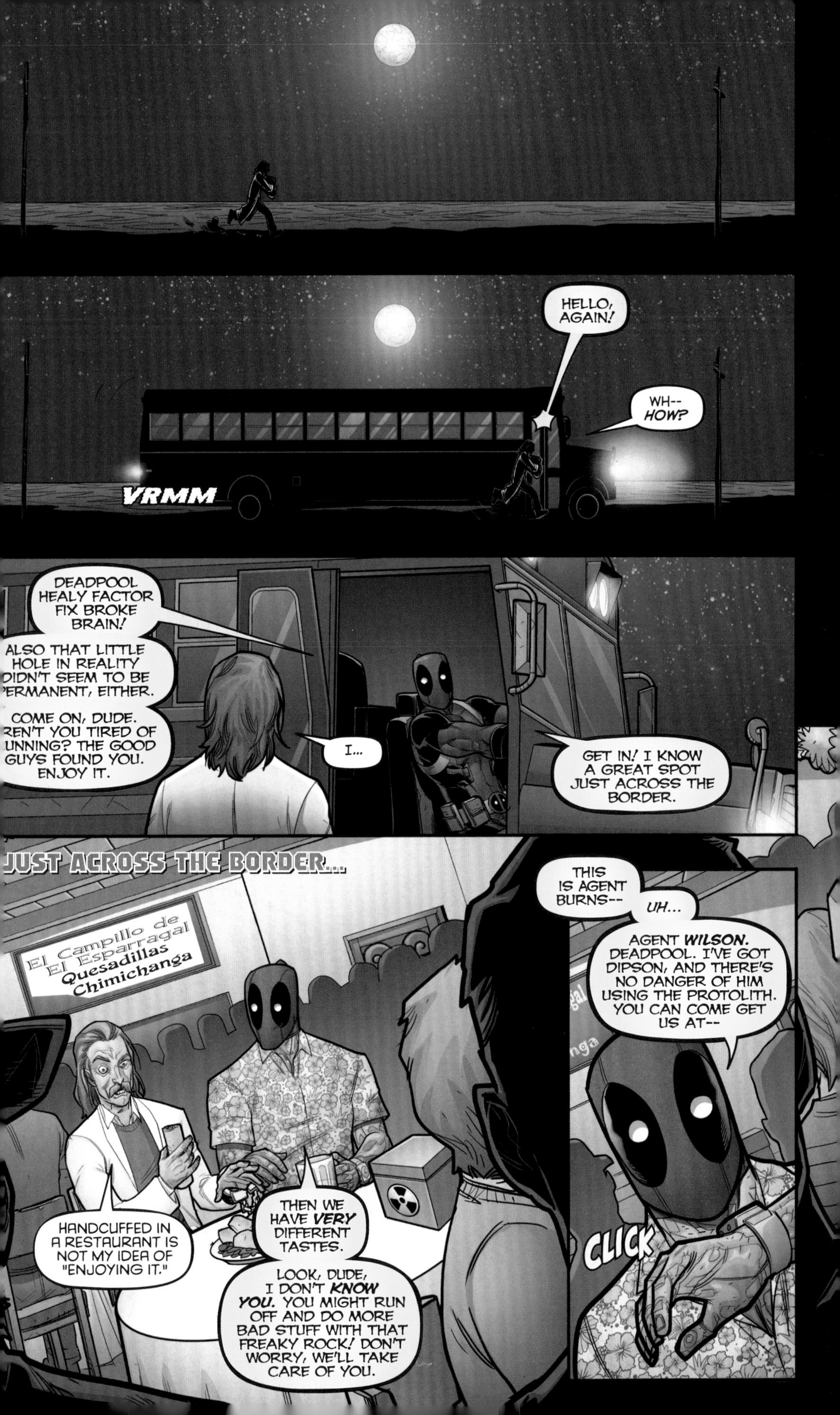
HELLO, AGAIN!
WH-- HOW?
VRMM
DEADPOOL HEALY FACTOR FIX BROKE BRAIN!
ALSO THAT LITTLE HOLE IN REALITY DIDN'T SEEM TO BE PERMANENT, EITHER.
COME ON, DUDE. AREN'T YOU TIRED OF RUNNING? THE GOOD GUYS FOUND YOU. ENJOY IT.
I...
GET IN! I KNOW A GREAT SPOT JUST ACROSS THE BORDER.
JUST ACROSS THE BORDER...
El Campillo de El Esparragal Quesadillas Chimichanga
THIS IS AGENT BURNS--
UH...
AGENT WILSON. DEADPOOL. I'VE GOT DIPSON, AND THERE'S NO DANGER OF HIM USING THE PROTOLITH. YOU CAN COME GET US AT--
HANDCUFFED IN A RESTAURANT IS NOT MY IDEA OF "ENJOYING IT."
THEN WE HAVE VERY DIFFERENT TASTES.
LOOK, DUDE, I DON'T KNOW YOU. YOU MIGHT RUN OFF AND DO MORE BAD STUFF WITH THAT FREAKY ROCK! DON'T WORRY, WE'LL TAKE CARE OF YOU.
CLICK

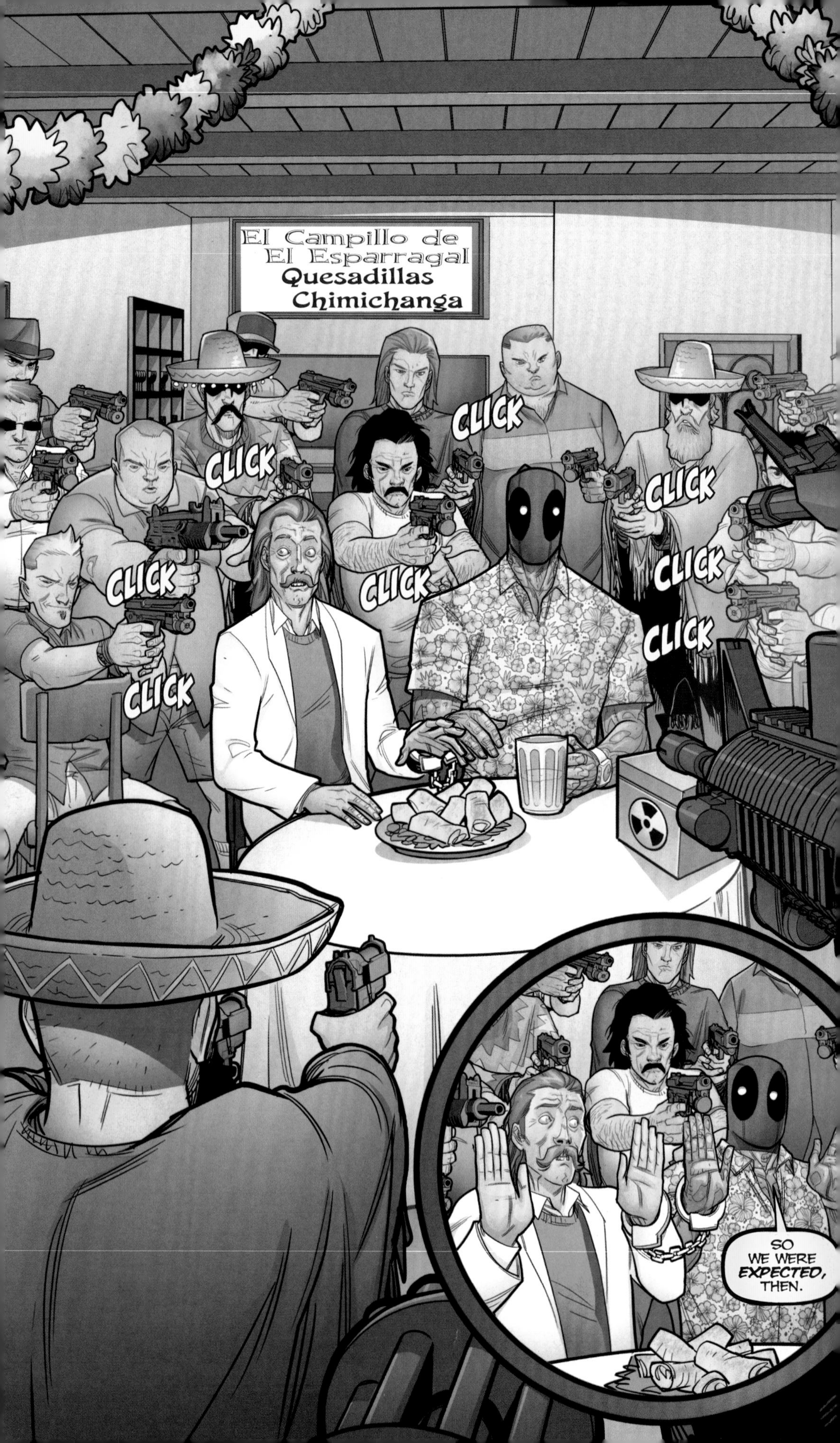
El Campillo de
El Esparragal
Quesadillas
Chimichanga
CLICK
CLICK
CLICK
CLICK
CLICK
CLICK
CLICK
CLICK
SO WE WERE *EXPECTED,* THEN.

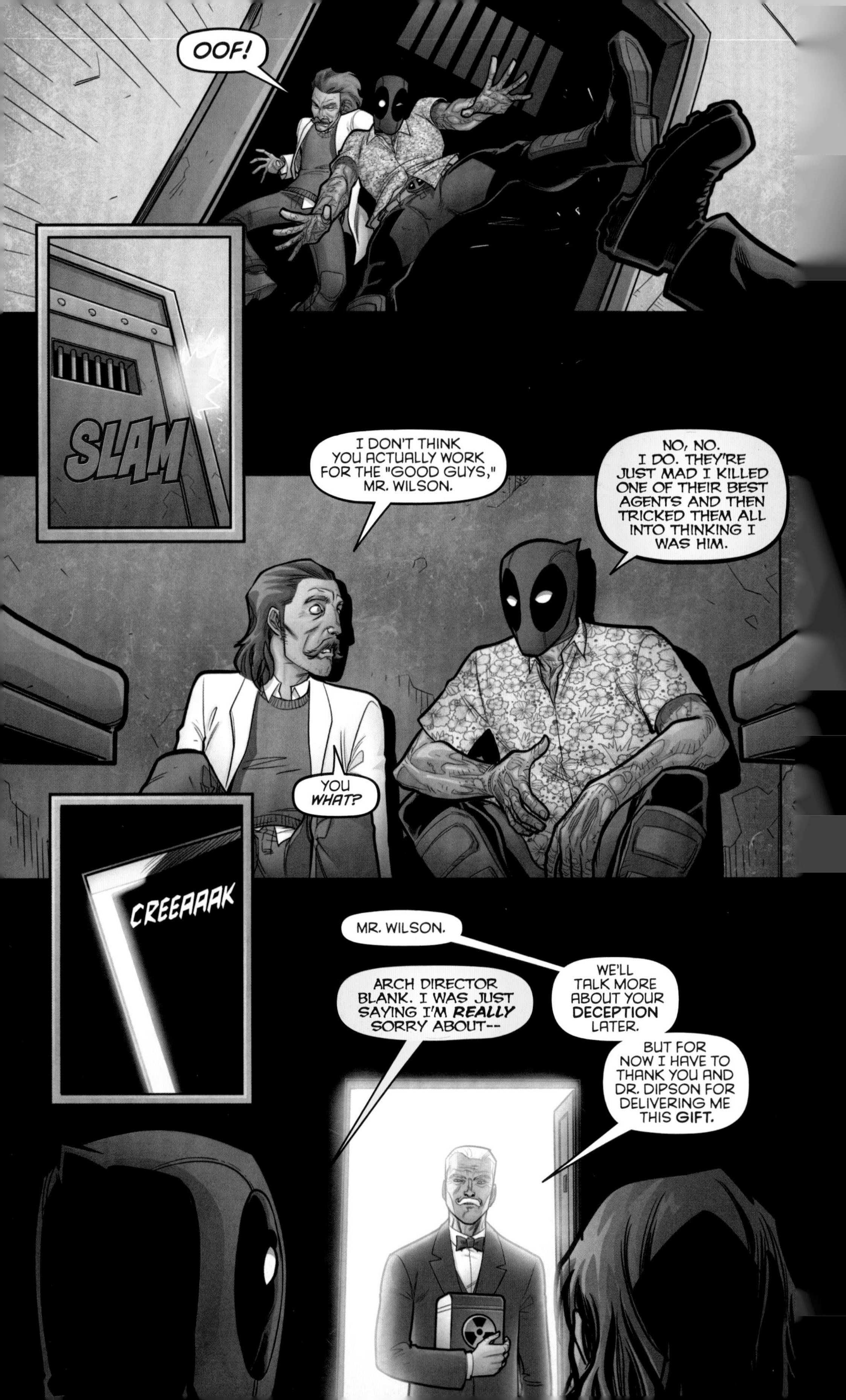
OOF!
SLAM
I DON'T THINK YOU ACTUALLY WORK FOR THE "GOOD GUYS," MR. WILSON.
NO, NO. I DO. THEY'RE JUST MAD I KILLED ONE OF THEIR BEST AGENTS AND THEN TRICKED THEM ALL INTO THINKING I WAS HIM.
YOU *WHAT?*
CREEAAAK
MR. WILSON.
ARCH DIRECTOR BLANK. I WAS JUST SAYING I'M *REALLY* SORRY ABOUT--
WE'LL TALK MORE ABOUT YOUR **DECEPTION** LATER.
BUT FOR NOW I HAVE TO THANK YOU AND DR. DIPSON FOR DELIVERING ME THIS **GIFT.**

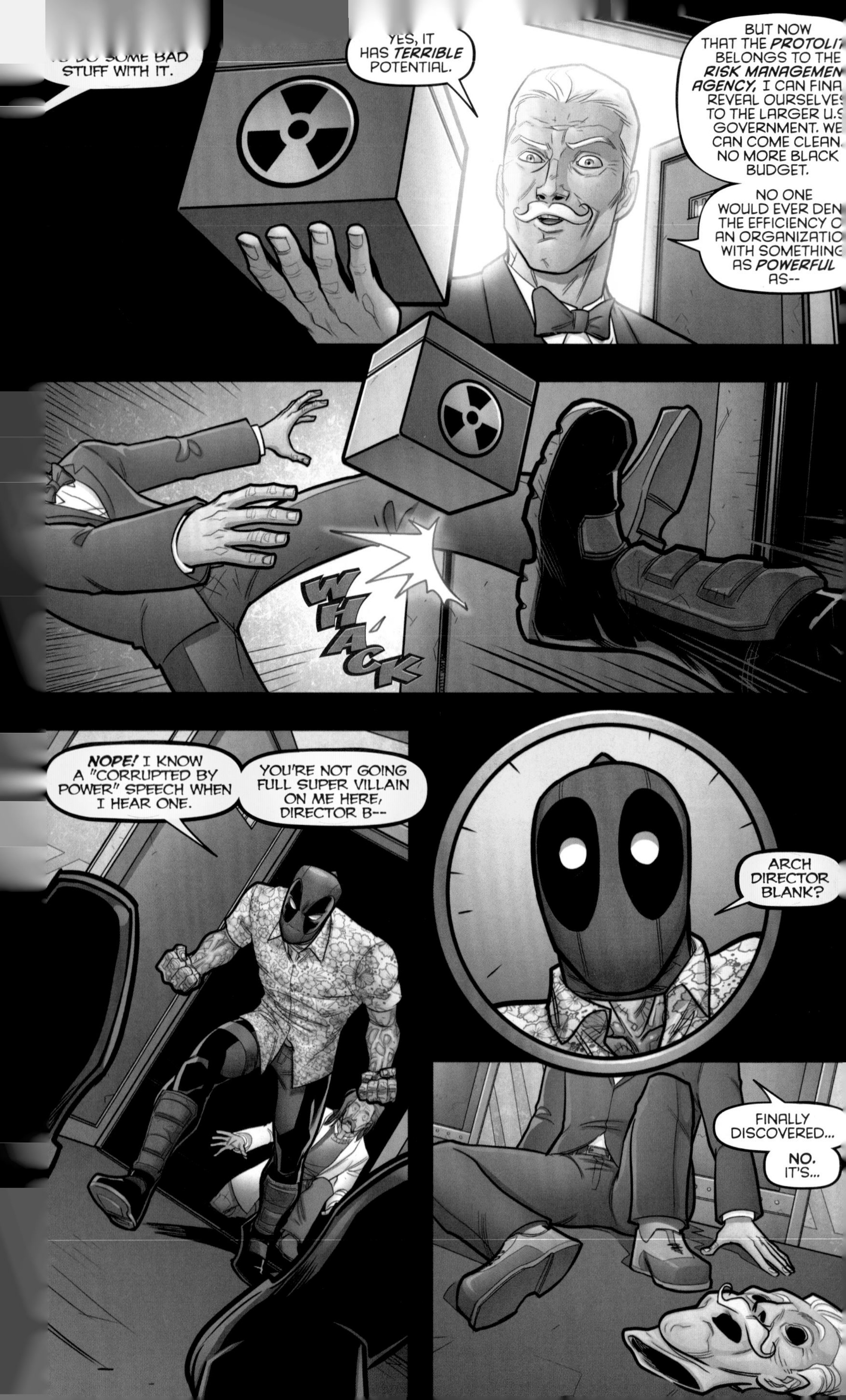

SOME BAD STUFF WITH IT.
YES, IT HAS *TERRIBLE* POTENTIAL.
BUT NOW THAT THE *PROTOLIT* BELONGS TO THE *RISK MANAGEMEN* *AGENCY,* I CAN FINA REVEAL OURSELVE TO THE LARGER U. GOVERNMENT. WE CAN COME CLEAN. NO MORE BLACK BUDGET.
NO ONE WOULD EVER DEN THE EFFICIENCY O AN ORGANIZATIO WITH SOMETHING AS *POWERFUL* AS--
WHACK
NOPE! I KNOW A "CORRUPTED BY POWER" SPEECH WHEN I HEAR ONE.
YOU'RE NOT GOING FULL SUPER VILLAIN ON ME HERE, DIRECTOR B--
ARCH DIRECTOR BLANK?
FINALLY DISCOVERED...
NO. IT'S...

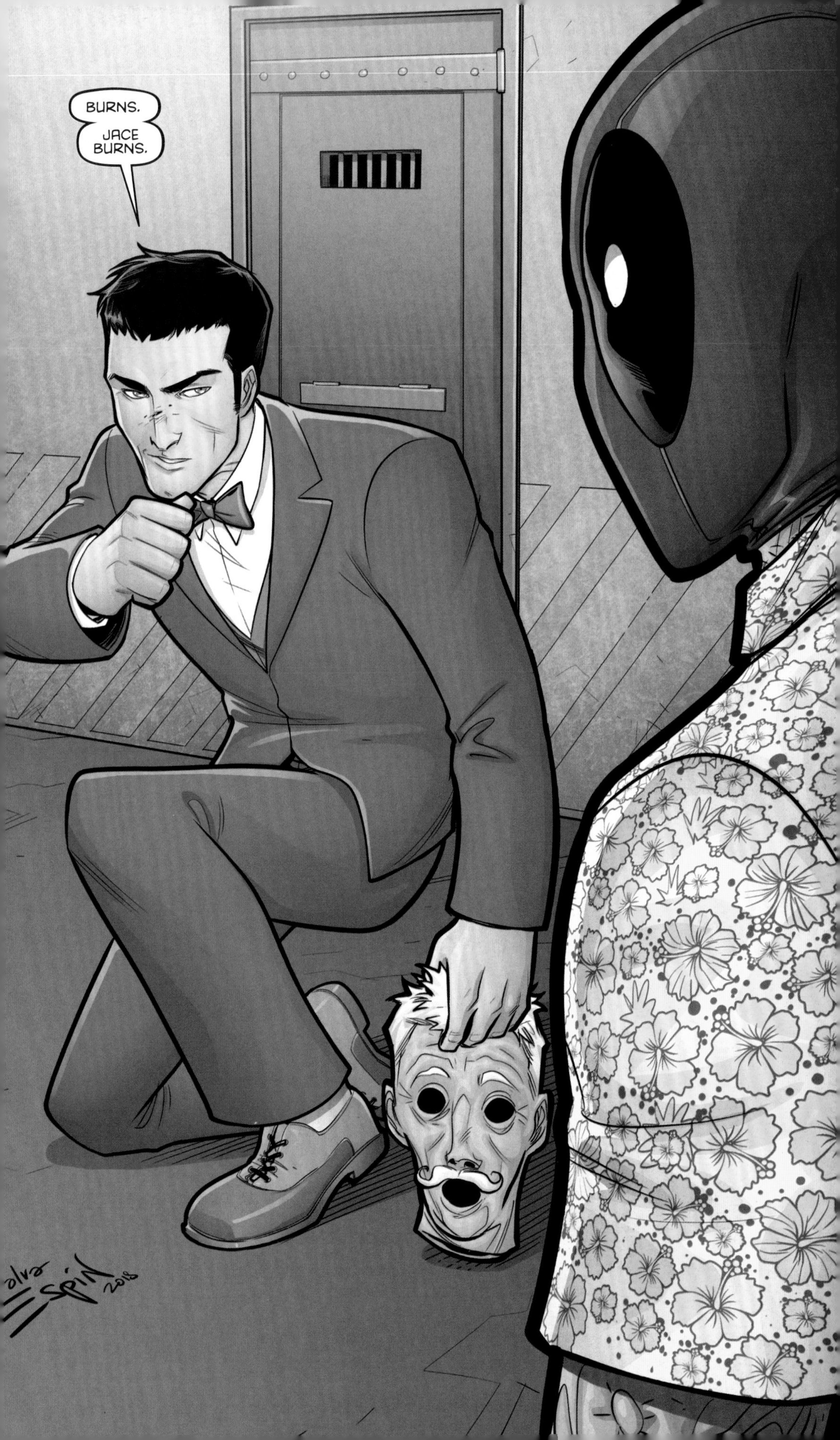
BURNS.
JACE BURNS.

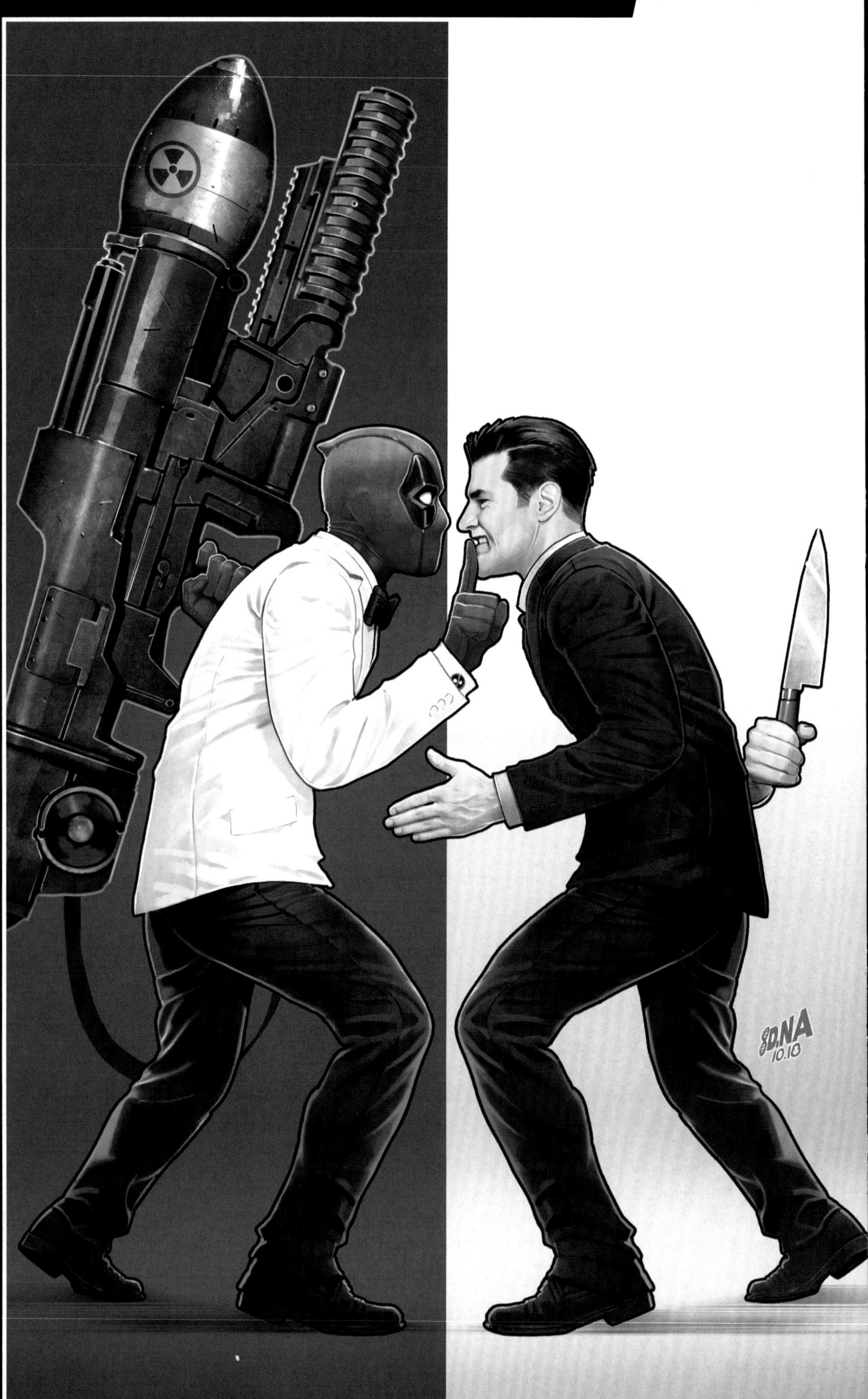
D.NA
10.18

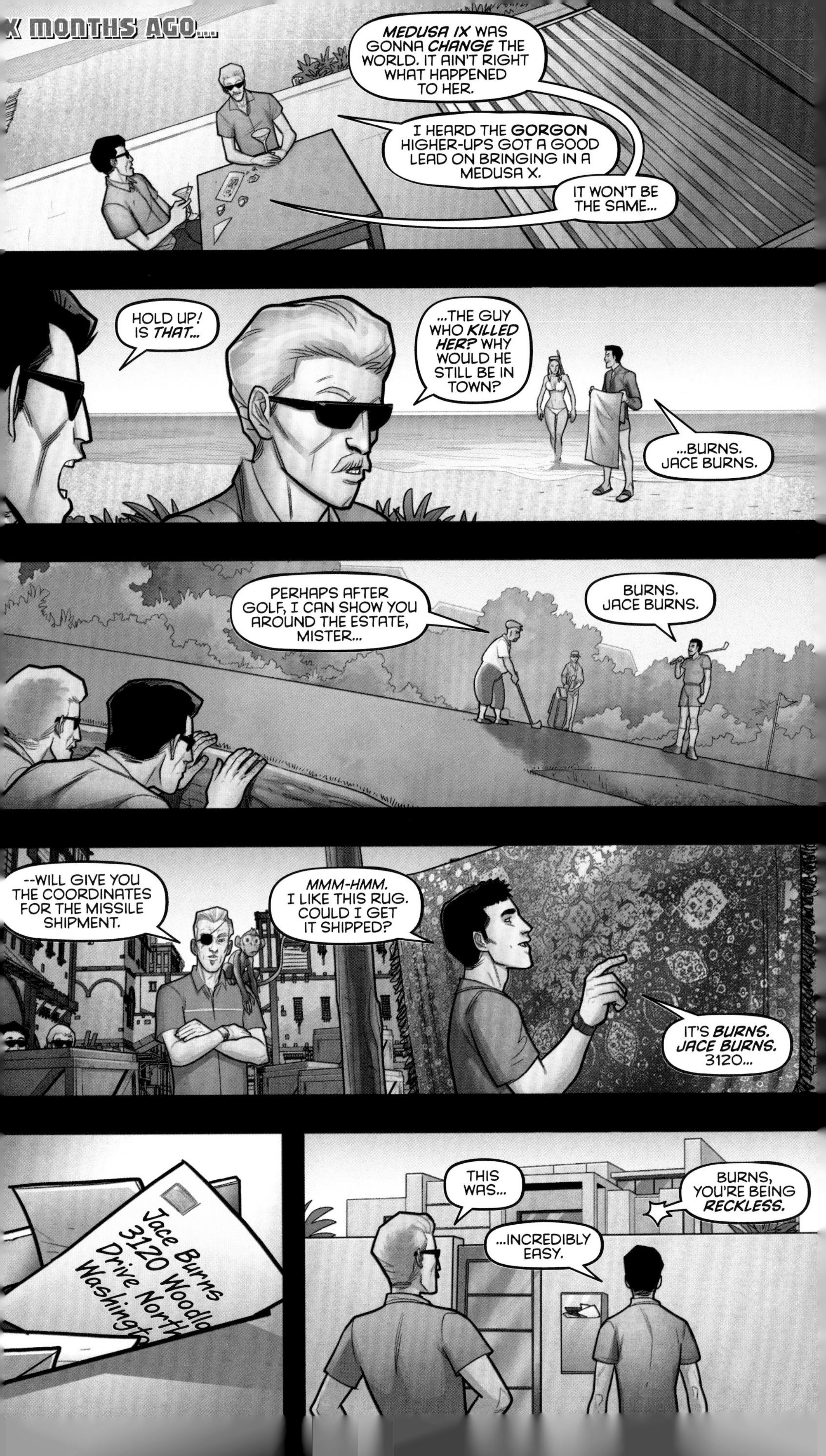
X MONTHS AGO...
MEDUSA IX WAS GONNA CHANGE THE WORLD. IT AIN'T RIGHT WHAT HAPPENED TO HER.
I HEARD THE GORGON HIGHER-UPS GOT A GOOD LEAD ON BRINGING IN A MEDUSA X.
IT WON'T BE THE SAME...
HOLD UP! IS THAT...
...THE GUY WHO KILLED HER? WHY WOULD HE STILL BE IN TOWN?
...BURNS. JACE BURNS.
PERHAPS AFTER GOLF, I CAN SHOW YOU AROUND THE ESTATE, MISTER...
BURNS. JACE BURNS.
--WILL GIVE YOU THE COORDINATES FOR THE MISSILE SHIPMENT.
MMM-HMM. I LIKE THIS RUG. COULD I GET IT SHIPPED?
IT'S BURNS. JACE BURNS. 3120...
Jace Burns
3120 Woodl
Drive North
Washingt
THIS WAS...
...INCREDIBLY EASY.
BURNS, YOU'RE BEING RECKLESS.

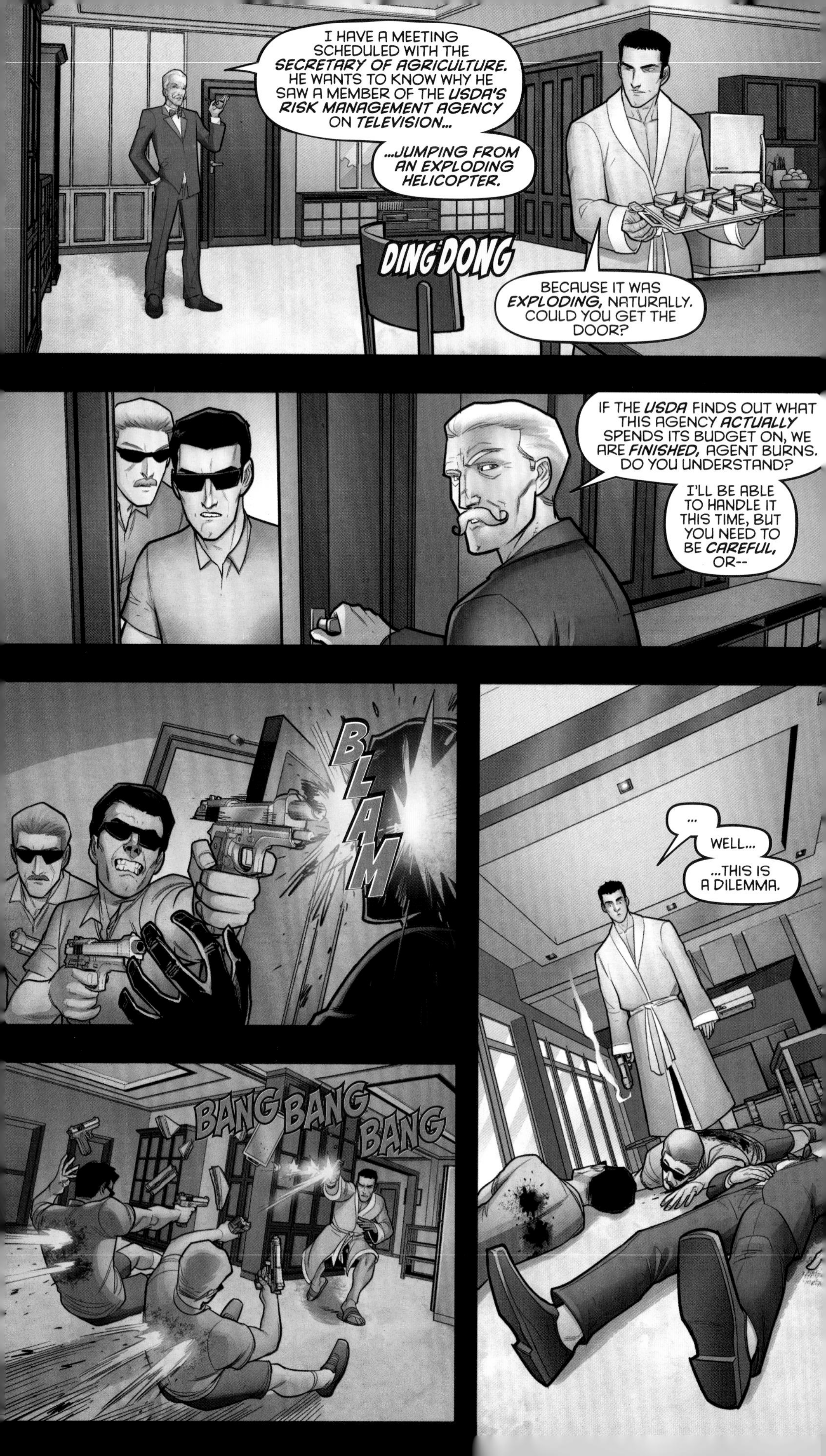
I HAVE A MEETING SCHEDULED WITH THE SECRETARY OF AGRICULTURE. HE WANTS TO KNOW WHY HE SAW A MEMBER OF THE USDA'S RISK MANAGEMENT AGENCY ON TELEVISION...
...JUMPING FROM AN EXPLODING HELICOPTER.
DING DONG
BECAUSE IT WAS EXPLODING, NATURALLY. COULD YOU GET THE DOOR?
IF THE USDA FINDS OUT WHAT THIS AGENCY ACTUALLY SPENDS ITS BUDGET ON, WE ARE FINISHED, AGENT BURNS. DO YOU UNDERSTAND?
I'LL BE ABLE TO HANDLE IT THIS TIME, BUT YOU NEED TO BE CAREFUL, OR--
BLAM
BANG BANG BANG
...
WELL...
...THIS IS A DILEMMA.

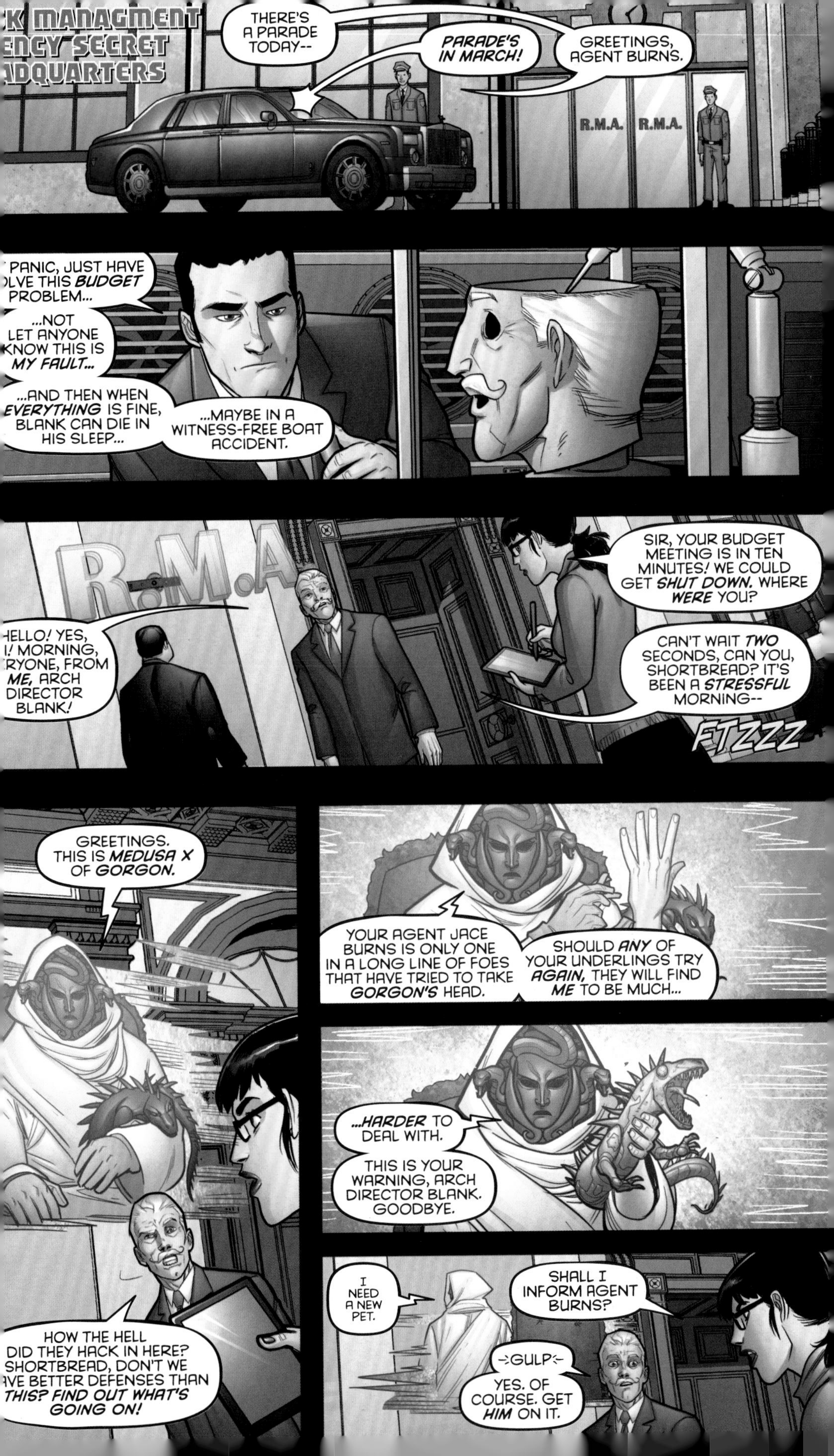

K MANAGMENT
ENCY SECRET
ADQUARTERS
THERE'S A PARADE TODAY--
GREETINGS, AGENT BURNS.
PARADE'S IN MARCH!
PANIC, JUST HAVE
LVE THIS BUDGET PROBLEM...
...NOT LET ANYONE KNOW THIS IS MY FAULT...
...AND THEN WHEN EVERYTHING IS FINE, BLANK CAN DIE IN HIS SLEEP...
...MAYBE IN A WITNESS-FREE BOAT ACCIDENT.
R.M.A.
ELLO! YES, ! MORNING, RYONE, FROM ME, ARCH DIRECTOR BLANK!
SIR, YOUR BUDGET MEETING IS IN TEN MINUTES! WE COULD GET SHUT DOWN. WHERE WERE YOU?
CAN'T WAIT TWO SECONDS, CAN YOU, SHORTBREAD? IT'S BEEN A STRESSFUL MORNING--
FTZZZ
GREETINGS. THIS IS MEDUSA X OF GORGON.
YOUR AGENT JACE BURNS IS ONLY ONE IN A LONG LINE OF FOES THAT HAVE TRIED TO TAKE GORGON'S HEAD.
SHOULD ANY OF YOUR UNDERLINGS TRY AGAIN, THEY WILL FIND ME TO BE MUCH...
...HARDER TO DEAL WITH.
THIS IS YOUR WARNING, ARCH DIRECTOR BLANK. GOODBYE.
HOW THE HELL DID THEY HACK IN HERE? SHORTBREAD, DON'T WE VE BETTER DEFENSES THAN THIS? FIND OUT WHAT'S GOING ON!
I NEED A NEW PET.
SHALL I INFORM AGENT BURNS?
GULP
YES. OF COURSE. GET HIM ON IT.

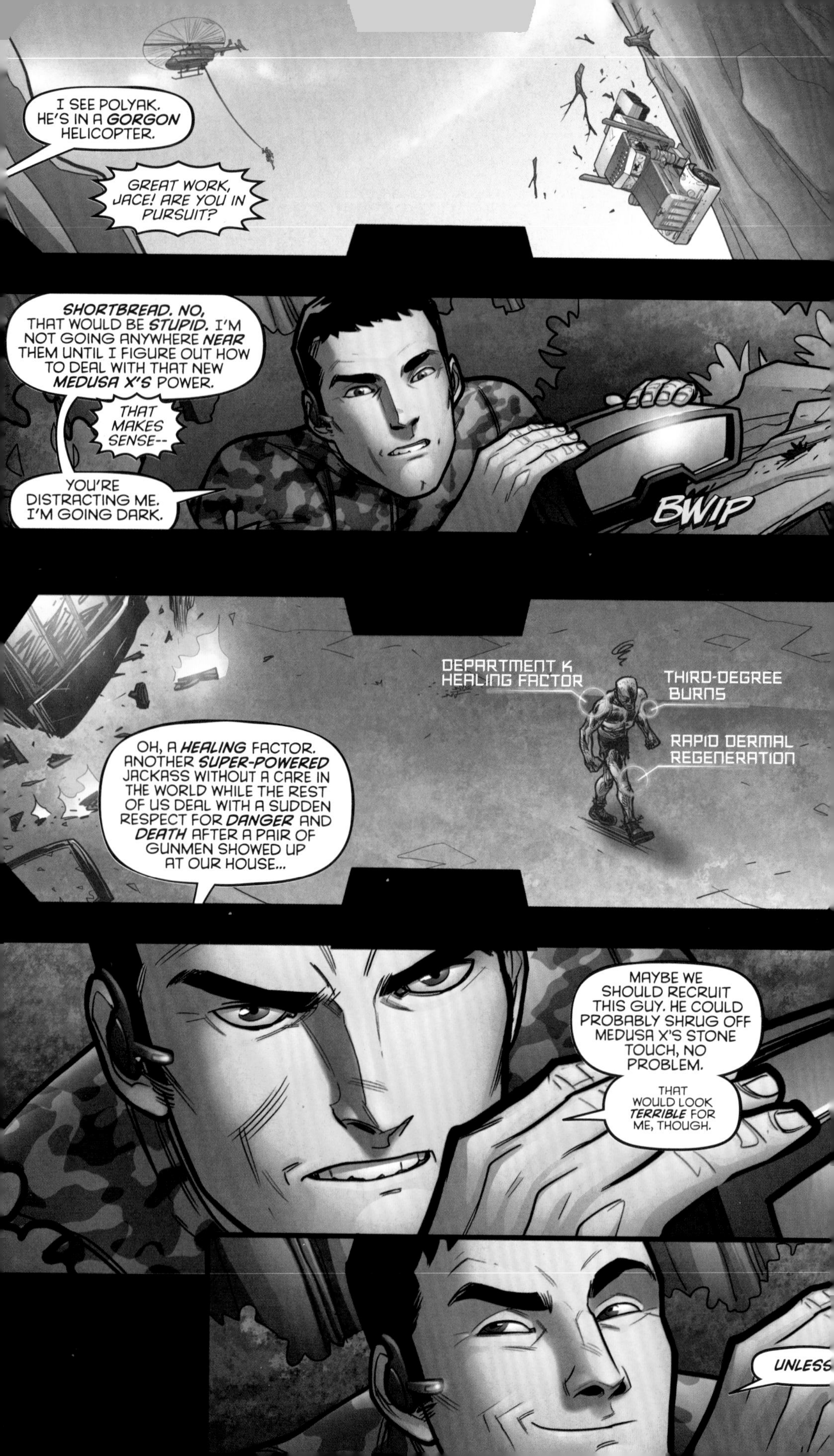
I SEE POLYAK. HE'S IN A GORGON HELICOPTER.
GREAT WORK, JACE! ARE YOU IN PURSUIT?
SHORTBREAD. NO, THAT WOULD BE STUPID. I'M NOT GOING ANYWHERE NEAR THEM UNTIL I FIGURE OUT HOW TO DEAL WITH THAT NEW MEDUSA X'S POWER.
THAT MAKES SENSE--
YOU'RE DISTRACTING ME. I'M GOING DARK.
BWIP
DEPARTMENT K HEALING FACTOR
THIRD-DEGREE BURNS
RAPID DERMAL REGENERATION
OH, A HEALING FACTOR. ANOTHER SUPER-POWERED JACKASS WITHOUT A CARE IN THE WORLD WHILE THE REST OF US DEAL WITH A SUDDEN RESPECT FOR DANGER AND DEATH AFTER A PAIR OF GUNMEN SHOWED UP AT OUR HOUSE...
MAYBE WE SHOULD RECRUIT THIS GUY. HE COULD PROBABLY SHRUG OFF MEDUSA X'S STONE TOUCH, NO PROBLEM.
THAT WOULD LOOK TERRIBLE FOR ME, THOUGH.
UNLESS

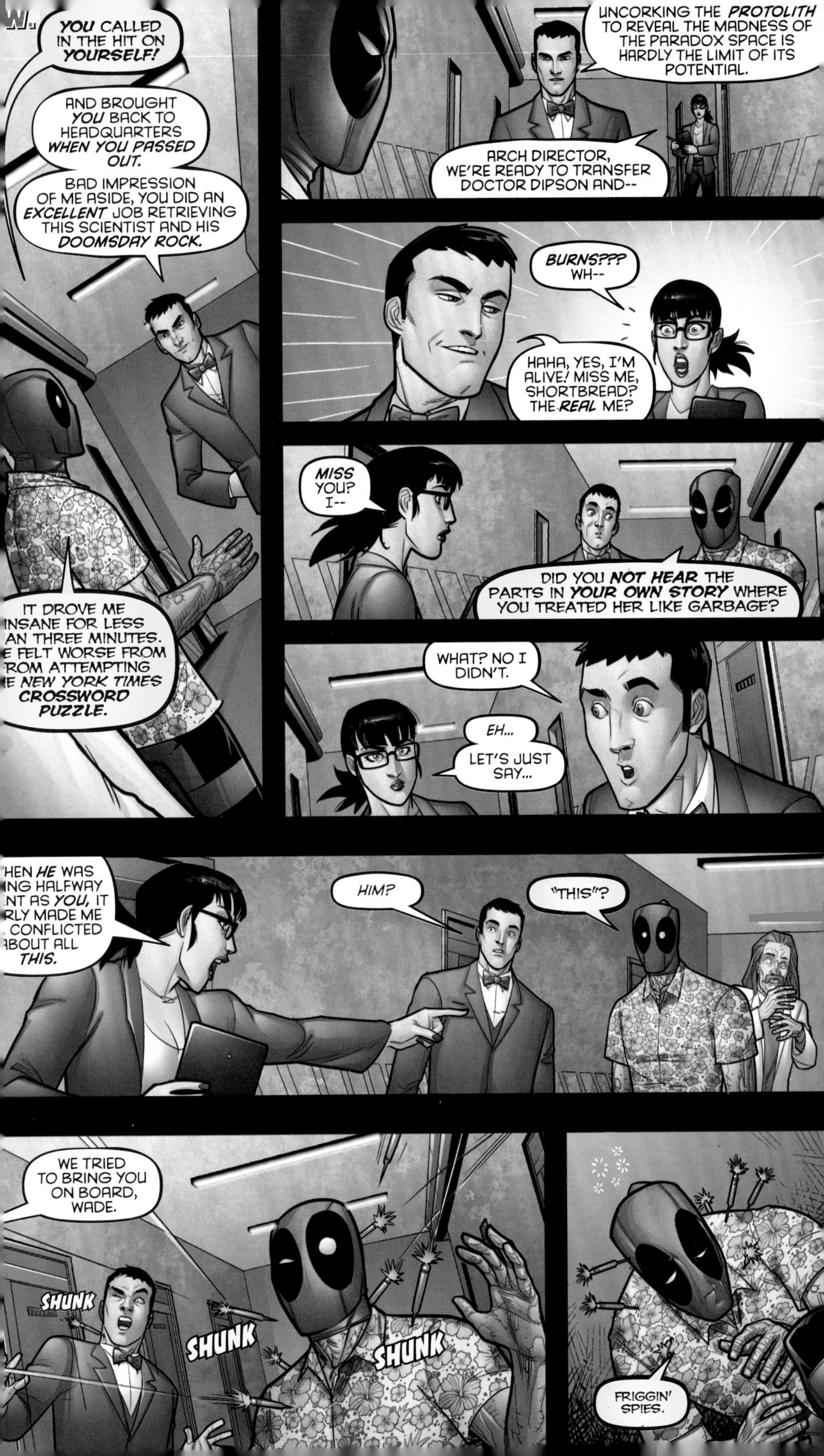
W--
YOU CALLED IN THE HIT ON YOURSELF!
AND BROUGHT YOU BACK TO HEADQUARTERS WHEN YOU PASSED OUT.
BAD IMPRESSION OF ME ASIDE, YOU DID AN EXCELLENT JOB RETRIEVING THIS SCIENTIST AND HIS DOOMSDAY ROCK.
IT DROVE ME INSANE FOR LESS AN THREE MINUTES. E FELT WORSE FROM ROM ATTEMPTING E NEW YORK TIMES CROSSWORD PUZZLE.
UNCORKING THE PROTOLITH TO REVEAL THE MADNESS OF THE PARADOX SPACE IS HARDLY THE LIMIT OF ITS POTENTIAL.
ARCH DIRECTOR, WE'RE READY TO TRANSFER DOCTOR DIPSON AND--
BURNS??? WH--
HAHA, YES, I'M ALIVE! MISS ME, SHORTBREAD? THE REAL ME?
MISS YOU? I--
DID YOU NOT HEAR THE PARTS IN YOUR OWN STORY WHERE YOU TREATED HER LIKE GARBAGE?
WHAT? NO I DIDN'T.
EH...
LET'S JUST SAY...
HEN HE WAS NG HALFWAY NT AS YOU, IT RLY MADE ME CONFLICTED ABOUT ALL THIS.
HIM?
"THIS"?
WE TRIED TO BRING YOU ON BOARD, WADE.
SHUNK
SHUNK
SHUNK
FRIGGIN' SPIES.

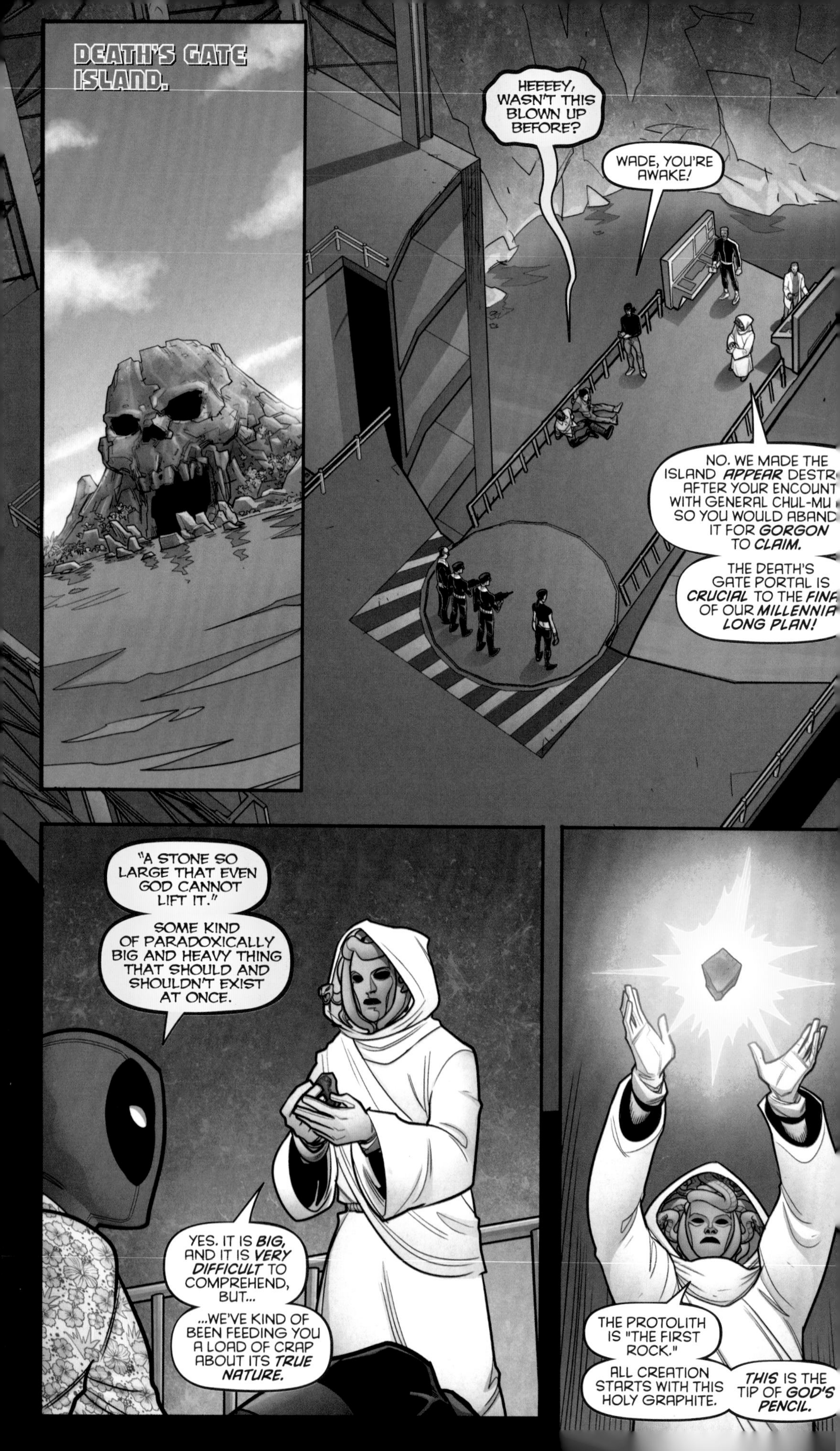

DEATH'S GATE ISLAND.
HEEEEY, WASN'T THIS BLOWN UP BEFORE?
WADE, YOU'RE AWAKE!
NO. WE MADE THE ISLAND APPEAR DESTR AFTER YOUR ENCOUNT WITH GENERAL CHUL-MU SO YOU WOULD ABAND IT FOR GORGON TO CLAIM.
THE DEATH'S GATE PORTAL IS CRUCIAL TO THE FINA OF OUR MILLENNIA LONG PLAN!
"A STONE SO LARGE THAT EVEN GOD CANNOT LIFT IT."
SOME KIND OF PARADOXICALLY BIG AND HEAVY THING THAT SHOULD AND SHOULDN'T EXIST AT ONCE.
YES. IT IS BIG, AND IT IS VERY DIFFICULT TO COMPREHEND, BUT...
...WE'VE KIND OF BEEN FEEDING YOU A LOAD OF CRAP ABOUT ITS TRUE NATURE.
THE PROTOLITH IS "THE FIRST ROCK."
ALL CREATION STARTS WITH THIS HOLY GRAPHITE.
THIS IS THE TIP OF GOD'S PENCIL.

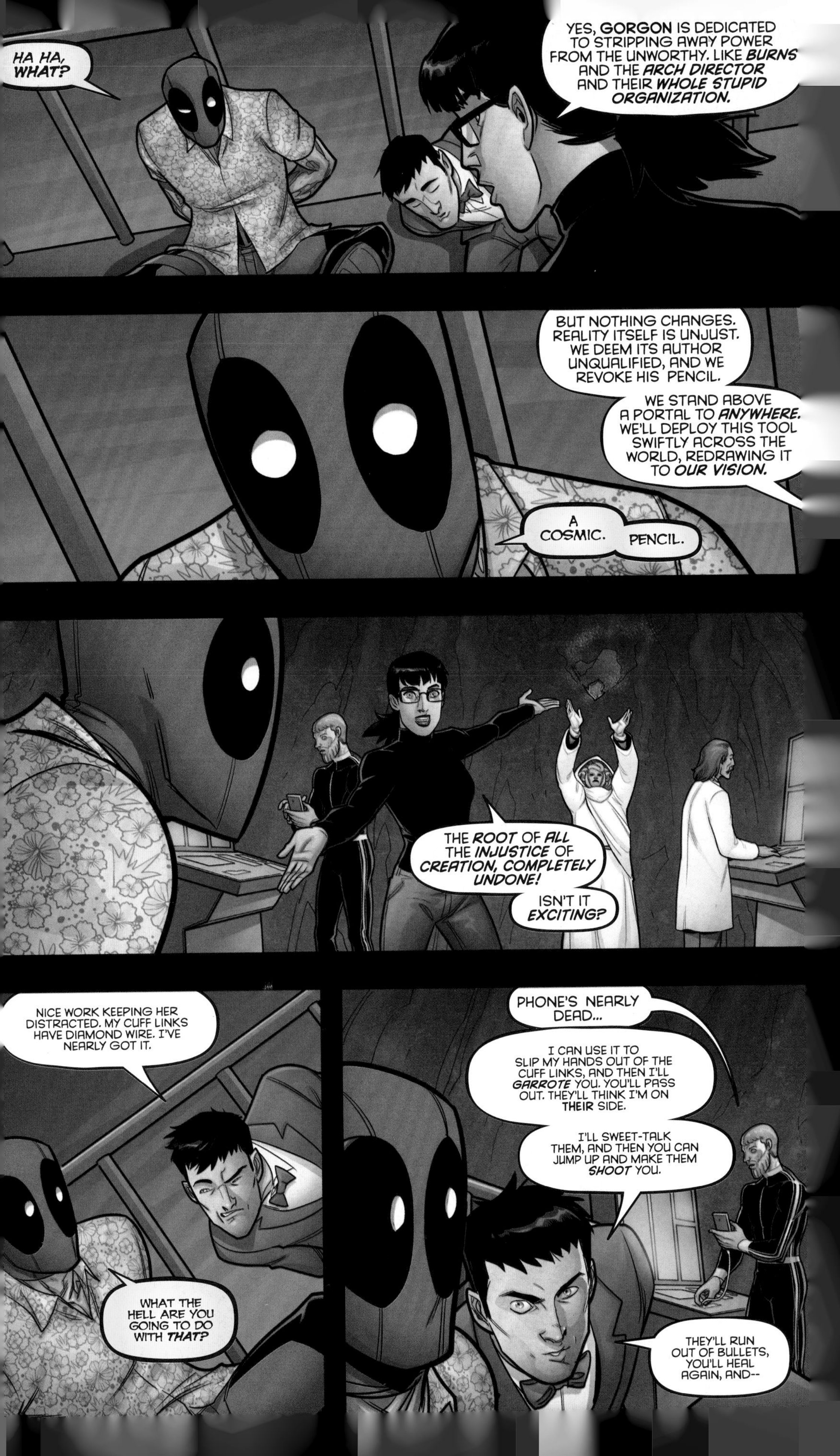
HA HA, WHAT?
YES, GORGON IS DEDICATED TO STRIPPING AWAY POWER FROM THE UNWORTHY. LIKE BURNS AND THE ARCH DIRECTOR AND THEIR WHOLE STUPID ORGANIZATION.
BUT NOTHING CHANGES. REALITY ITSELF IS UNJUST. WE DEEM ITS AUTHOR UNQUALIFIED, AND WE REVOKE HIS PENCIL.
WE STAND ABOVE A PORTAL TO ANYWHERE. WE'LL DEPLOY THIS TOOL SWIFTLY ACROSS THE WORLD, REDRAWING IT TO OUR VISION.
A COSMIC.
PENCIL.
THE ROOT OF ALL THE INJUSTICE OF CREATION, COMPLETELY UNDONE!
ISN'T IT EXCITING?
NICE WORK KEEPING HER DISTRACTED. MY CUFF LINKS HAVE DIAMOND WIRE. I'VE NEARLY GOT IT.
WHAT THE HELL ARE YOU GOING TO DO WITH THAT?
PHONE'S NEARLY DEAD...
I CAN USE IT TO SLIP MY HANDS OUT OF THE CUFF LINKS, AND THEN I'LL GARROTE YOU. YOU'LL PASS OUT. THEY'LL THINK I'M ON THEIR SIDE.
I'LL SWEET-TALK THEM, AND THEN YOU CAN JUMP UP AND MAKE THEM SHOOT YOU.
THEY'LL RUN OUT OF BULLETS, YOU'LL HEAL AGAIN, AND--

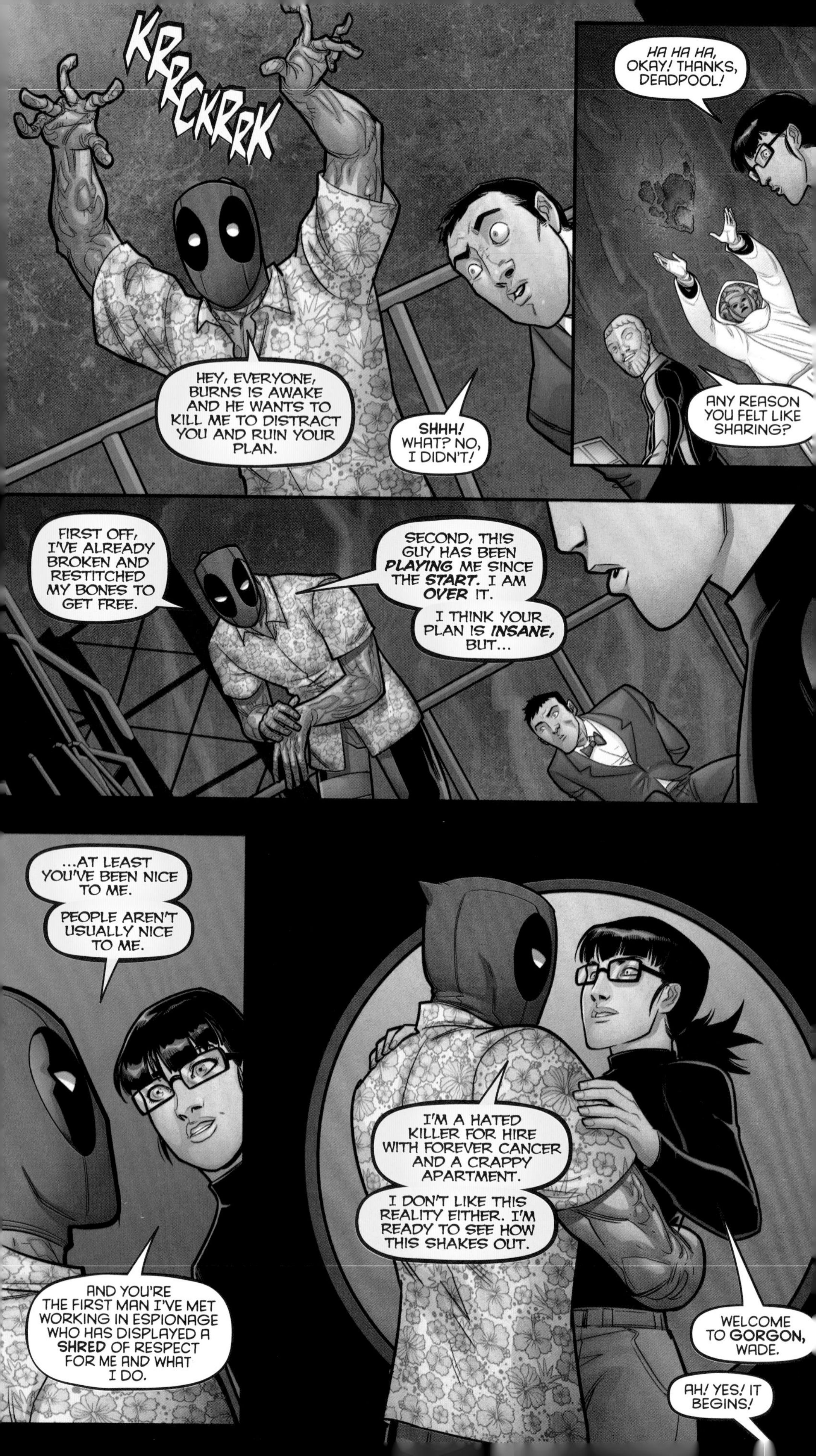
KRRCKRRRK
HEY, EVERYONE, BURNS IS AWAKE AND HE WANTS TO KILL ME TO DISTRACT YOU AND RUIN YOUR PLAN.
SHHH! WHAT? NO, I DIDN'T!
HA HA HA, OKAY! THANKS, DEADPOOL!
ANY REASON YOU FELT LIKE SHARING?
FIRST OFF, I'VE ALREADY BROKEN AND RESTITCHED MY BONES TO GET FREE.
SECOND, THIS GUY HAS BEEN PLAYING ME SINCE THE START. I AM OVER IT.
I THINK YOUR PLAN IS INSANE, BUT...
...AT LEAST YOU'VE BEEN NICE TO ME.
PEOPLE AREN'T USUALLY NICE TO ME.
AND YOU'RE THE FIRST MAN I'VE MET WORKING IN ESPIONAGE WHO HAS DISPLAYED A SHRED OF RESPECT FOR ME AND WHAT I DO.
I'M A HATED KILLER FOR HIRE WITH FOREVER CANCER AND A CRAPPY APARTMENT.
I DON'T LIKE THIS REALITY EITHER. I'M READY TO SEE HOW THIS SHAKES OUT.
WELCOME TO GORGON, WADE.
AH! YES! IT BEGINS!

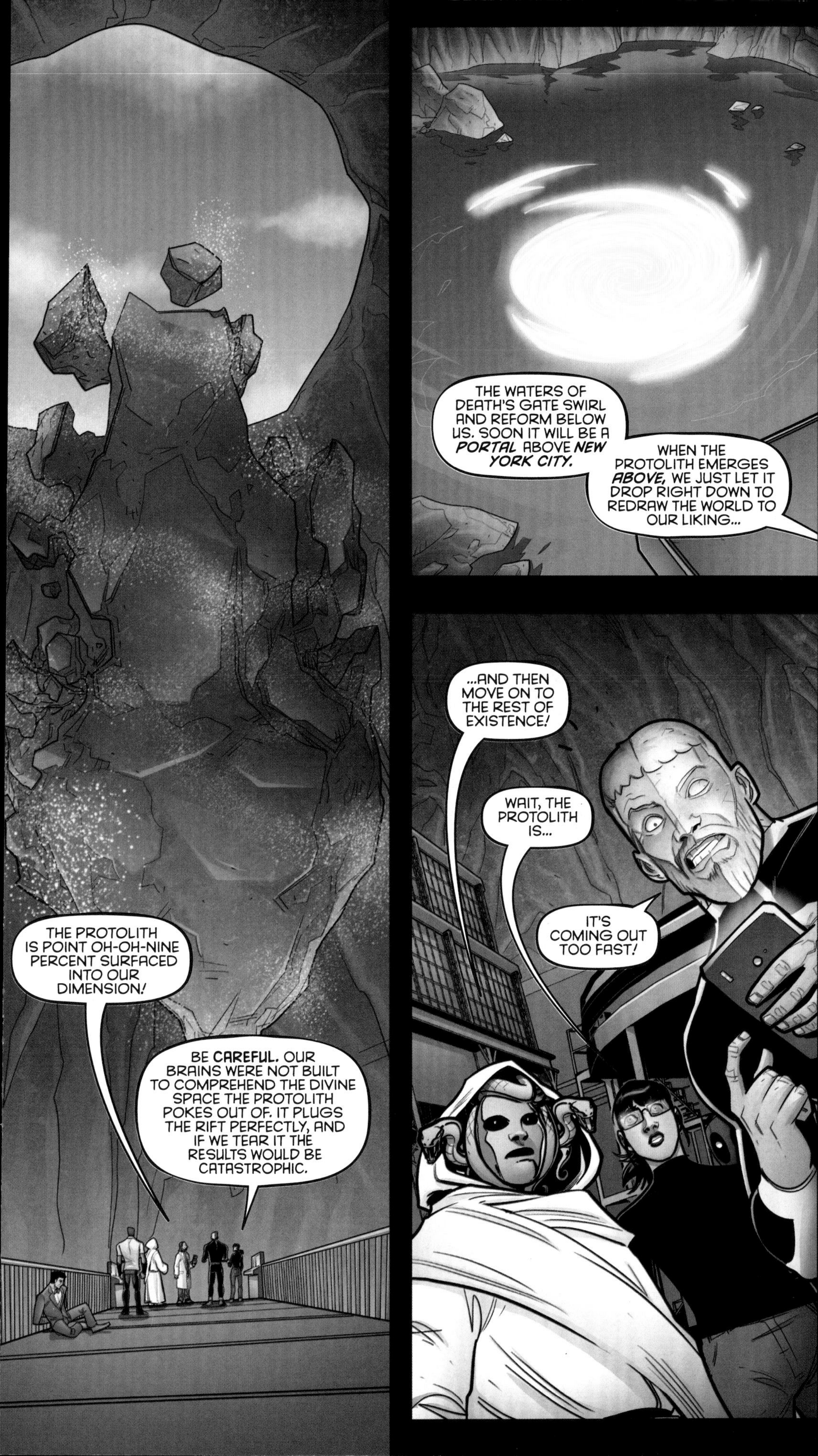

THE PROTOLITH IS POINT OH-OH-NINE PERCENT SURFACED INTO OUR DIMENSION!
BE CAREFUL. OUR BRAINS WERE NOT BUILT TO COMPREHEND THE DIVINE SPACE THE PROTOLITH POKES OUT OF. IT PLUGS THE RIFT PERFECTLY, AND IF WE TEAR IT THE RESULTS WOULD BE CATASTROPHIC.
THE WATERS OF DEATH'S GATE SWIRL AND REFORM BELOW US. SOON IT WILL BE A PORTAL ABOVE NEW YORK CITY.
WHEN THE PROTOLITH EMERGES ABOVE, WE JUST LET IT DROP RIGHT DOWN TO REDRAW THE WORLD TO OUR LIKING...
...AND THEN MOVE ON TO THE REST OF EXISTENCE!
WAIT, THE PROTOLITH IS...
IT'S COMING OUT TOO FAST!

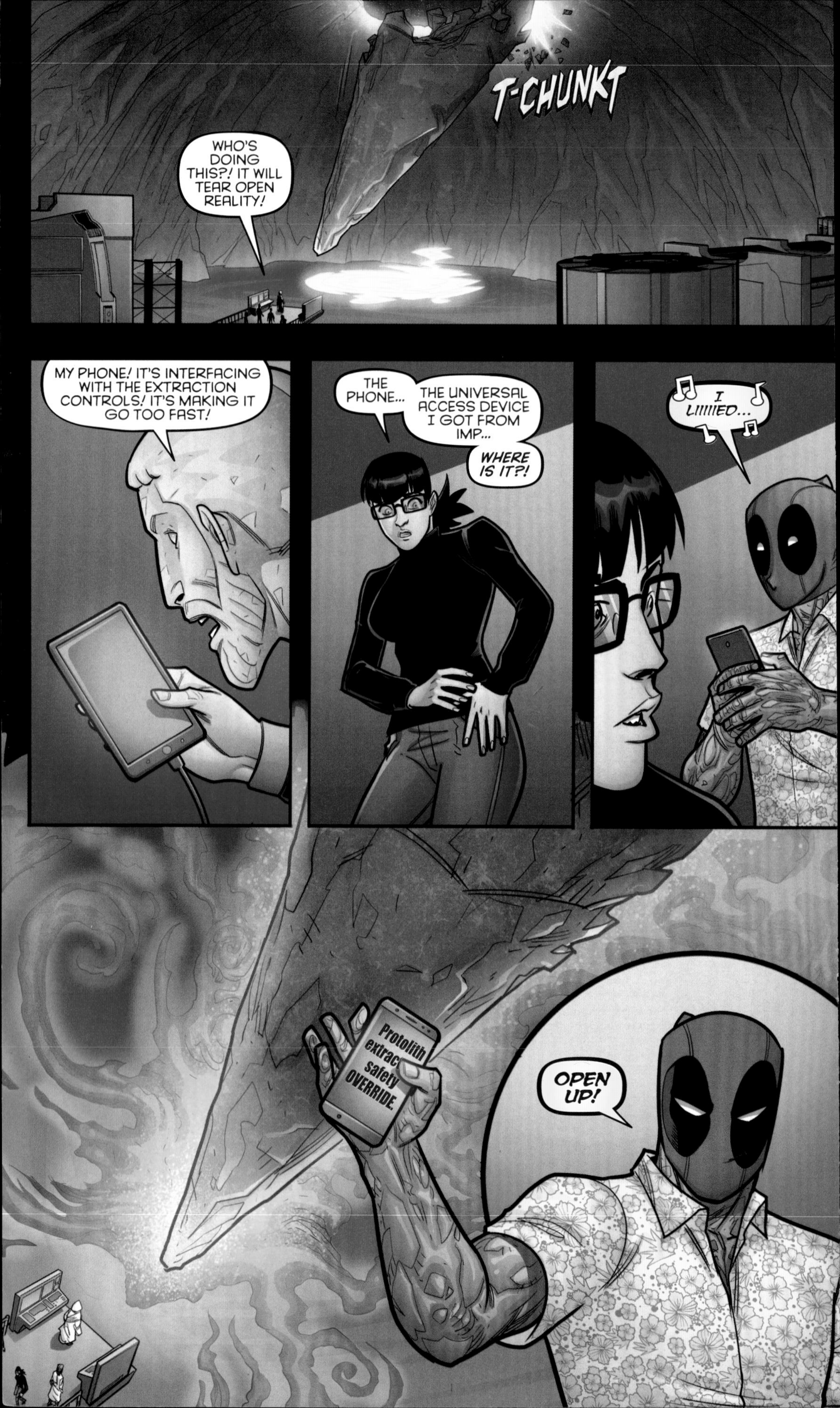

T-CHUNKT
WHO'S DOING THIS?! IT WILL TEAR OPEN REALITY!
MY PHONE! IT'S INTERFACING WITH THE EXTRACTION CONTROLS! IT'S MAKING IT GO TOO FAST!
THE PHONE...
THE UNIVERSAL ACCESS DEVICE I GOT FROM IMP...
WHERE IS IT?!
I LIIIIIED...
Protolith extrac safety OVERRIDE.
OPEN UP!

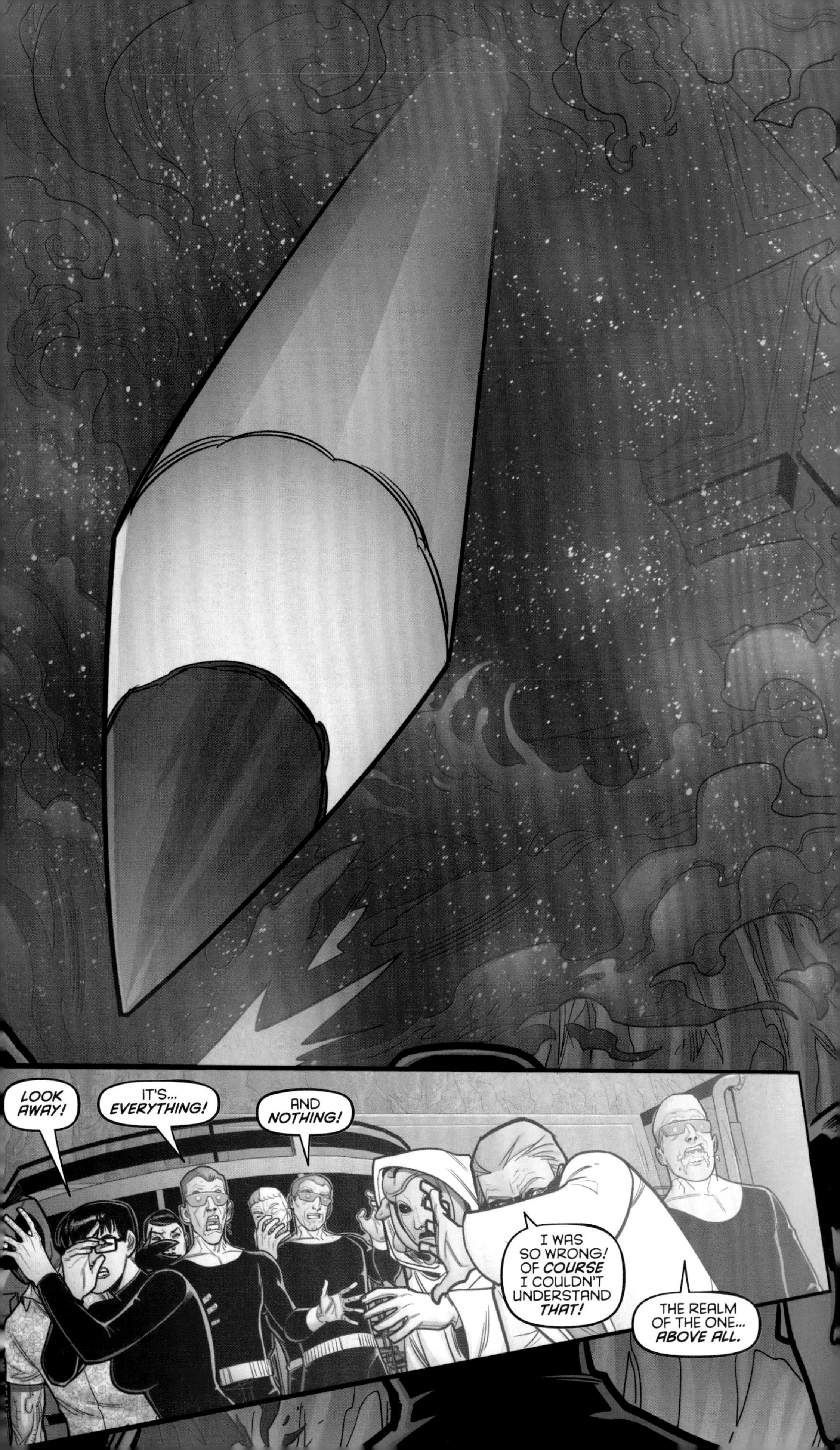
LOOK AWAY!
IT'S... EVERYTHING!
AND NOTHING!
I WAS SO WRONG! OF COURSE I COULDN'T UNDERSTAND THAT!
THE REALM OF THE ONE... ABOVE ALL.

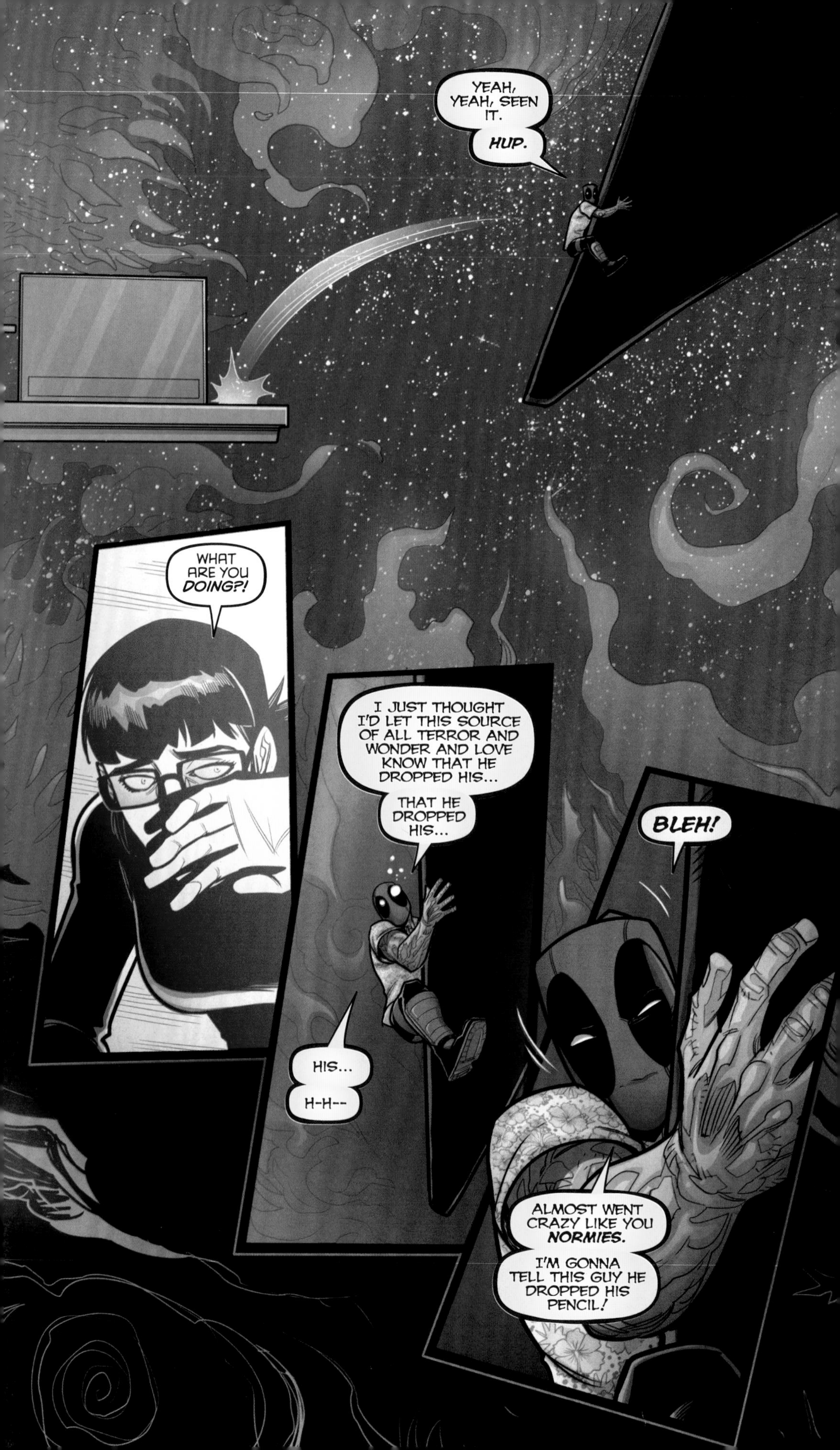

YEAH, YEAH, SEEN IT.
HUP.
WHAT ARE YOU DOING?!
I JUST THOUGHT I'D LET THIS SOURCE OF ALL TERROR AND WONDER AND LOVE KNOW THAT HE DROPPED HIS...
THAT HE DROPPED HIS...
HIS...
H-H--
BLEH!
ALMOST WENT CRAZY LIKE YOU NORMIES.
I'M GONNA TELL THIS GUY HE DROPPED HIS PENCIL!

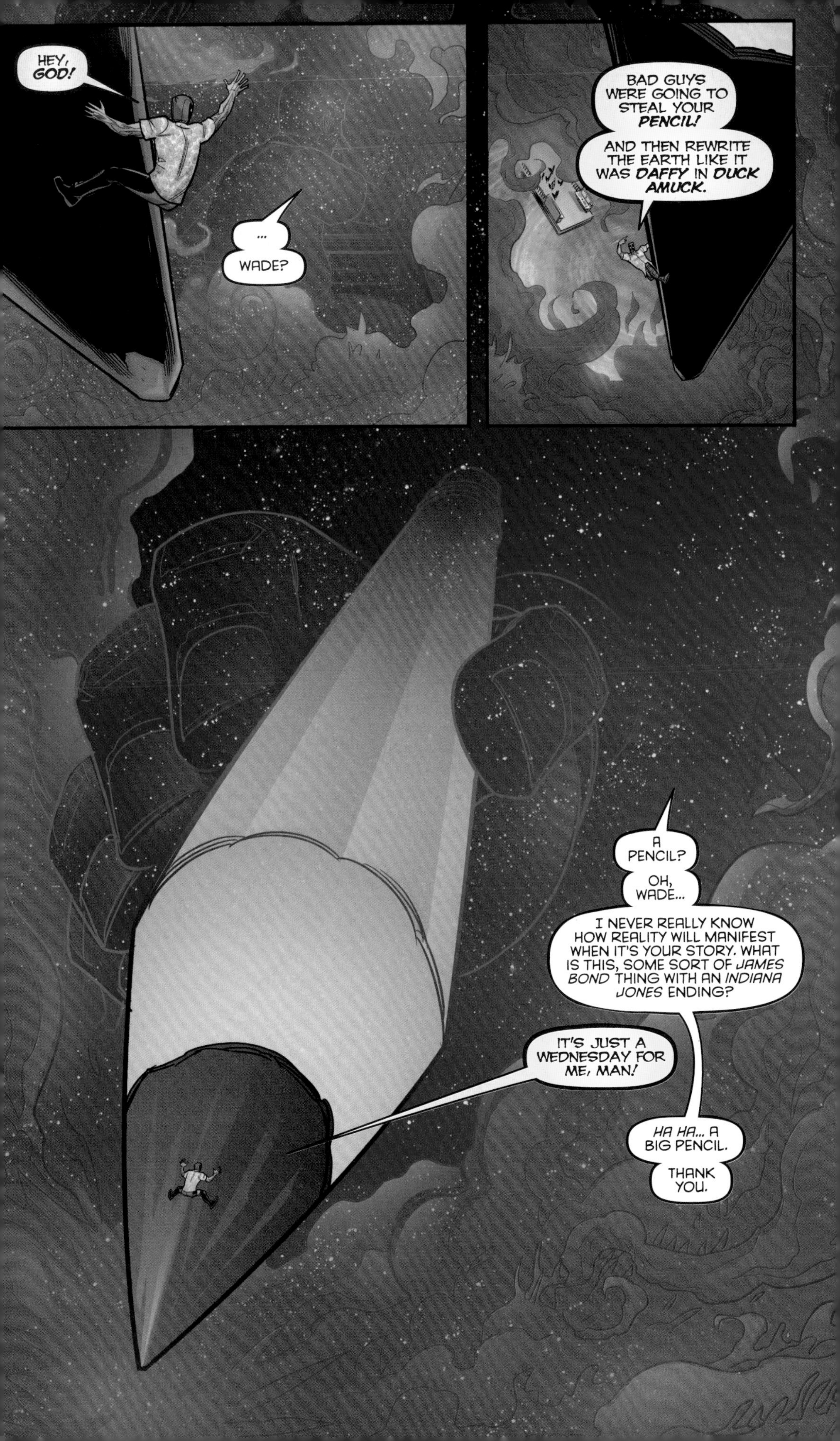
HEY, GOD!
...
WADE?
BAD GUYS WERE GOING TO STEAL YOUR PENCIL!
AND THEN REWRITE THE EARTH LIKE IT WAS DAFFY IN DUCK AMUCK.
A PENCIL?
OH, WADE...
I NEVER REALLY KNOW HOW REALITY WILL MANIFEST WHEN IT'S YOUR STORY. WHAT IS THIS, SOME SORT OF JAMES BOND THING WITH AN INDIANA JONES ENDING?
IT'S JUST A WEDNESDAY FOR ME, MAN!
HA HA... A BIG PENCIL.
THANK YOU.

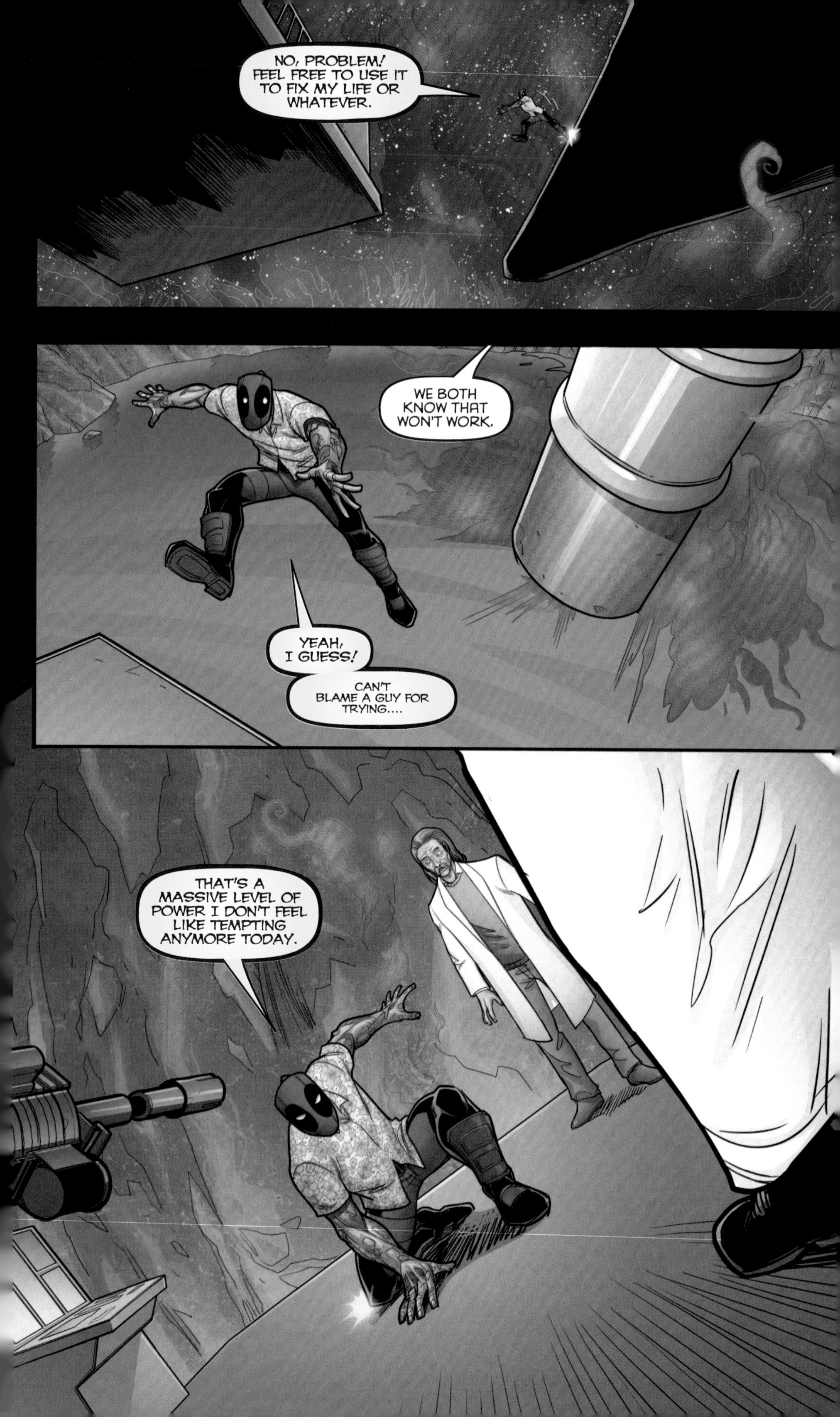
NO, PROBLEM! FEEL FREE TO USE IT TO FIX MY LIFE OR WHATEVER.
WE BOTH KNOW THAT WON'T WORK.
YEAH, I GUESS!
CAN'T BLAME A GUY FOR TRYING....
THAT'S A MASSIVE LEVEL OF POWER I DON'T FEEL LIKE TEMPTING ANYMORE TODAY.

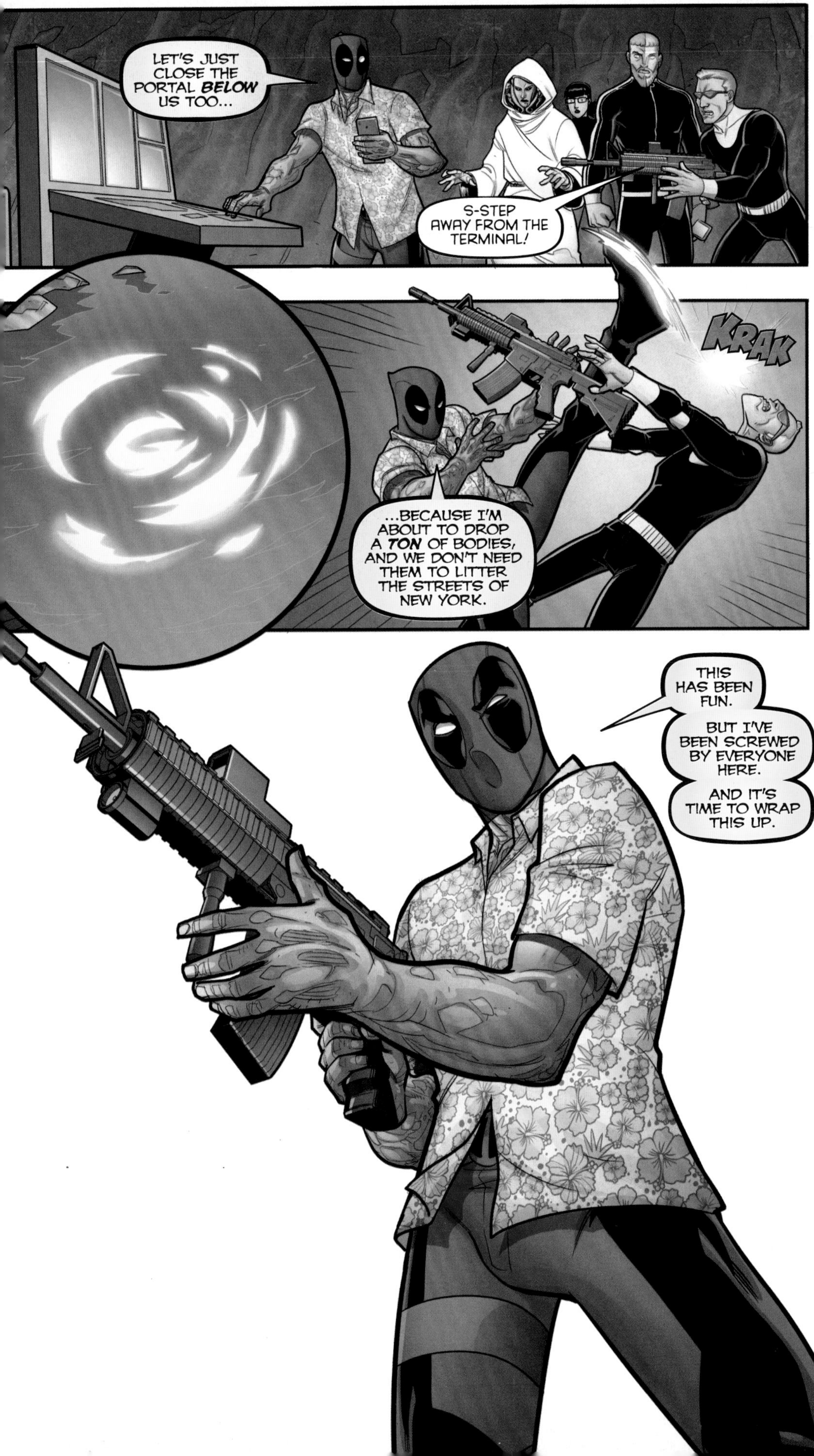
LET'S JUST CLOSE THE PORTAL BELOW US TOO...
S-STEP AWAY FROM THE TERMINAL!
KRAK
...BECAUSE I'M ABOUT TO DROP A TON OF BODIES, AND WE DON'T NEED THEM TO LITTER THE STREETS OF NEW YORK.
THIS HAS BEEN FUN.
BUT I'VE BEEN SCREWED BY EVERYONE HERE.
AND IT'S TIME TO WRAP THIS UP.

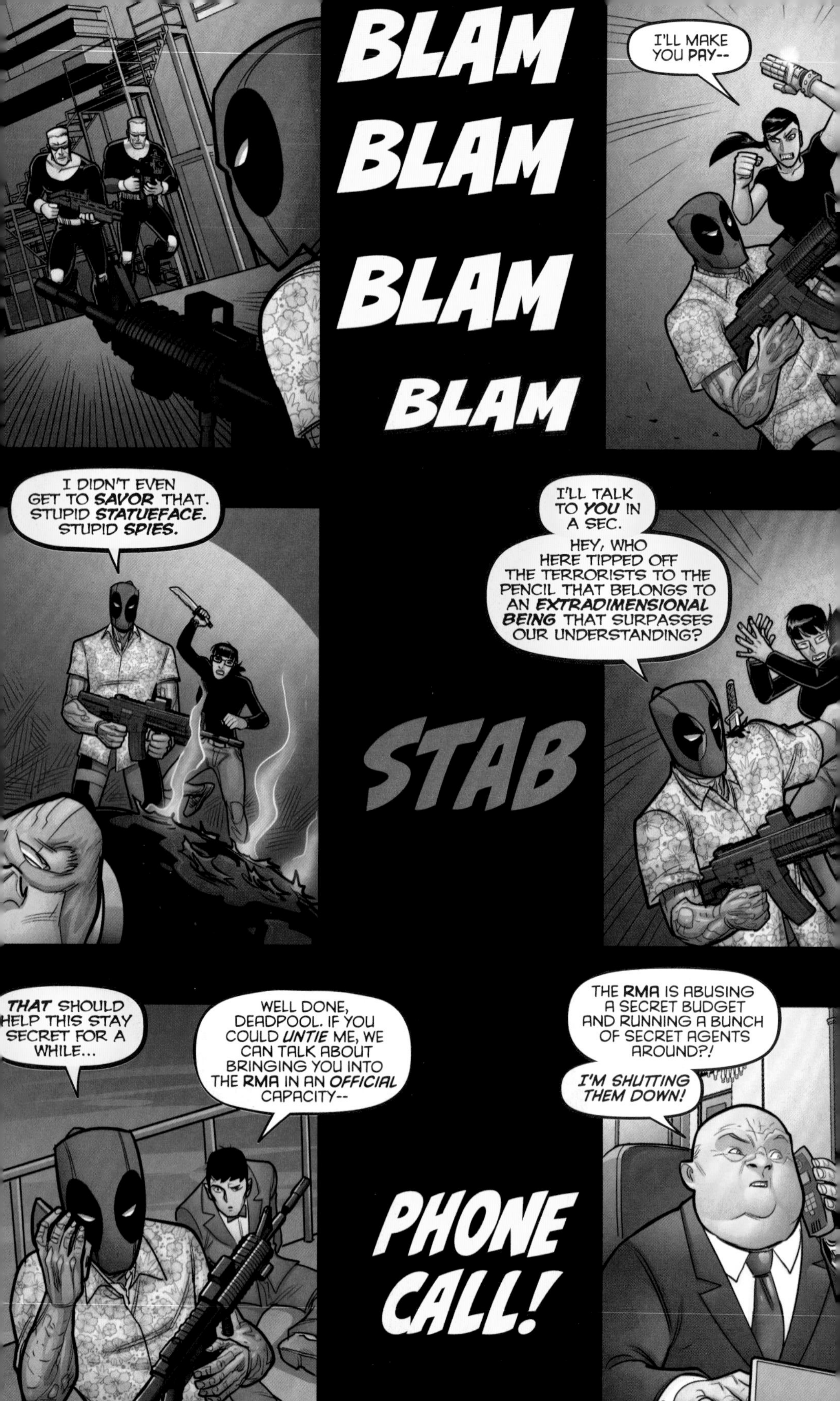
BLAM
BLAM
BLAM
BLAM
I'LL MAKE YOU PAY--
I DIDN'T EVEN GET TO SAVOR THAT. STUPID STATUEFACE. STUPID SPIES.
STAB
I'LL TALK TO YOU IN A SEC.
HEY, WHO HERE TIPPED OFF THE TERRORISTS TO THE PENCIL THAT BELONGS TO AN EXTRADIMENSIONAL BEING THAT SURPASSES OUR UNDERSTANDING?
THAT SHOULD HELP THIS STAY SECRET FOR A WHILE...
WELL DONE, DEADPOOL. IF YOU COULD UNTIE ME, WE CAN TALK ABOUT BRINGING YOU INTO THE RMA IN AN OFFICIAL CAPACITY--
PHONE CALL!
THE RMA IS ABUSING A SECRET BUDGET AND RUNNING A BUNCH OF SECRET AGENTS AROUND?!
I'M SHUTTING THEM DOWN!

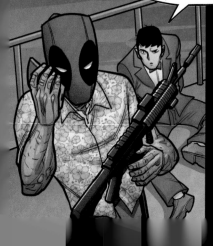

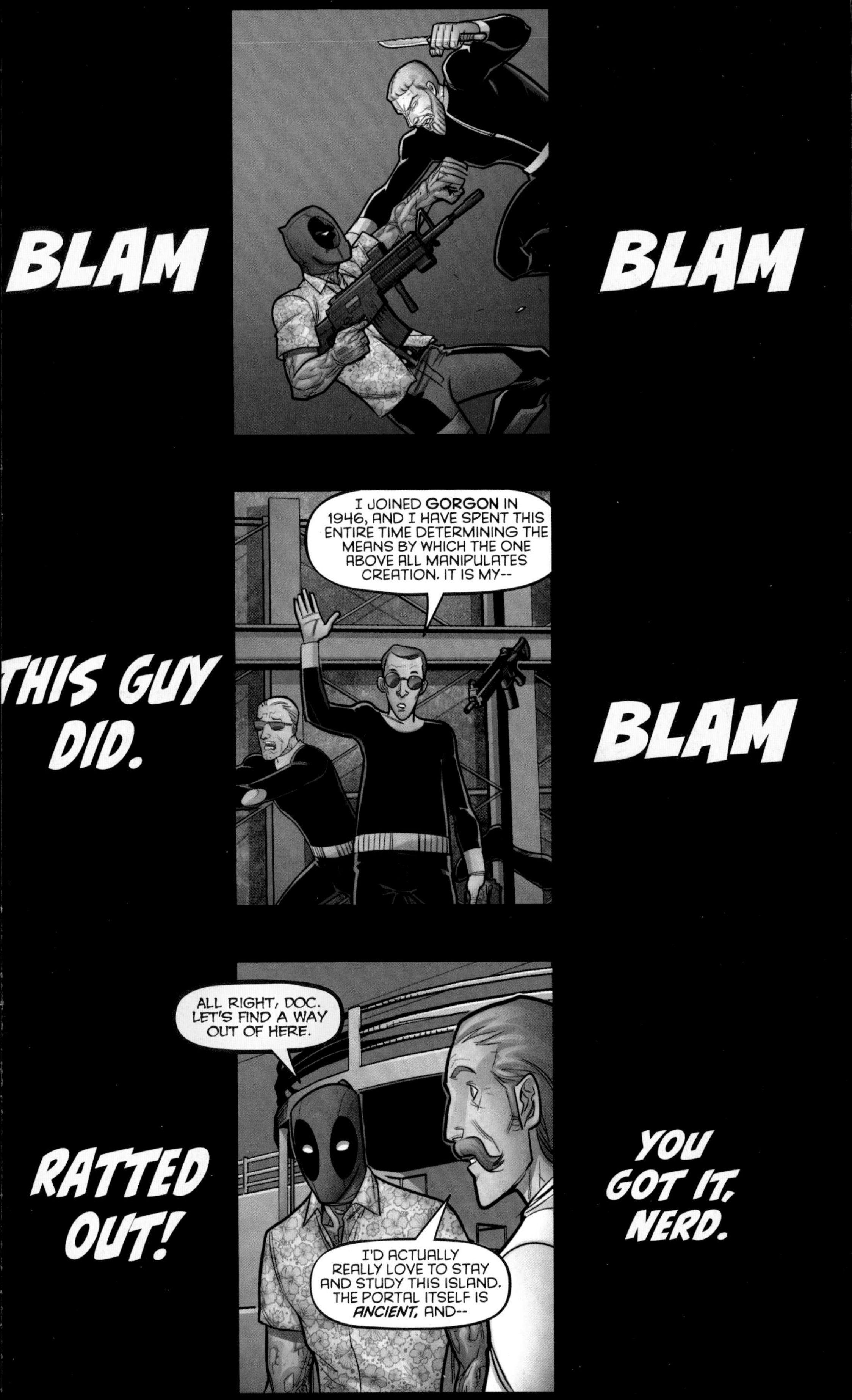
BLAM
BLAM
THIS GUY DID.
I JOINED GORGON IN 1946, AND I HAVE SPENT THIS ENTIRE TIME DETERMINING THE MEANS BY WHICH THE ONE ABOVE ALL MANIPULATES CREATION. IT IS MY--
BLAM
RATTED OUT!
ALL RIGHT, DOC. LET'S FIND A WAY OUT OF HERE.
YOU GOT IT, NERD.
I'D ACTUALLY REALLY LOVE TO STAY AND STUDY THIS ISLAND. THE PORTAL ITSELF IS ANCIENT, AND--

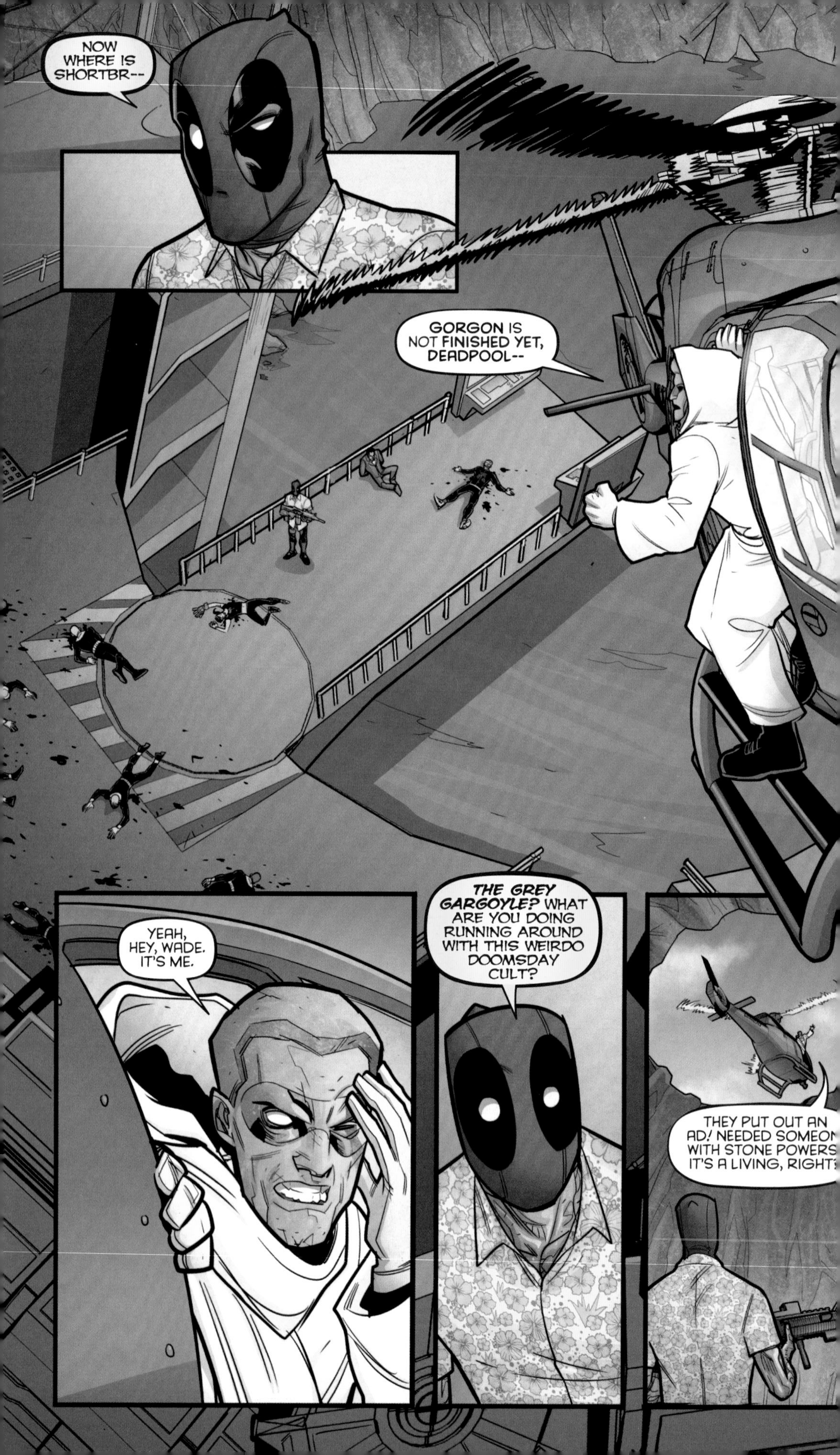
NOW WHERE IS SHORTBR--
GORGON IS NOT FINISHED YET, DEADPOOL--
YEAH, HEY, WADE. IT'S ME.
THE GREY GARGOYLE? WHAT ARE YOU DOING RUNNING AROUND WITH THIS WEIRDO DOOMSDAY CULT?
THEY PUT OUT AN AD! NEEDED SOMEON WITH STONE POWERS IT'S A LIVING, RIGHT

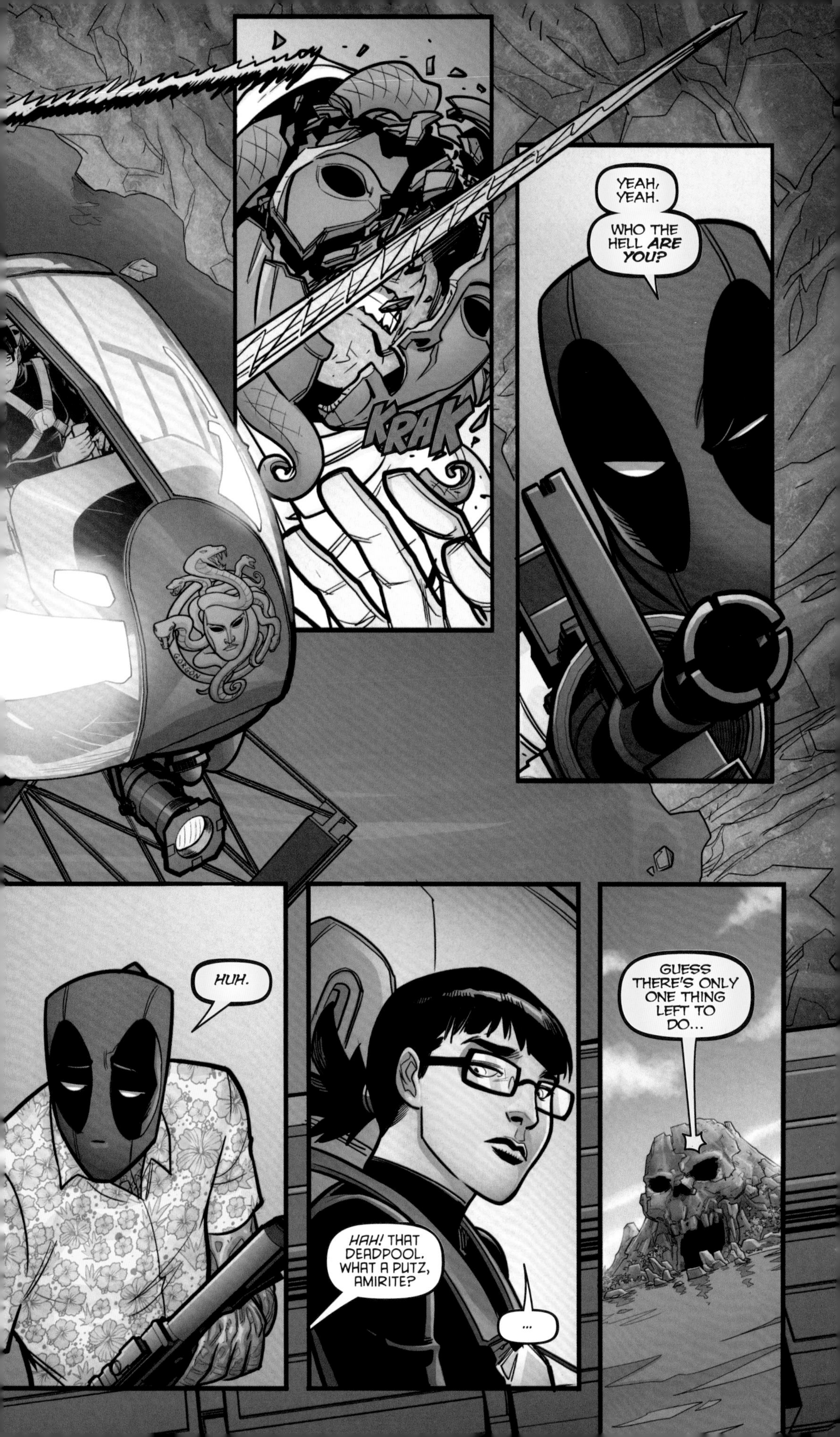
KRAK
YEAH, YEAH.
WHO THE HELL ARE YOU?
GORGON
HUH.
HAH! THAT DEADPOOL. WHAT A PUTZ, AMIRITE?
...
GUESS THERE'S ONLY ONE THING LEFT TO DO...

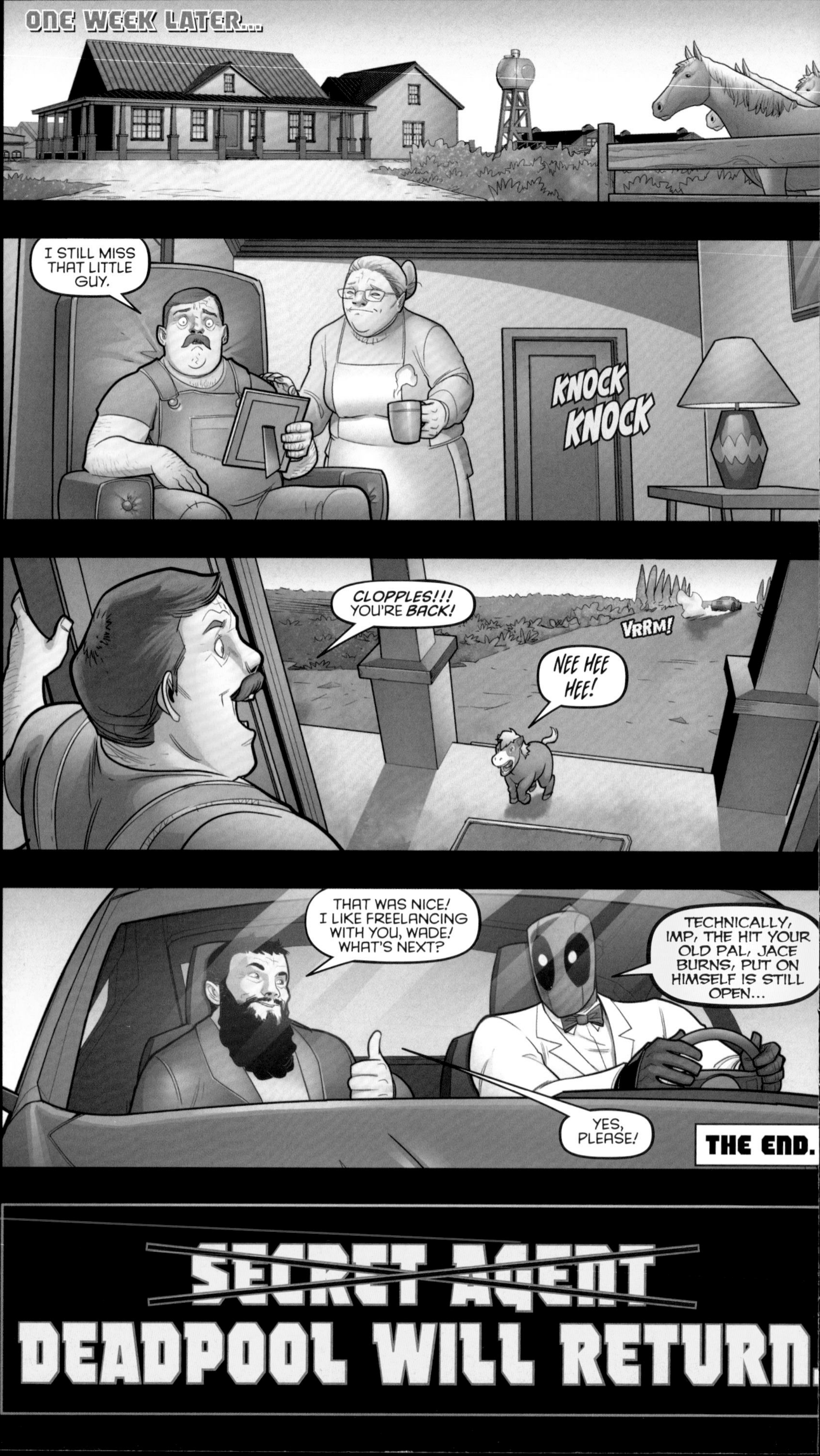
ONE WEEK LATER...
I STILL MISS THAT LITTLE GUY.
KNOCK KNOCK
CLOPPLES!!! YOU'RE BACK!
VRRM!
NEE HEE HEE!
THAT WAS NICE! I LIKE FREELANCING WITH YOU, WADE! WHAT'S NEXT?
TECHNICALLY, IMP, THE HIT YOUR OLD PAL, JACE BURNS, PUT ON HIMSELF IS STILL OPEN...
YES, PLEASE!
THE END.
SECRET AGENT
DEADPOOL WILL RETURN.

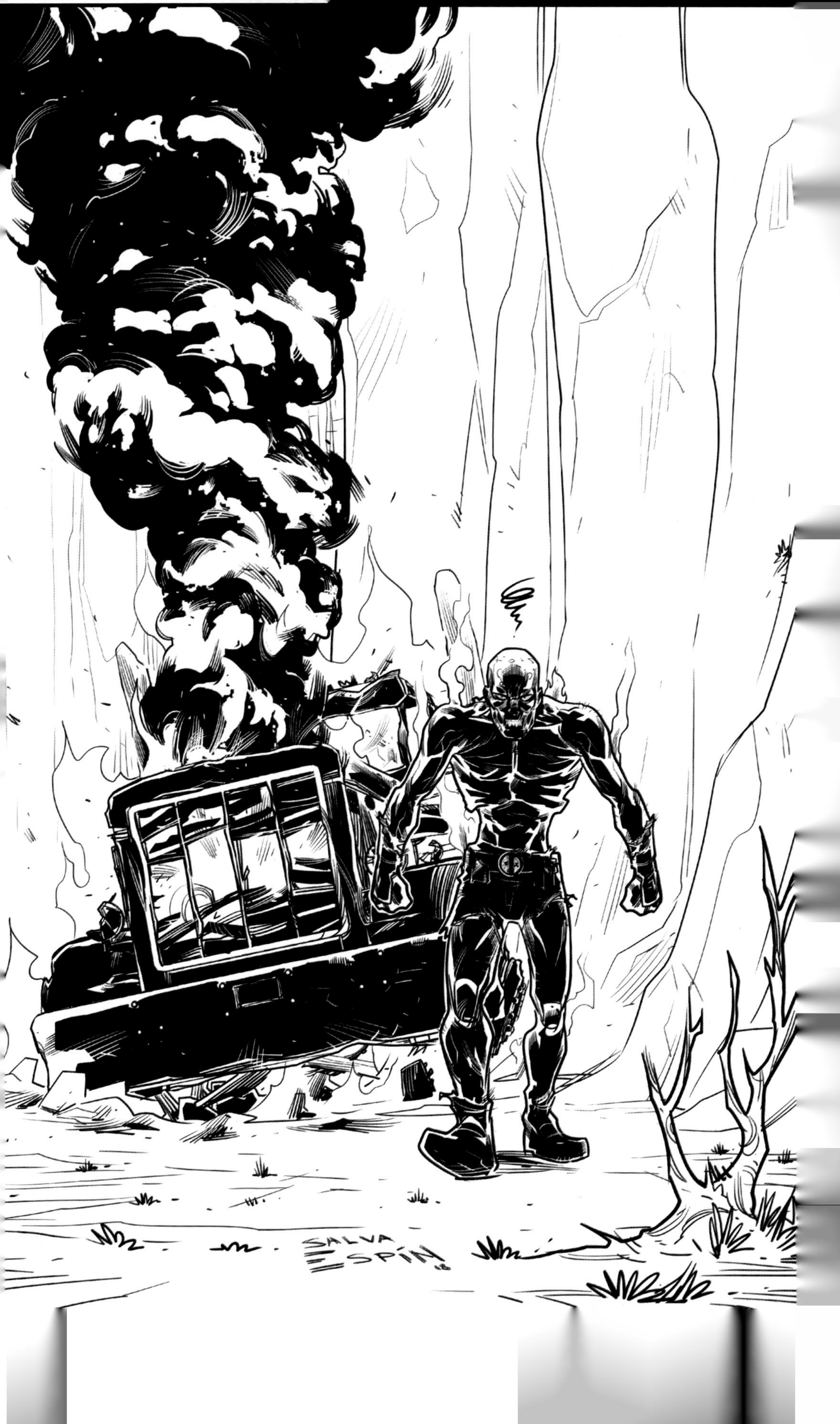
SALVA
ESPÍN

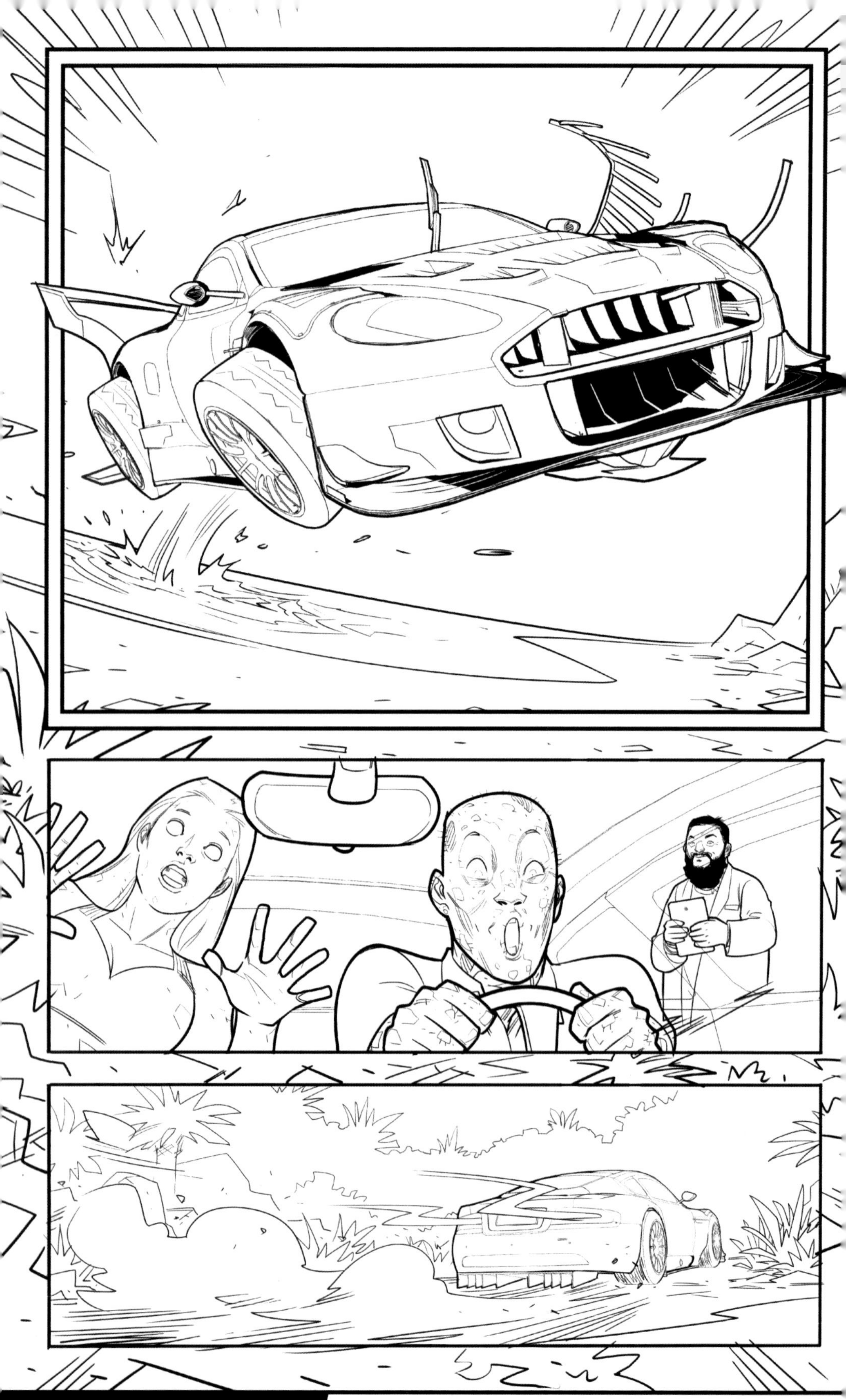

ISSUE 2, PG. 7 ART BY SALVA ESPIN

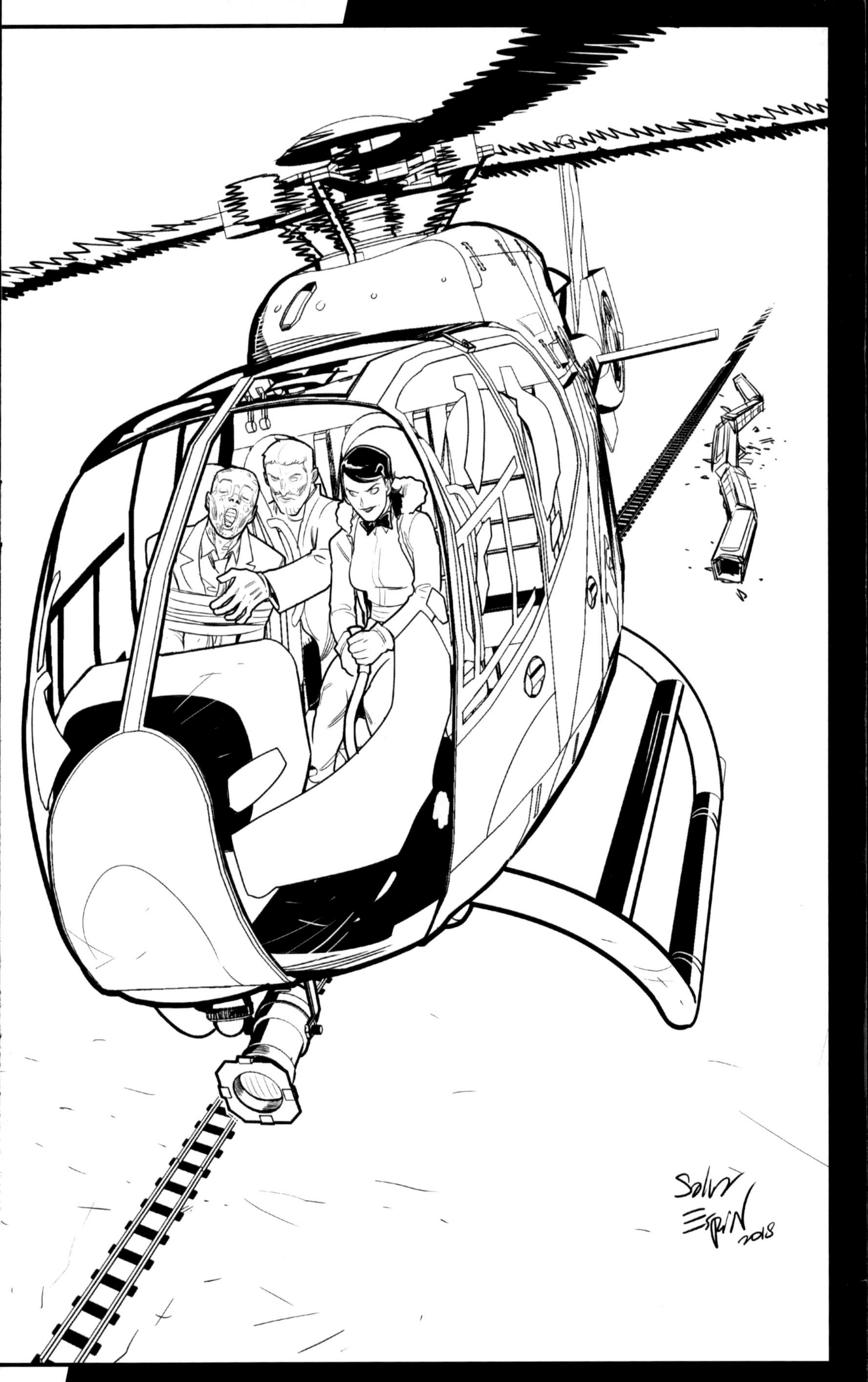
Salva
Espin 2018

ISSUE 3, PG. 20 ART BY SALVA ESPIN

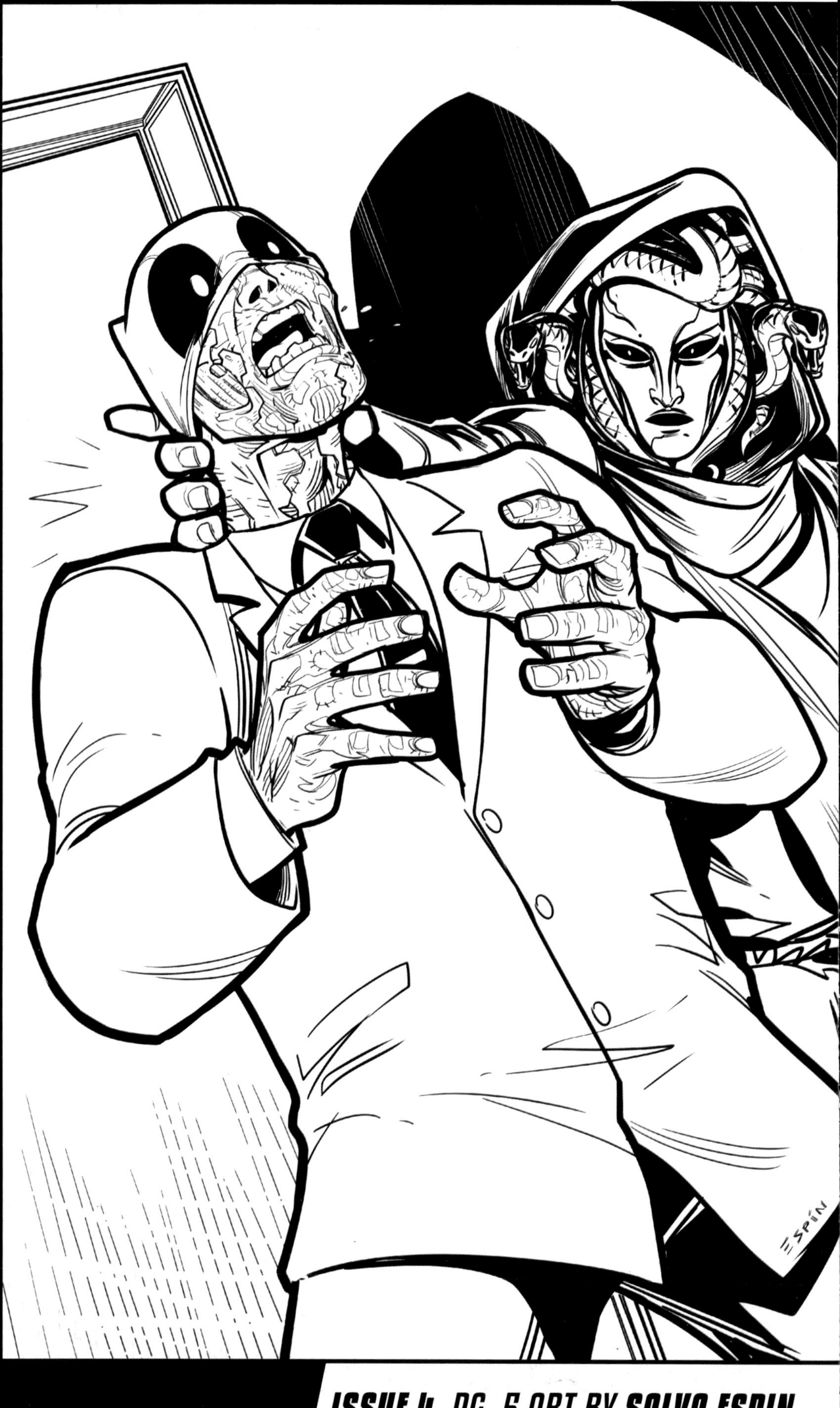

ISSUE 4, PG. 5 ART BY **SALVA ESPIN**

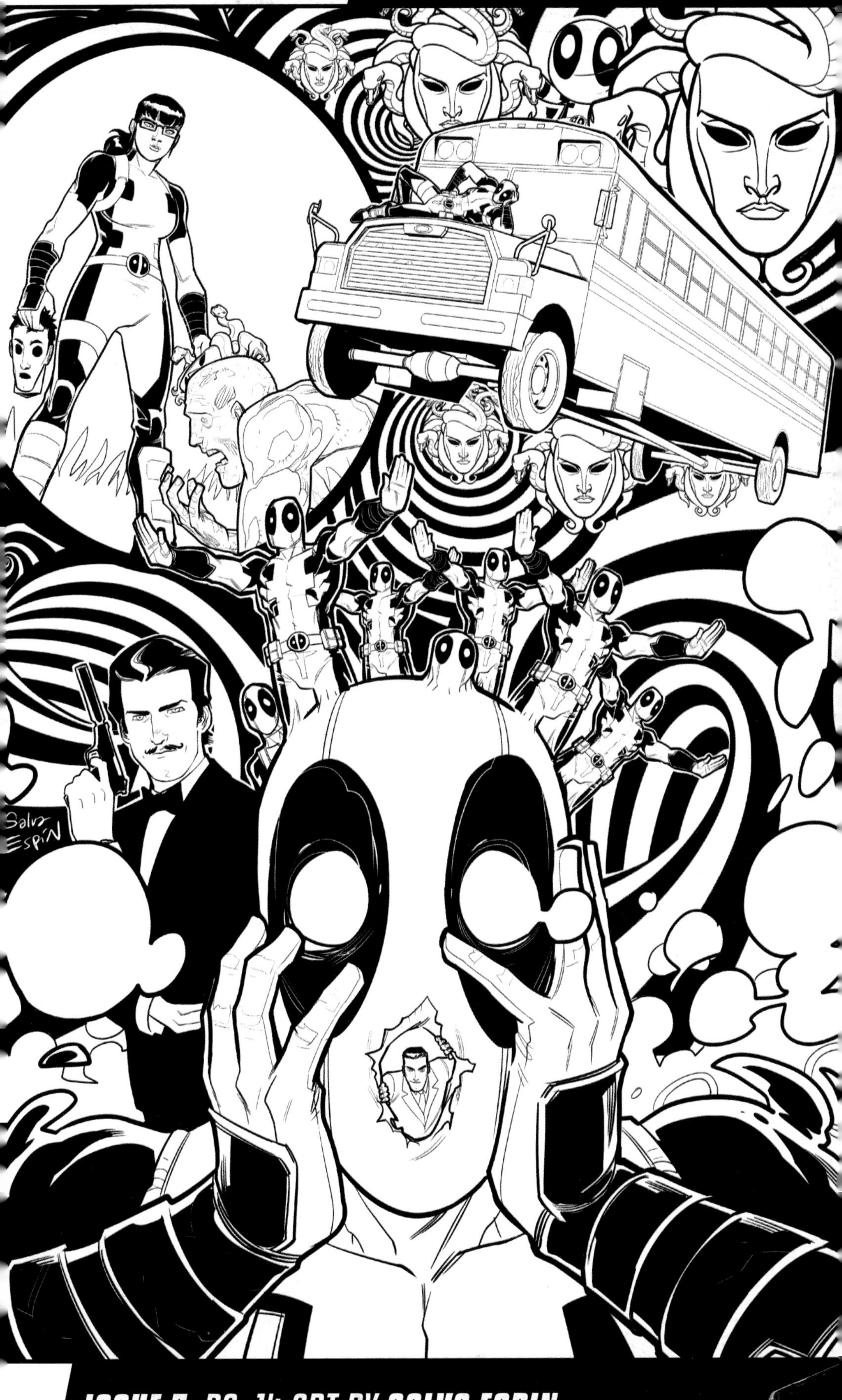
Salva ESPIN

ISSUE 5, PG. 14 ART BY SALVA ESPIN

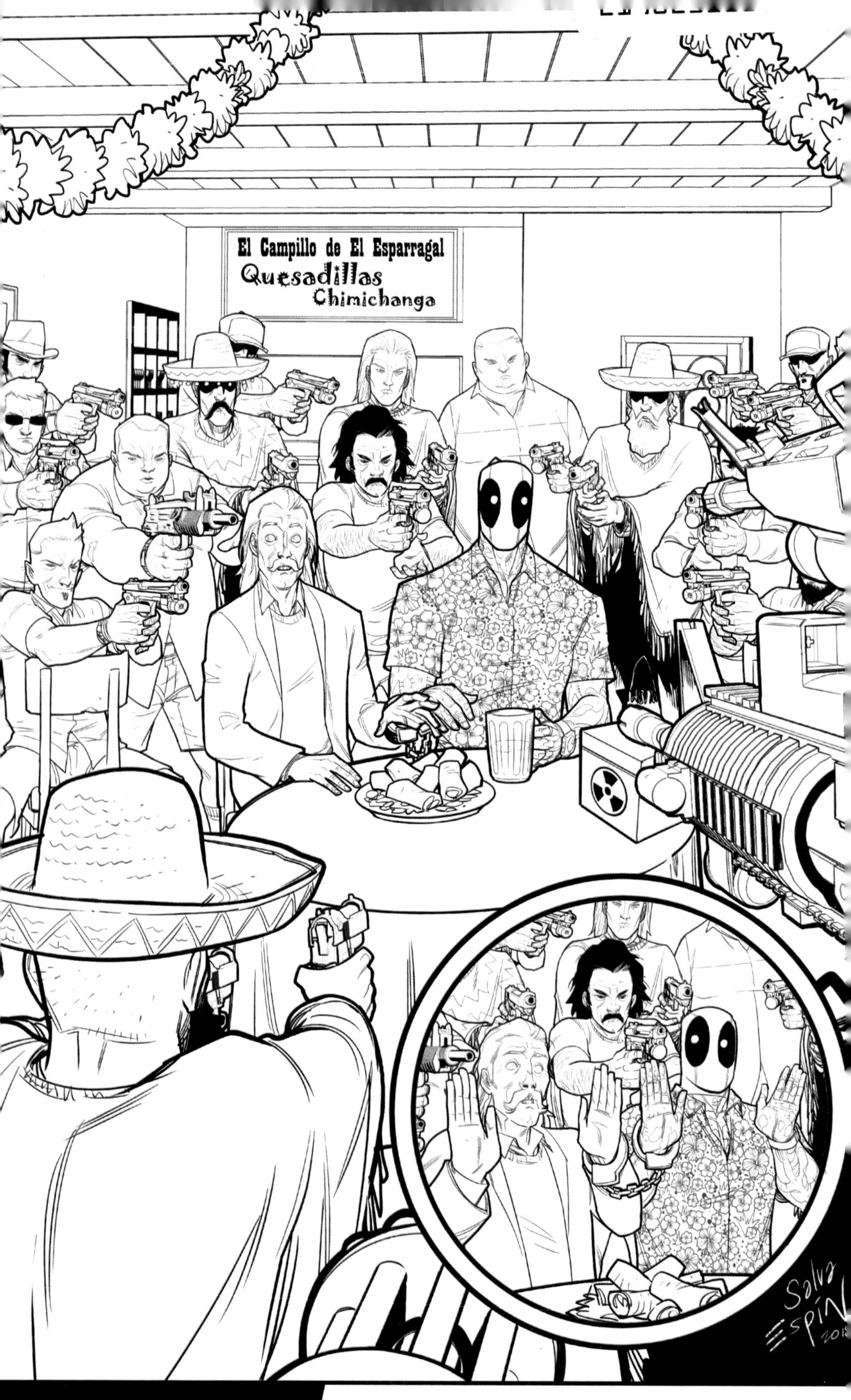
El Campillo de El Esparragal
Quesadillas
Chimichanga
Salva ESPIN

ISSUE 5, PG. 17 ART BY **SALVA ESPIN**